"I Didn't Want to Do It. Gretchen Made Me."

Dolores suddenly jumped up and ran to the bathroom, shouting "I've had it! I'm going to put an end to this nonsense right now!"

I shuddered—"Has she gotten into the tranquilizers?" Desperately I prayed, "O God, no! Surely they're too much for her!"

Running to the bathroom I couldn't get in—she had locked the door!

"Go away!" she ordered. "Besides, there's nothing you can do—it's too late!"

"Did you get the medicine?" I demanded loudly, scared.

"Ich kann nicht sprechen! Es ist verboten! Du musst jetzt weggehen!" screamed the woman who didn't know a word of German. . . .

❖━━━━━━━━━❖

LIFE AFTER DEATH
Is this the final proof?

(Turn page . . .)

CAN THE DEAD COMMUNICATE WITH THE LIVING?

Here for the first time is the shocking story behind one of the most celebrated and documented cases ever recorded of life after death.

The Washington Post reported:

"Dolores Jay, the 52-year-old wife of a United Methodist minister, has never learned German or come in contact with anyone who speaks it. Yet, under hypnosis, she speaks German in the voice of a little girl, becomes agitated at long-forgotten dangers, calls herself Gretchen Gottlieb, and tells questioners how she was murdered in a German wood a century ago."

Newsweek noted:

"Dolores Jay, under hypnosis, has disclosed what seems to be the memory of another lifetime."

Ian Stevenson, M.D., professor of psychiatry at the University of Virginia, investigated the case for five years. He arranged for a lie detector test for Mrs. Jay. Writing in the Journal of the *American Society for Psychical Research,* he concluded that the Gretchen case is "evidence of the survival of human personality after death."

GRETCHEN, I AM

REVEREND CARROLL E. JAY

AVON
PUBLISHERS OF BARD, CAMELOT AND DISCUS BOOKS

All events in this account are authentic and can be fully documented. However, most names and identifying details have been disguised to assure the privacy of those concerned.

The excerpt on pages 281-283 from the *Journal of the American Society for Psychical Research* is published with permission of the American Society for Psychical Research.

AVON BOOKS
A division of
The Hearst Corporation
959 Eighth Avenue
New York, New York 10019
Copyright © 1977 by Rev. Carroll E. Jay
Published by arrangement with Wyden Books.
Library of Congress Catalog Card Number: 77-13784
ISBN: 0-380-42820-2

First Avon Printing, March, 1979

To my wife, Dolores, and my children: Carol Lynne, Vonda Rhee, Mary JoAnn, and Jesse Lee—and my son-in-law, Larry, and yes, to our only granddaughter, Erin Beth, with love unending and gratitude unbounded, I dedicate this, my first published volume.

ACKNOWLEDGMENTS

The possibility of anyone writing a book such as this without the generous and sometimes self-sacrificing help of others is nil. Thus, not only do I thank my Maker and Creator for endowing me with inspiration and talent (however limited it may be); I shall forever be grateful to the many persons who came to me for help and in turn helped me by granting me permission to include their stories in this book. I am especially thankful to all the members of Anderson Memorial United Methodist Church for lessening their demands on my time so that I could write with a minimum of interruptions—not many people or institutions would have been so kind and thoughtful. Certainly, I am indebted to Dr. Ian Stevenson and all his associates; especially am I thankful for his helpful advice and gracious introduction to this book. To Hans Ruppel of the Darmstadt Archives, who made our visit to Germany most profitable and enjoyable, a mere thank you can never truly express our heart-felt appreciation.

To the hundreds of people who encouraged me to write and helped in ways too numerous to mention, the words thank you are also too small a reward. Nevertheless, to Jim and Judy Jay, Lana Sammons, Kim, Charlotte and Harold Hamlett, Susan and Jane Hunt, Clem and Joel Shelton, Rachel del Campo, and Rita Jefferson, I thank you for reading the original manuscript and giving me much needed evaluation and editorial help. And last, but not least, without Ruby Poindexter's nimble fingers at the typewriter, and her uncanny ability to decipher my scribbles, this book would never have reached the editor's desk on time. Thank you, and God bless you each and everyone.

CARROLL E. JAY
September 1, 1977

time in her life!"

...ated to learn that she had actually spoken German,
... hagrined at the ... that Dolores and I
... conspired to perpetrate a hoax. I departed the profes-
... office in the full belief that the professor had found a
... acle, that his conclusion had something to do with his
... him to explain the strange phenomenon I had deemed

CONTENTS

ACKNOWLEDGMENTS   vii

INTRODUCTION *by Ian Stevenson, M.D.*   xi

  I   *The Vision*   1
  II   *Gretchen Speaks: Voices from the Unknown*   18
  III *Whence the Voices?*   35
  IV *The Heavenly Portal*   55
  V   *A Brief Journey into Gloryland*   69
  VI *Christmas, a Beautiful Interlude*   83
  VII *Life's Injustice—God's Justice*   99
  VIII *Kicked Out of Church*   113
  IX *Back Home in Virginia*   134
  X   *The Dead Do Live*   149
  XI *Our Ancestors Speak*   175
  XII *Gretchen Goes Worldwide*   199
  XIII *Our Life an Open Book*   210
  XIV *How Do the Dead Communicate?*   232
  XV *Searching for Gretchen's Roots*   256
  XVI *To Know Is to Believe*   273

BIBLIOGRAPHY   287

INTRODUCTION

Carroll Jay has written an account of the development of the case of Gretchen that is both interesting and informative. It gives me pleasure to recommend it and to express the hope that it will have many readers. I consider the case of Gretchen one of the more important parapsychological cases that I have studied. I shall try to explain why I believe this.

Of one aspect of the case I can speak with absolute certainty: During the sessions at which Gretchen manifested, Dolores Jay, through the personality of Gretchen, unquestionably spoke German. Moreover, she spoke it in an intelligible way, by which I mean that she gave sensible answers in German to questions put to her in German. Gretchen's German was imperfect; indeed, at times it was quite bad. It was, however, definitely German, and that is the important point.

I have been speaking German for many years and think I know what I am talking about in this matter. I did not, however, wish to rely solely on my own knowledge of the language. I therefore invited three native speakers of German to attend sessions with Gretchen and speak German with her. Two of them concurred with my judgment that Gretchen spoke German intelligibly and gave sensible answers in German to our questions spoken to her in German; the third had some reservations about how much Gretchen understood of the German she was speaking, but, in my opinion, an examination of the tape recording of the session in which this colleague participated showed that during it Gretchen understood what was said to her in German and gave a not-inconsiderable number of sensible replies in German.

When someone speaks a foreign language in an intelligible conversation and has not learned the language normally, we parapsychologists refer to the case as one of responsible xenoglossy. (This should not be confused with the phenomenon of "speaking in tongues," which is known in our jargon as glossolalia; the two types of experience are, however, somewhat related.) A case of responsive xenoglossy acquires its significance from the phrase "not normally learned." We must be confident that the subject who shows the ability to speak a foreign language never learned it normally prior to its later manifestation in trances or otherwise.

For the case of Gretchen, only two living persons know whether it is a hoax or not. These are Carroll and Dolores Jay. I cannot claim to have the direct knowledge they have on this matter. If, however, there is somewhere a third person who has a right to say whether the case is authentic or not, this could be myself. I can claim that I made every reasonable effort, and some efforts that may have exceeded the reasonable (and that certainly strained the patience of the Jays), to learn whether Dolores Jay had ever learned German—or, indeed, could have learned German—before the first manifestation of Gretchen, in 1970. My inquiries may have been tedious and vexatious, but at least they permit me now to say confidently that I am convinced Dolores Jay had no normal knowledge of German before the first appearance of Gretchen. I think this equally true of Carroll Jay. (I am excepting here the few words of German, such as "nein" and "ja," that almost every American learns; what we are concerned with is a capacity for intelligible conversation in the language.)

Who was Gretchen? We do not know. She did not give sufficient detail of proper names and dates to permit identification of a person corresponding to her statements. Although the information she gave has permitted some plausible conjectures about when and where she may have lived, we have made no positive identification of her through records in Germany. I regard this as regrettable, but it by no means diminishes the importance of the case. For me, that lies not in the identification of Gretchen as an actual person who once lived—interesting as that would be —but in the responsive xenoglossy.

Cases of responsive xenoglossy provide some of the best

evidence for survival of human personality after death that we have so far obtained. Much of the other evidence of our survival after death has been explained, and therefore explained away, as due to the manifestation of extrasensory perception on the part of a living person. It is supposed that certain psychically gifted persons, usually called mediums or sensitives, may acquire unlimited amounts of detailed information about dead persons from living ones or from printed sources, such as books and documents. (This is not a ridiculous idea even though persons who can accomplish such feats are extremely rare.) Thus equipped with information about a dead person, the medium or sensitive may then present it in the dramatized form of a communication from that person. Thus, a case that includes only information about a deceased person may derive from processes of extrasensory perception between living persons, or from written sources.

There is, however, more to a few cases. I refer to those in which subjects demonstrate skills not normally learned. I claim that skills, of which the ability to speak a foreign language is one, cannot be communicated by extrasensory perception.* If I am correct in this, the (not normally learned) foreign language spoken by a trance personality, such as Gretchen, must have its origin in some deceased person still capable of somehow manifesting through a living body. Opinions may legitimately differ as to the type of manifestation of a deceased person we are observing, and we cannot always choose between alternative interpretations. That we are concerned in such cases with a communication from *some* deceased person who has survived death is, however, my own firm conclusion.

I think that I owe it to readers of this book, and to myself, to distinguish the case of Gretchen as I know it and the present book reporting it by Carroll Jay. This book narrates many occurrences to which I was not a witness, and I have neither the right nor the wish to comment on them. It also contains reports of events, such as sessions with Gretchen and interviews, in which I did participate directly. Concerning the details of most of these, my mem-

---

* For an exposition of the reasons that I think justify this statement, I refer interested readers to my book *Xenoglossy* (Charlottesville: University Press of Virginia, 1974).

ories and notes accord with what Carroll Jay has written.

I am bound to say, however, that there are some matters of attitude and interpretaion, and even a few questions of fact, about which I disagree with him. If I believed that any of these were important to a judgment concerning the interpretation of the case of Gretchen, I would describe them in detail. I do not think this. The matters on which we disagree are subsidiary and in no way lessen the great value of the case. I am happy to give it an unqualified endorsement.

There is one thing more to be said. Carroll Jay's book actually develops two stories threaded together. He describes the development of the case of Gretchen, which is interesting enough by itself. In addition, however, the reader learns about the extraordinary difficulties the Jays had when they tried to present the case to people in the communities in which they lived, and others as well. The Jays were subjected to the sort of harassment that we are inclined to associate with past centuries and are shocked to find occurring in our own. We cannot say that the antagonism Carroll Jay aroused derived exclusively from the development of the case of Gretchen. He was, after all, practicing hypnotism, a phenomenon still poorly understood by scientists and even less well understood by most of the general public. The very word "hypnosis" can generate strong emotions in many persons who hear it. Unfortunately, we often try to deny, and even eliminate, what we do not understand. And some people are willing to persecute anyone who appears to challenge accepted patterns of thinking.

Not everyone would have persisted as earnestly as Carroll and Dolores Jay did in developing the case of Gretchen and exposing it to public scrutiny. The Jays had the option, everyone should understand, of keeping the case of Gretchen entirely to themselves. This would have been an understandable course. It would have spared them much inconvenience (and not just from me). Instead, they decided to offer the case first for scientific investigation and then for the education and instruction of the general public.

Their decision to do this led to consequences that have made this book not only the report of an unusual case, but also a record of exceptional courage. The Jays will have the usual reward of virtue: the sense of having done what one believes to be right. In addition, they may have the gratification of finding that through their sacrifices they have encouraged others who have had a similar experience, perhaps in some cases even better than that of Gretchen, to come forward and offer it also for scientific investigation.

—IAN STEVENSON, M.D.
Carlson Professor of Psychiatry

Division of Parapsychology
Department of Psychiatry
School of Medicine
University of Virginia
Charlottesville, Virginia

June 1977

"No, in time I will ahhhuuuh speak of great mysteries. I will bring others, ahhhuuuh others' knowledge as the vibrations of this soul attune to us."

But Marjorie had no desire to attune to whoever or whatever spoke through her. When she later listened to the tape of the recorded growler who claimed to "have never lived on the earth plane," she wanted to have as

CHAPTER I

The Vision

April 21, 1970, was a glorious day for me and my family. Dolores had prepared a meal fit for a king, Vonda and Mary Jo had baked and decorated a birthday cake, Jesse had helped me transplant a couple of young maple trees, and our oldest daughter, Punky (Mrs. Carol Cain), phoned our home in Greenbush, Ohio, from Philadelphia to wish me a happy birthday.

To say that I was a happy man is to put it mildly: I was a fortunate man, most fortunate! Despite sickness and tribulation over the past few years, life had been good, and I rejoiced in my blessings, as I should have. After all, it is a rare man who has survived seven near-fatal heart attacks, then sat back to bask in the love and companionship of his wife and children on his forty-ninth birthday.

But if life was good that day, all the tomorrows were going to be better. Of that I was sure—I felt it in my bones—but never did I dream that fate (if that be the correct word) would choose that night to propel my wife and me onto a pathway of exotic adventure which, to our great surprise, generated worldwide attention.

The initial event began shortly after Dolores and I had retired for the night: The resounding echoes of a feminine voice roused me from the mists of a twilight sleep. After quickly glancing at my wife and seeing that she was sleeping comfortably, I assumed that the cries came from outside the house. However, after getting out of bed to peer out the window, I was quickly drawn back to my life mate's side, because she exclaimed in a strange, lilting voice, "Oh, what a beautiful horse!"

Never before had I heard her utter a single word in her sleep, and, titillated by the heady prospects of being

1

made privy to her most intimate thoughts (don't we all love to listen to our spouse's uncontrolled thoughts?), I quickly curled up on the bed and waited anxiously for her to speak again. But disappointment was my only reward: She failed to say anything more. So, with nothing better to do, I slipped under the bedcovers and resigned myself to the night's only other alternative: sleep.

But sleep eluded me, and again I got up, intending to go to the kitchen for a midnight snack. After donning my robe and slippers and starting for the door, I was pulled up short, frozen in my tracks by the chilling intuition that Dolores and I were not alone in the room. Quivering with spine tingles (I am not normally afraid of man or beast, but the unseen—that's another story), I frantically searched under the bed, behind the curtains, and in the clothes closet for whoever or whatever had stealthily invaded the privacy of our bedroom. And even though my search proved fruitless, there was no way I could overcome the disquieting feeling that we were not alone; the presence of the unseen eyes was as real as the darkened shadows.

The uninitiated may snicker at my cowardliness, but you can feel terribly alone, even abandoned, even though you know that your children are asleep in their rooms down the hall and your wife is lying but a few feet away. Be that as it may, without apologies for my fear, I made a hasty plunge for the bed to huddle close beside my sleeping wife. And there's a joke in that: I stand an even six feet and weigh one hundred eighty; Dolores, whom I sought for protection, rises only on a bright sunny day to four foot eleven and a scant one hundred pounds.

To be near Dolores was all the strength and comfort I needed. In the thirty years of our marriage we had waded the troubled waters of life and had kicked aside the hard rocks of misfortune by loving, working, and clinging to each other in mutual dependency. Outside of the good Lord and His legion of holy angels, I know of no one whom I would rather have at my side in a time of need than my Dolores.

From the day when we first dated, when she was a little girl of fourteen, we immediately discovered that we were soul mates, in perfect harmony. As such, we had a meeting of the minds, a sort of synchronization—a tuning in to each other's thoughts, à la mind reading, as it was called then; "telepathy" is the modern term. When I was in the Army, and separated from her by several hundred miles, we corresponded frequently, always beginning our letters by noting the exact time and date. On innumerable occasions we wrote to each other on the same day, at the same time, about the same subject, often answering specific questions the other was then putting on paper.

One day I was inexplicably worried about Dolores and wrote to her, "Punkins [yes, that's what I called her in the old days], something tells me that you are not quite up to par physically, so please make an appointment with Dr. Mills immediately, and if need be, have your tonsils removed." Two days later I received a letter from her: "Ked, honeybunch, please don't get alarmed, but today I went to see Dr. Mills and he suggested that I enter the hospital for a tonsillectomy." The letters had been written at exactly the same time.

Thankfully, our interplay of telepathy has continued unabated down through the years. A more recent example occurred during a lull in my psychology class at Lynchburg-Clay High School in Lynchburg, Ohio, where I taught a few years ago. Sitting at my desk while the students were supposedly studying, I blurted without thinking, "Oh no, Dolores! Please, not that!" Naturally, the students laughed and inquired about my embarrassing outburst. I explained: For at least twenty years my family and I had gargled with a popular red mouthwash, but at that precise moment I had clearly envisioned Dolores, in a supermarket some forty miles away, purchasing a large bottle of green mouthwash which had recently come on the market. I had sampled the new mouthwash and didn't like it. As any students would, those in my class hooted and hawed and pooh-poohed my vision, but the last laugh was on them: When I got home that evening a large bottle of green mouthwash sat prominently on a cabinet in the bathroom. Dolores rationalized, "Well, it was on sale and I just couldn't pass up a good buy." Then she added laughingly, "Had I known you were going to monitor my shopping trip with ESP, I'd have sought your advice through ESP before buying."

GRETCHEN, I AM

That fateful night of April 21, 1970, I was hoping that
by being close to Dolores I could rid myself of the feeling
that prying eyes were watching me, so I bundled closer,
thinking she might psychically perceive my fears and
awaken to explain away the presence of the eerie in-
truder. But I was grasping at straws. Even if she had
awakened, it is highly doubtful that she could have done
anything except cower closer to me. Dolores is not di-
vinely endowed with psychic gifts; besides, it is seldom
that ESP will respond on command. Too, simply because
we have an excellent ESP relationship in no way gives us
cause for believing that either of us has the power to
discern and explain away the paranormal. Nevertheless,
hoping to draw comfort from her, I sought tenderly to
pull her closer to me, but, to my consternation, an invisible force seemed to grip my right arm, rendering me helpless.

This was not a new experience. A few months earlier,
during the pastoral visiting that was a duty of my ministry, I had gone to the home of a parishioner who apparently had suffered a stroke shortly before I knocked on
his door. Getting no response, I opened the door and
called out, "Anybody home?" I heard a moan from the
dining room. Quickly, I rushed in and found Old Joe lying on the floor, unconscious. I checked his pulse, then
made a dash for the door to summon help—there was no
phone in the house—but when I got to the door I found
I couldn't lift my hand to the doorknob. Desperately I
willed my arm to move, but it was no go. Frustrated, I
turned, went back to kneel beside Old Joe, and began to
pray. Soon he opened his eyes, sought my hand with his,
and smiled a fond farewell. "I knew you wouldn't leave
me, Preacher. I just couldn't go to my Maker without
someone at my side."

Remembering Old Joe's last moments, I looked at Dolores lying beside me and was seized by apprehension.
Was Dolores ill? Clearly the restraining force on my arm
was the same that I had experienced with Old Joe—
would she too open her eyes and tell me that she was de-
parting this world to be with her Maker?

Several minutes passed as I sat looking at Dolores.
Then the strangest of all things happened: I heard a

voice, and oh, I shuddered, what a night! It was unreal—
incredibly unbelievable! And now I tell you a secret: A
thousand times I assured myself that never would I tell a
soul, not even my wife and children, about that night, but
. . . well, I had done nothing wrong; I was not ashamed.
Besides, there is no way anyone could possibly understand the truth of that night without knowing the complete story.

So—yes, I heard a voice, but, paradoxically, not a
word was spoken, not a sound was made—not a normal
sound, anyway. Still, I had heard something. Who or what
made it, I don't know. I had become so confused by the
bizarre events that I even considered the possibility that
the Lord had spoken to me in a "wee, still, small voice,"
which is not too far removed from my final conclusion:
that I had perceived paradisiacal vibrations which made
me know that a transcendent power had borne Dolores's
spirit on the wings of night to a realm far beyond the con-
fines of our bedroom.

Although I was terribly frightened at first, the memory
of that night is most precious. Never can I forget the
heavenly aura that enveloped Dolores's angelic beauty as
she lay with hands clasped in an attitude of prayer, her
moon-bathed face reflecting a luminous light, pure and
holy. Equally dear to my heart is the memory of her shining eyes slowly opening to emit a radiance which could
only come from one who beheld things celestial.

"Such a lovely girl," she rhapsodized, lips barely moving.

Ah, Dolores, surely the skeptics will insist that you
spoke merely the words of a dreamer, but I shout loud
and clear, "No!" As I live and breathe, I know that all
the powers of heaven were in the room that night, and in
no way can our experience be explained by mouthing
commonalities! It was as if heaven itself came down and
lifted you to heights unknown while transforming my fear
into reverential awe, an alteration as complete as it was
miraculous. God's goodness and mercy had given me
pleasure and joy beyond measure in times past, but never
will I know a more peaceful moment of serenity than was
mine for a short while that night. The old gospel hymn
describes my moments of blissfulness best:

When peace like a river attendeth my way,
When sorrows like sea billows roll;
Whatever my lot, Thou hast taught me to say,
It is well, it is well with my soul.

When Dolores waxed ecstatic about the girl's loveliness, my fears that she might walk the Glory Road with Old Joe were quickly forgotten, and I wondered only about the girl's identity.

"I don't know her name," Dolores said airily.

Even her response to my unasked question added to my elation, indicating that our telepathy was still in good order, sleep or no sleep. But I could not help wondering further: Was she actually asleep? Clearly the exotic conditions surrounding that night lent credence to the belief that she was not experiencing a run-of-the-mill dream or nightmare, and I momentarily questioned whether she was indeed engaging in ESP.

"She's just a girl," Dolores continued. "So beautiful, tiny . . . brown hair braided in a bun, and . . . she's wearing a weskit, you know, laced down the front."

The words were quite ordinary, but the empyreal quality of her voice was a further indication that she communicated from a spiritual realm completely foreign to our world. The atmosphere was electric—phantasmal! Curiosity overwhelmed me, and even though I was reluctant to risk awakening her, because a sense of the eternal was now present, I asked softly, "Dolores, is the girl in your dream actually in the room with us?"

"No," she answered, still looking as though seeing things not meant for mortal eyes while languidly lifting an arm to point. "There! She's there in the meadow."

For the next thirty minutes Dolores recounted the events in her dream, and I hung on every word and expression. (Subsequent knowledge and events taught us that Dolores had experienced a retrocognitive vision in which she saw a young German girl named Gretchen Gottlieb, who lived in the nineteenth century, and who rode a beautiful bay mare side-saddle, her long dark skirt draping to her ankles. For a while, though, I shall use the words "dream" and "vision" interchangeably.) Dolores had never seen the girl before, but from the moment

Gretchen first appeared in the dream Dolores felt a kinship which she said was impossible to describe. Also in the dream was an elderly man, whom she identified only as the girl's uncle; they sat together in a pastoral setting "on the bank above the road," until a scraggly man crept stealthily from the woods behind them and grabbed the horse's reins.

It had been a beautiful dream, and Dolores glowed rapturously until the appearance of the scraggly man transformed her ecstatic joy into instant terror.

"Run, Uncle! Run!" she screamed.

Dreams filled with strangers are commonplace, as are those in which the dreamer is an active participant, yet I was surprised when she referred to the man as "Uncle."

"Watch out, Uncle!" she called frantically. "There's more of them coming up over the bank!"

To my way of thinking, Dolores was getting too involved in the dream, and as I looked into her frightened eyes and tear-stained face I tried to awaken her, fearful of traumatic effects. But she would not awaken. Instead, she began to lash and flail as though fighting for her life before grabbing her head in her arms and collapsing in moans and sobs: "My head! Ohhhh, my head hurts!"

"Dolores, wake up! It's only a dream."

Stirring to look up at me with perplexed eyes, she asked incredulously, "Wake up? I am awake!"

Relieved, I started to get out of bed, calling back, "Good! I'll get a cool cloth to wipe away the tears of your dream."

"Oh, no! Uncle—run—run!" she screamed, and again began to fight her invisible assailant.

Distressed because I had failed to awaken her, I grabbed her by the shoulders and shook her. "Wake up! Do you hear me, wake up!"

"I can't!" she lamented in a sweet, angelic voice, then collapsed to lie inert. "I cannot awaken, not now— never!"

"Oh, come now!" I chided. "Why can't you awaken?"

Dolores did not answer. "Oh, Uncle," she whimpered, "he's . . . he's dead! They . . . they've killed him!"

Suddenly I was tired, so very tired. It had been a long night. Desperately I fought against a fainting weariness;

7

the many heart attacks and my emotional involvement that night had sapped too much of my strength. I simply could not stand the stress, so I lay back to recapture my strength. When I later opened my eyes and looked around, Dolores had sat up and was looking at me as though seeing me for the last time. Softly, gentle as the mist that was settling in those early-morning hours, she spoke ethereally from her hallowed plane: "Always you have been my love, but now—I am not, therefore I do not exist."

"But you do exist!" I reasoned sensibly. "You live as my wife! You are the mother of my children! Here"—I extended my hand and called from the depth of urgency and fear—"take my hand. See! It is flesh and blood! You are flesh and blood! You do exist!"

Deaf to my plea and oblivious to the things of this world, she closed her eyes, slowly bowed her head, and clasped her hands in an attitude of prayer before looking heavenward to petition pleadingly, "Wait, Uncle! Wait! I come—I go with you!"

Finally, with voice trailing on the cool air, she lay back on the bed, turned onto her side, and began to breathe in the deep, even rhythm of natural sleep. Quietly, patiently, hoping that the strangest night of our lives was done, I waited to make certain that her nocturnal excursion in dream had come to an end.

Suddenly there was a knock on the door, scaring me half to death—my nerves were truly frazzled. But it was only Vonda, who called out, "Daddy, is Momma all right?"

"Yes, honey. She . . ." I searched for an answer. I don't lie to my children, but I didn't want to alarm Vonda, then twelve years old. "She's just been talking in her sleep. You go back to bed and don't worry. Everything is fine!"

But was it, really? After twisting and turning in confused thought, I finally got up. The long night of Dolores's strange dream surrendered to dawn as I sat over a cup of coffee, attempting to fathom all that I had seen and heard.

Had Dolores merely dreamed? Something within me shouted, No! Never had anything seemed so out of this world, yet real. Her assertion that she did not exist bothered me tremendously. And what about the presence of that third party which I had sensed so strongly in the room just before the dream began to unfold? And the mysterious force which held my hand back? Ah, yes —that force! Why would it not let me hold my Dolores close to me?

Apparently, as I have reasoned in later years, I do have a guardian angel which keeps me from fouling up more often than usual. In Old Joe's case, calling an ambulance would have done him no good; it was too late— he needed me at his side in his last moments. On other occasions when I have been unable to raise my arm although there was nothing wrong with me physically, a need for my services was present; this will be seen more clearly in subsequent chapters. But that night with Dolores a history-making event was taking place, and I feel certain that future chronicles will record that Dolores's retrocognitive vision was of tremendous importance. Had I been able to move her that night by drawing her close to me, she might have awakened and destroyed the link between events of that night and the subsequent events in our life that can be described only as paranormal if not supernatural.

No matter. The many unanswered questions swarming through my mind that night made me determine to hypnotize Dolores at the first opportunity so that I could make her reexperience her bizarre dream, if indeed it was merely a dream. Enabling people to "redream" is one of hypnotism's strange but wonderful qualities.

For twenty years I had practiced hypnotism, and Dolores was my most willing subject, a human guinea pig. She was a somnambulist (a person who readily enters a deep trance), an excellent subject, and I knew that she would not consider unusual a request that she submit to another session on the couch. Already we had performed almost every experiment known to hypnosis. And since she knew that I viewed hypnosis as both an art and a science, she would not automatically assume I had ulterior motives for wanting to probe her subconscious.

Hypnotherapy had served her and hundreds of others well under my ministration. They had been cured or at least afforded effective relief from migraine headaches, functional hypertension, insomnia, ulcers, backaches, fears and phobias, depression, and other conditions. Probably my most dramatic use of hypnosis occurred on New Year's Day, 1970, when Dolores cut her finger on a knife while washing the dishes and severed an artery. Seeing the blood spurt from the deep, inch-long gash on her right forefinger, Punky screamed for me to come quickly. Dashing to the kitchen, I immediately touched Dolores on the forehead with three fingers, activating a posthypnotic suggestion for trance induction, and commanded, "Relax! As you relax, the bleeding will stop, your finger will not hurt, and it will heal rapidly." As Dolores lapsed into a trance, the spurting blood stopped as if I had turned a valve which cut off circulation, all in a matter of seconds. When I brought her out of the trance she wrapped a bandage around her finger and resumed washing the dishes. There was no more pain or bleeding.

This dream was something else, and as I sat idly stirring my coffee, I looked up and saw Dolores emerge from the bedroom, in high spirits, never indicating that she remembered the traumatic events of the night. When I asked if she had had any good dreams, she smiled.

"No, I slept soundly."

Later that afternoon, without mentioning the dream, I asked her to submit to hypnosis, and after she had made herself comfortable on the couch I induced hypnosis with the usual posthypnotic suggestion. As the trance deepened and the heavy, rhythmical breathing and relaxed muscles indicated that she was in the somnambulistic state, I began the process of having her re-create the dream. Soon REM (Rapid Eye Movement), increased pulse, and fluttering hands indicated that the dream was in progress.

"Dolores, you are now able to speak clearly. You will tell me everything that you are experiencing right now."

With a slight thickness of tongue, a sleep inflection normal for most people in hypnosis, she observed, "There is a girl in the meadow. She's young, beautiful."

"Do you know the girl?"

"No, not really. And yet . . ." She paused reflectively. "There's something about her that is terribly familiar."

"How old is she? Can you guess her age."

"No need to guess"—she smiled—"she's sixteen." Then she added, as if reading my thoughts, "I know that you're wondering how I know her age, but—well, she is sixteen, believe me."

Although I did wonder how she could have known the girl's age, I did not think it strange that she knew. The experienced hypnotist soon learns that the knowledge exhibited by some people when in hypnosis often seems incredible. But a subject in hypnosis does not have an increase in latent knowledge; it only seems that way sometimes, because everything a person ever sees, hears, or thinks is recorded in the brain's memory bank, and an entranced person has easier access to those memories than someone in the walking state, because the hypnotized person's active, conscious mind is at rest, permitting the unencumbered subconscious to call forth specific data on command.

Too, some hypnotized subjects are more susceptible than others to receiving psychic information, such as telepathy, spirit communion, etc. Dr. Ian Stevenson, Carlson Professor of Psychiatry at the University of Virginia School of Medicine, states in "New Cases of Xenoglossy" that "under the special circumstances provided by hypnosis, a previous personality could come to the surface." He believes that both reincarnation and spirit possession can be sources of new information for people in hypnosis.

In other words, if someone in hypnosis begins imparting information about another, quite distinct life, it might very well be that that person has been regressed and is recalling the events of a former life. If that be true, obviously the reincarnated entity is privy to the knowledge gained in a former life as well as in this one, which would make the entity seem extra-intelligent. If a discarnate spirit chooses to enter into or speak through a person in hypnosis, the hypnotized person appears to have inexplicable knowledge. In fact, no information coming from a spiritual entity through a person in hypnosis can be credited to that person, because the entranced person is merely a channel through whom the spirit speaks.

Prior to Dolores's strange dream I had regressed hundreds of people in an attempt to disprove the theory that hypnosis could be used to prove scientifically the reality of reincarnation, yet now I did not even consider the possibility that her dream had any relationship to a prior life, possibly because she was not hypnotized at the time; nor did I consider the possibility that a spirit might be speaking through her, even though I was fairly certain that the unknown presence in our bedroom was a spirit from another world.

I began regressing persons simply because I had read several books in which the authors had attempted to prove that evidence of a former life was revealed in stories told by subjects in regression. While a few of the stories reflected what some persons considered evidence of a prior life, the majority seemed to provide very flimsy evidence for such suppositions. But I will discuss this in greater length in later chapters.

As Dolores lay on the couch re-creating the previous night's dream, she slowly clasped her hands in an attitude of prayer and breathed admiringly, "Such a lovely horse."

Although Dolores eventually became an active participant when the original dream unfolded, it would have been improper for me to suggest while she was in hypnosis that her subconscious go directly to the point at which she assumed the role of the girl in her dream. The re-creation had to be a spontaneous emission from her subconscious. However, there have been occasions when I did give instructions to subjects which encouraged them to elaborate on certain events which, awake, they might have considered extraneous material. It was with that purpose that I asked Dolores to reveal intimate details about the girl in her dream.

"Dolores, describe the girl. Tell me what she looks like and how she is dressed."

Tilting her head back as though looking up at the girl sitting sidesaddle on her horse, she responded studiously, "She's petite, brown hair—braided in a bun—and she's wearing a weskit, you know, laced down the front. Oh!" She blanched. "She's leaving! She's going into the forest."

"That's all right, Dolores. Relax! Go into the forest with her. Go along and tell me everything you see and hear."

Immediately Dolores sat up and looked around, then rose to walk to the end of the room, at times stepping around or stumbling over objects invisible to me, possibly tree stumps or brush which were a part of her dream. Then, stopping and turning with a gasp, she buried her face in her hands and sobbed uncontrollably.

"Dolores, what happened? What did you see?"

Gaining a measure of control and wiping her tears on her sleeve, she exclaimed in relief, "Thank God you've come!" Obviously she was referring to her uncle. But her relief was short-lived, and she returned to the couch, sat down heavily, and began to struggle.

"Let go, you beast!" she screamed. "Get your hands off the bridle!"

Sometimes it is hilarious to be a spectator at the wild imaginings of another person's dream, but I assure you it can be dreadfully painful to watch the one you love suffer the torments of hell at your request.

"Run, Uncle, run! Ohhhhh, there's more of them coming up over the bank!" she shrieked before doubling over in pain, holding her head, and calling weakly, "Speak to me, Uncle! Talk to me, please!"

I felt callous just sitting there, not offering to help her, yet it was imperative that I remain objective even when the strongest tugs of my emotions urged me to intervene. So I submerged my feelings and placated my conscious by reasoning "It's just a dream."

"Murderers!" Dolores charged, slipping to the floor, her face mirroring sheer agony.

I could take no more—I was not nearly so tough as I had thought. Overcome by pathos, and realizing that nothing really new was coming from her subconscious, I decided to bring her out of the trance.

"Dolores, relax! In a few minutes you will awaken; you will forget the dream; you will have absolutely no remembrance of the dream after awakening."

Seeming to obey my instructions, she went limp and lay on the floor.

"Now, I want you to get up, go to the couch, and lie down."

"No," she responded meekly, "I shall not awaken."

"But you will! You are merely dreaming."

"No! No dream," she protested dogmatically. "This is real, very, very real!"

"How can it possibly be real, not being able to awaken when you are merely in a trance—asleep, so to speak?"

Sitting up and brushing away the tears, she smiled as a teacher might in addressing a dull child. "You still don't understand, do you?"

"Understand what?"

"That I am that girl!"

"So," I agreed, "you were that girl, but only in a dream." Then, noting her glazed eyes, I added, "You're still dreaming."

"Impossible!" she insisted, the smile fading. "I am that girl!"

Realizing the futility of arguing with her, I began a process of progression. "All right, Dolores, relax! You may be that girl, but for now I want you to move ahead in time. You will move ahead until you become my wife, Dolores Jay, living with me and our children in the parsonage at Greenbush, Ohio."

Slowly she relaxed and lay on the floor, again clasping hands in an attitude of prayer. "Now," I instructed her, "get up, go to the couch, lie down, and make yourself comfortable."

Obediently she did as instructed, and after she had reclined on the couch I continued to instruct her. "You will sleep for thirty minutes; you will forget the dream and you will awaken rested and refreshed. The memory of the dream will be completely gone."

Thirty minutes later Dolores awoke and felt chipper. But not me. The events of the past twenty-four hours had taken their toll; her actions haunted me, and as I took my afternoon stroll her statement "I am that girl" plagued me. Had she really just been dreaming? Was she merely recalling the events of her life as a teenager?

For the first time I began to consider whether it was possible that she might have lived in another lifetime, in another place as another person. But nothing she had said lent credence to the belief that anything more substantial than a dream had occurred. She had not given the girl or her uncle a name; no locale other than the meadow and forest was given; even the description of the clothing was not all that unusual, especially in a dream. Obviously it was just a dream, and it would not be bothering me so except for my feeling that an uninvited guest had been present in our bedroom. But even the phantasmal atmosphere could have been nothing more than my own emotional fantasy. Still, why hadn't she awakened, especially when I shook her?

Clearly, the answer to all the questions that swarmed through my mind would not come easy, other than the one concerning her youth. Dolores and I first met when she was thirteen. As I previously stated, we began dating when she was fourteen. But nothing in her dream tallied with her actual life. True, like the girl in her dream, she was small and had brown hair, but to my recollection she had never worn a weskit or braided her hair in a bun; and she had never ridden a horse, although she had always had a strange love and fascination for horses. And if the girl really was sixteen, it could not have been Dolores, because she had not had an uncle die while she was in her teens. There was always the possibility that in the dream she was re-creating a novel she had read or a movie she had seen. But, if so, her fantasizing was extremely vivid.

As if I had not had enough of the paranormal for a while, that evening Vonda added spice to an already overly rich day. After dinner she went across the road to the Greenbush School with some friends to watch the Greenbush Little League Bombers practice baseball. It was a delightfully warm spring evening, and a good-size crowd had gathered to sit in folding chairs and in the bleachers. Soon, growing tired of the practice session, she and her friends went for a walk. Directly in back of the school was a large maple tree, and as the girls walked past it Vonda saw a ball of shiny gray mist hovering about head high on the tree trunk.

Fascinated but not frightened, she stared at it for quite some time before looking around to see if anyone else was looking at it. No one else seemed to be paying any attention. Drawn to the glistening phenomenon, she turned back to look at the hovering mass, which had moved away from the tree. She continued to marvel at the incredible sight until one of her friends tugged at her arm and said, "C'mon, Vonda, let's go over to the swings." When she got to the swings, some seventy-five feet away, she again looked to the tree for the "shiny gray ball that floated." It was gone.

"Daddy," she queried reverently later that evening, "I didn't say anything to anyone about it because I was afraid they wouldn't believe me, but it was real, and—oh, I wonder if it was a sign from heaven, if it had some important meaning for us."

Whether it was a sign or not I'll never know. I do know that from that day on paranormal occurrences have never been far removed from us.

Not long after Vonda's experience, Cid Posey, a friend from Batavia, Ohio, and the father of three young sons, came to my study "just to talk," he said. Cid was extremely nervous and gave every indication that he had a specific problem he wanted to discuss. Finally he said, "Preacher, the strangest thing happened the other day, and, well—I've got to talk to someone about it or go crazy. Remember a couple of weeks ago when Charlie Weston died and was buried— But you'll never believe me . . ."

"Try me and see." I smiled, hoping to put him at ease. He looked paler than usual.

"This past Saturday morning," he began, "we were all still in bed—it was about six A.M.—when my wife and I heard Jud, our youngest boy [he was about seven or eight years old at the time] making a terrible racket. Well, Lana jumped out of bed and ran to his room, where she found him leaning out the window yelling, 'Where'd you go? What did you want?' Jud was wide awake, mind you, and when Lana asked, 'What in the world are you doing, boy?' Jud told her that something had woke him up and when he opened his eyes he saw Charlie standing at the foot of his bed, pleading, 'Help me! Help me!' "

Cid smiled nervously. "Of course, Jud yelled at Charlie, 'Hey, how'd you get in here? What you want?' And 'Mister, you better get out of here quick before my dad finds you! Get out! If you don't go I'm gonna call my dad!' And, Preacher, believe it or not, Charlie started to leave through the window, but as he was crawling out his foot tripped on the sill, and he fell out. Naturally, Jud jumped up and ran to the window, thinking Charlie had hurt himself in the fall, but when Jud got to the window, ol' Charlie was gone." Cid leaned back and relaxed, with the palms of his hands turned up. "Now what do you make of that?"

"Maybe Jud had been grieving over Charlie's death. Maybe he—"

"No, Preacher, that can't be it! You see, Jud didn't even know Charlie other than to see him on the street a time or two, and we didn't tell the boys that Charlie was dead. We never discuss death in front of the children; we don't want to scare them, you know."

Well, to each his own thoughts about Vonda and her shiny gray ball, about Jud and Charlie's mysterious appearance, but this much I know: Some of us in this world have been permitted to see and hear things not common to the natural eye and ear—things of the spirit world—and whether we can understand or explain those things is immaterial. They do exist! They have always existed!

CHAPTER II

Gretchen Speaks:
Voices from the Unknown

Three weeks had slipped by rapidly, and the strange dream was all but forgotten when Dolores was laid low with a severe backache, the result of a childhood tumbling-class accident. As I had done so many times in the past, I hypnotized her to induce analgesia. After waiting a few minutes to ascertain that she was sleeping soundly and the pain was completely gone, I left the bedroom. It was my custom after treating her with hypnotherapy to make the suggestion that she would slip from a hypnotic trance into natural sleep. It always worked, producing beneficial rest and comfort.

When I returned to the bedroom, about thirty minutes later, Dolores moved ever so slightly on the bed and shouted in a strange and alien voice something that sounded like "Geen veck! Geen veck!" At first I dismissed the outburst as nonsense syllables uttered in her sleep. Second thoughts made me realize that she might be suffering from a recurrence of pain, and I inquired, "Hon, are you all right?"

"Ja. Ja!" she drawled in that same strange, alien voice.

Amused at her response, I smiled. "Does your back still hurt?"

"Nein." She sighed, and nestled against the pillows.

Now, I am not a student of languages—I have never studied a foreign language other than high-school Latin—but a knowledge of languages was not a prerequisite for understanding the German words "ja" and "nein," which I had learned mean "yes" and "no" during my younger days, in World War II. Looking at my wife lying quietly on the bed, my curiosity began to grow, and I wondered:

Was she actually speaking a foreign language? Possibly German? *

I was inclined to think it impossible. In fact, it seemed sheer nonsense to even think such a thing. Dolores had never studied a foreign language. But those words, "ja" and "nein"—she had spoken them clearly, and I was certain I had heard her correctly. So although I was filled with ambivalence, there was but one thing to do: set up the tape recorder and ply her with questions.

The possibility that she was speaking a foreign language was not so farfetched as it first seemed. Of the hundreds of people I had hypnotized, several had surprised me by speaking in a foreign language while in the trance state. However, after coming out of the trance all had admitted to having learned the language previously. Dolores could have learned the language as a child or even later in life and forgotten it. Since I had not regressed her that day, or made an effort to determine the depth of her trance state, it was also possible that she was playing a game with me. She knew that I could not speak a foreign language, that it would be comparatively easy to fool me by mouthing foreign-sounding gibberish.

Not really knowing what to expect, I cautiously inquired, "What is your name?"

Moistening her lips and swallowing a couple times, Dolores responded, in a soft, girlish voice, "Ich bin Gretchen."

Still thinking she might be playing a game, I continued, with great hesitation. "How old are you?"

"Neun," she answered after a pause of several seconds.

If Dolores was putting me on, she was doing a good job of it. There was nothing to indicate that her answers were anything but sincere, so I went on. "Where do you live?"

Frowning and lifting her hands as if frustrated, she hesitated. "Ich . . . Ich verstehe nicht. [I . . . I don't understand.]"

Neither did I. Completely at a loss as to what she was saying, but judging from her facial expressions that she

* To avoid confusion for readers, Gretchen's German has been clarified in some passages. Also, the sequence of events in the case (though not the events themselves) has been altered on two occasions to insure clarity.

was confused, I rephrased the question. "In what town do you live?"

Smiling like a child proud of her home town, she almost cooed, "Ich lebe in Bergenstrasse [I live in Bergenstrasse.]"

"And in what country is Bergenstrasse located?" I followed through, understanding only the word "Bergenstrasse."

"Deutschland. [Germany.]"

Dolores's responses were incredible and I must again emphasize that I found it almost impossible to believe what I was hearing. She could not speak a foreign language—that I knew for sure!—yet she seemed to be doing exactly that. I blurted out testily:

"C'mon, Dolores! You've had your fun! Let's call it a day."

Quickly she shot back, "Ich verstehe nicht! [I do not understand!]"

I was sobered by the sincerity of her exclamation. My skepticism abated, and I continued with the questions:

"Is there a street in front of your house?"

Relieved that I had softened my voice, she replied happily, "Ja. Ich lebe in Birkenstrasse. [Yes. I live on Birch Street.]"

"And does your house have a number?"

Wrinkling her brow: "Ich weiss nicht. [I do not know.]"

Still unable to understand her, I continued blithely, "What is your mother's name?"

With lips pursed and face clouding as though she were about to cry, she uttered sadly, "Meine Mutter tot sein. [My mother is dead.]"

One thing was certain: Dolores was either the world's greatest actress or she was coming on with the real thing. Despite a twinge of pity, I barged on. "What is your father's name?"

"Hermann," she answered with filial devotion.

"Gretchen—that is your name, isn't it?"

"Ja, Gretchen, ich bin. [Yes, Gretchen, I am.]"

"Gretchen, what is your last name?"

"Gottlieb."

"What kind of work does your father do?"

"Mein Vater, der Bürgermeister. [My father, the mayor.]"

"Do you have any brothers or sisters?"

"Nein, kein Schwester, kein Bruder. [No, no sister, no brother.]"

All through the interview Dolores had shown no sign of nervousness, but now she began to exhibit great fear and placed a forefinger to her lips and shushed me. "Mehr sagen sehr schlecht, verboten! [More talking is very bad, forbidden!]"

In ignorance, I attempted to continue. "Gretchen—"

"Nein! Nein!" she exploded, before lowering her voice and whispering fearfully, "Der Bundesrat! Sie hören. Sie zuhören! [The National Council! They hear. They listen!]"

Alarmed by her tense expression, I began to probe for an explanation.

"What are you trying to say, Gretchen?"

Opening her eyes and frantically searching the room, she whispered, "Sie hören zu! [They are listening!]"

Aggravated because I could not understand anything she said apart from the proper nouns, I tried to frame the questions in a logical sequence, presuming that she understood me and would give sensible answers to my questions. Thus, guided by her facial expressions, I continued. "Where is the Bundesrat?"

"Der ist überall. [It is everywhere.]"

"Oh . . ."

"Überall! Sie hören zu. Das ist gefährlich. [Everywhere! They listen. That is dangerous.]"

The questioning had gone on for more than an hour, and Dolores was becoming restless. When I asked if she was all right, she sighed, said "Gretchen ist sehr müde [Gretchen is very tired]," and refused to answer any more questions.

The emerging personality calling itself Gretchen was extremely slow to answer the questions, but that was not altogether unusual; many regressed subjects exhibit the same trait, though not to the same degree. I wasn't concerned about the length of time she took to respond—just hearing her talk was more than enough to make me know that perhaps something strange and wonderful had happened in our bedroom that April night.

After Dolores awoke, sat up, stretched, and yawned, as most people do following an extended session of deep hypnotic sleep, I asked, "Feel better?"

"Wonderful!" She continued to yawn, stretch, and rub her eyes. "Ohhhh, I slept so soundly—I must have been clear out of this world."

Dolores can never remember anything she says or does while in a hypnotic trance, and I thought, "Oh, girl! If you only knew just how far out you really were, you might never sleep again." If the things Dolores/Gretchen said actually had substance—if it could be verified that she spoke a true foreign language—then it was a foregone conclusion that I had stumbled on the greatest phenomenon of the century, and I tingled from head to toe with excitement.

Even before the questioning ended I was making plans to find someone who spoke German; I wanted to verify my impression that Dolores actually had spoken a foreign language before informing her of the tape's content. Incidentally, since I had not regressed her (taken her back in time), she must have spontaneously regressed—another first for Dolores. Regression is not an automatic function of hypnosis; normally it must be induced.

I took the tape to school the next day hoping to locate a teacher who could speak German. Regrettably, no one at the school could speak the language, but Miss Mary Muntz, the French teacher, had studied German in high school and remembered just enough to confirm my suspicion that Dolores had actually spoken German. Anxious to assist me in unraveling the mystery, she suggested that I contact Dr. Jacob Langert, a professor at the University of Cincinnati who was acknowledged to be an authority on both hypnosis and the German language. My spirits soared when Dr. Langert agreed to see me that afternoon in his office.

I was on cloud nine until partway to the university, the seriousness of my mission began to dawn on me. What would I do if the good professor agreed with Miss Muntz that Dolores actually had spoken German? The question was of vital importance, because most authorities on hypnosis were adamant in their belief that no one in hypnosis could speak a foreign language without having learned that language in this life. In response to a question posed in his thesis, Dr. F. L. Marcuse asked, "Can a person in hypnosis play a piano or speak a foreign language if these are suggested to a person in hypnosis?" He answered, "Yes, providing they could do so before they were hypnotized." Leslie LeCron and Jean Bordeaux report that "all hypnotic accomplishments are in accordance with natural laws, and . . . no one in hypnosis can speak a foreign language which is not already known." They then add, "nothing in hypnosis can be done that is contrary to natural law." Clearly, although they did not know that Dolores had spoken German in hypnosis, or that she had never learned the language, they were saying that she could not do what Miss Muntz and I knew she had done.

But, and this is vitally important: In the waking state Dolores could not speak a foreign language! She had never studied a foreign language! No one in her family had ever spoken or studied a foreign language, and she had never lived near anyone who spoke German as a normal means of conversation. Logically there was no reason to believe that she could speak a foreign language. Her newly discovered ability, if it was real, was contrary to everything I knew of her past life as well as contrary to all scientific supposition. Yet I had heard her speak German with my own ears, and it was all there on tape for anyone to hear!

When I first arrived at the university, Dr. Langert affected a jovial mood that belied his skepticism. With what seemed to me a cynical smile and arched eyebrows expressing doubt, he said, "You say that she cannot speak German, eh?"

"Not unless she is in a hypnotic trance," I countered while leaning over to turn on the recorder.

Lounging in his high-backed chair with an air of sophistication, the learned professor quickly swung forward and glared at the recorder as Dolores's sleepy utterances flowed from the tape. Flushing, he scowled. "Dammit! Just this morning I taught my psychology class that this was impossible!"

"So she does speak German!" I chimed.

"Yes, apparently!" he railed. "But only because she learned the language. She had to have learned it at some time in her life!"

Elated to learn that she had actually spoken German, but chagrined at the veiled insinuation that Dolores and I had conspired to perpetrate a hoax, I departed the professor's office in the full belief that the professor had heard a miracle, that his conclusion had something to do with his inability to explain the strange phenomenon I had dumped in his lap.

During the forty-mile ride home I made plans for discussing with Dolores her new-found abilities. Obviously, if Dr. Langert's retort was prophetic, when the world heard of her ability they would do as he did: accuse us by innuendo of trickery, or accuse her of deceiving me.

I knew in my heart that there was no deceit on my part, and I found it impossible to believe that Dolores would do such a thing. Thirty years of togetherness through thick and thin had made me know that she was a woman honest beyond measure. Still, I must confess that that old devil, Satan, made me wonder if she had secretly learned the language. And if so, why?

Try as I might, I could not imagine when or where she could have learned the language without my knowing it; neither could I conceive of any reason why she would want to. It didn't make sense!

The only time Dolores and I had been separated for any length of time was during my stint in the Army in World War II. Perhaps she could have learned the language then—but no! She had lived with my parents during that time, and had she spent any extended time away from home for study, or secreted herself in her room for any long periods of study, my parents would have known. No, I was convinced that she had never conspired to deceive me, but that would not prevent me from making a concerted effort to learn where the language came from.

That evening after dinner, after the children had gone out to play, I cautiously inquired of Dolores, "When did you learn how to speak German?"

Surprised by my question, she exclaimed, "When did I do what?"

Flustered by her genuine surprise, and ashamed of

even having thought that she might have learned the language, I had to force myself to repeat the question.

"Me?" she laughingly scoffed. "Me speak German? Oh, that'll be the day!"

"No, hon, I'm serious."

"But you can't be!" she challenged. "There is no way! Besides, when did you ever hear me speak even one word in German?"

"Yesterday, in hypnosis."

"I don't believe it," she argued, somewhat subdued. "It's all so ridiculous! Is this some kind of a joke?"

Getting the tape recorder and setting it on the coffee table, I confronted her with the evidence. "Here, you listen and then deny that you can speak German."

"Sie hören zu," the childish voice whispered from the tape.

Tensing at the sound of the strange, alien voice, Dolores leaned forward on the edge of the couch. Staring intently at the recorder, her brow creased and clenched fists showing whitened knuckles, she stammered, "I—I don't understand!"

". . . ist gefährlich." the voice droned.

Dolores protested, "That's not my voice!"

So it wasn't, and yet the voice coming from the tape had come through her lips.

Dolores was not convinced. She knew that it was not unusual to hear a strange voice come from the recorder; regressed persons describing another life often speak with a different voice. Males sometimes speak in a feminine soprano and females in a deep, male bass. Young people can speak with an aged huskiness, and older folk have talked of their younger days in a childish lilt.

Again I wondered: Was it possible that she had learned the language as a child and then forgotten it? Well, yes, it was possible. Several persons have spoken a foreign language in hypnosis, a language they earnestly believed they had not learned. However, subsequent investigations have shown that they learned the language when they were children and, possibly because of a lack of someone to converse with, ceased speaking it; people can even forget that they ever learned a language. This is especially true in immigrant families; infants learned to imitate the Old

25

World language of their parents, but when their parents learned English and ceased to speak the old language, the children naturally followed suit.

While it was possible Dolores could have learned the German language as a child, it was highly improbable because no one in her family had ever spoken a foreign language.

There was always the possibility that she had learned the language subconsciously. There is recorded the case of a young man who demonstrated the ability to speak a few phrases of Oscan, an ancient dialect spoken in Italy in the third century B.C. In the waking state the young man had no knowledge of the language—he swore he had never learned the language. Still, in hypnosis he clearly spoke the words that were ultimately identified as Oscan. Stranger still, he was correct in believing that he had not consciously learned the language. Investigation revealed that he had visited a library and seen an open Oscan grammar, and while looking at the strange language, he subconsciously memorized the words—an acquisition of knowledge he did not know of until it was displayed in a hypnotic trance.

Learning subconsciously is rather common. The specific ability exhibited by the young man is less common. He exhibited a trait comparable to that of eidetikers, who mentally "photograph" a page or pages of written material and at a later date are able to recall the optical impression in vivid, minute detail. That is, they recall the pages as mental pictures and thus are able to read the material recorded in the mental image.

As I watched Dolores sitting on the couch in rapt attention, listening intently to every syllable emanating from the recorder, I began to really realize for the first time that something bordering on the supernatural had occurred if —and that was a big if—she had not learned the language at one time, either consciously or subconsciously.

When the tape ended, I inquired, "What are you thinking?"

"I still don't believe it!" she exclaimed. "This is impossible! I cannot speak German in the waking state, so how could I possibly do so when asleep, in a trance?"

"Maybe you're a second Bridey Murphy," I teased.

"Maybe you've been reincarnated and that voice is your old self come back to see how you're making out in this life."

"Fun-ny!" she quipped with a faint trace of a smile. "Very funny, especially when you know I don't believe in reincarnation."

"Neither do I," I hastened to assure her, "but the mere fact that you and I don't believe in reincarnation does not in any way lessen the fact that it may indeed be a reality." In a lighter vein, I added to reduce the tension, "Maybe a longlost spirit is speaking through you."

"Now you're really talking nonsense." She laughed before adding soberly, "Unless . . . ohhhh, surely you don't think I'm spirit-possessed, do you?"

"Of course not! I was merely joshing."

"But it is possible, isn't it?" she searched uneasily. "I mean, well, there's been so much talk about demons lately, and—"

"Oh, c'mon now!" I interrupted. "You're letting your imagination run wild!"

"But I'm serious," she continued. "If a spirit spoke through me, wouldn't it first have to possess me?"

Too late I realized that my attempted levity had gotten me into hot water. Common sense should have told me that under the circumstances spirits would be a touchy subject.

"Whoa, wait!" I pleaded. "Surely you realize that I have no idea as to what this is all about, that there is a whole lot of homework to be done before we can arrive at an answer, so please, don't go jumping off the deep end too quickly."

For several days Dolores lived in a world of deep thought. She neither ate well nor slept well, and it soon became apparent that she was becoming more and more upset by the disquieting material that flowed from her subconscious.

Several times I reasoned, "Dolores, try to keep calm. 'All things do work together for good to them that love God, and are called according to His purpose.' Besides, if this is real, if other language experts confirm your ability to speak German, and if it can be proven that you never learned the language, then—"

"What do you mean, if I never learned the language?" she challenged testily. "You know very well that I never learned the language."

"Well, yes, I do know that you never made a conscious effort to learn it, but—"

"Are you intimating," she interrupted with a sardonic smile, "that I learned to speak German while I was out cold, unconscious?"

"Oh, c'mon now! You know what I mean!"

"Do I, really?"

"Well, don't you?"

"To be perfectly honest, no!"

For quite some time Dolores sat silently brooding; then: "No! I don't see how anyone could be unconscious and learn anything!"

"But I didn't say that you learned German while you were unconscious, out cold! I meant, well—maybe, just maybe there was a time when someone around you spoke German, and without your knowing it, your subconscious recorded it somewhere in the deep recesses of your mind."

The explanation seemed to momentarily satisfy, but then she responded, "No, I don't recall ever hearing anyone speak German except on television, possibly *Hogan's Heroes.*"

"Whether you recall any such person is immaterial," I countered. "The fact remains there may have been such a person, and it is imperative that we check with all our friends, neighbors, and relatives to see if they remember anyone who might have spoken German in your presence."

With growing apprehension she asked, "But what if we don't find anyone from whom I might have learned the language?"

"Well, then, I'll hypnotize you and pry out all your most precious secrets!"

"You wouldn't dare!" she bristled.

"Well," I hedged, "it's either that or search for another means of determining how you learned to speak German."

"How many times must I tell you that I did not learn to speak German!" she retorted in exasperation.

"But those people out there, the world doesn't know

that! And this means that you and I must be willing to do anything, and I mean anything, even undergo any kind of a test necessary to prove that neither of us ever learned the language!"

With a guarded look she asked, "What kind of a test?"

"Well, a lie detector—"

"I'll take it!" she interrupted joyfully. "I've not lied! I don't know where the German comes from!"

The following day I again regressed Dolores, fully intending to communicate with the Gretchen personality, but Dolores did not respond as I had expected. After apparently passing back beyond the realm of this life, her spirit seemed to halt in a continuum of time which some parapsychologists have described as a plane of existence between earthy lives.

Never before had Dolores exhibited fear of the unknown while in a hypnotic trance, but that night she was so tense that her skin flushed a purplish-blue and the veins of her neck and temples were so grossly extended that her rapid pulse could be visually counted from a distance.

"Dolores, speak to me! Tell me, what is wrong?"

Through dry lips faded a pale gray, she rasped agonizingly, "Oh, those poor souls . . . nameless faces . . . thousands of them . . . pleading, screaming!"

Although deeply touched by the dreadful horror in her voice, I nonetheless pressed for more information:

"What people? Where are you?"

"I don't know," she lamented. "Oh, the torment! They're reaching out to me and I can't help them. Oh God! Mercy! Have mercy on them!"

In previous regressions the outreach of Dolores's spirit had occasionally become suspended in that sphere where entities supposedly exist between lives, but never before had she indicated that anyone was in torment; and although this is not to debate the question of a literal hell in the afterlife, we confess that the possibility of torment in hell became especially real for the both of us in that moment.

In my many years as a minister ordained in the United Methodist Church, I had developed an aversion to overzealous ministers who resorted to the threat of literal hellfire and brimstone in their attempt to win souls for Christ.

29

Still, I did and do believe in hell: "Vengeance is mine; I will repay, saith the Lord." But although I believed there would be torment for all the unfortunates who had become separated from God (that is hell!), never had I conceived that the torment of hell could be so agonizingly awful until I heard Dolores plead for the salvation of those nameless, faceless, anguished souls. And I wondered: Was Dolores actually granted providentially a fleeting peek into hell? Was it possible for mortals still on this side of the grave to ascend into the heavenly abode of the redeemed, or—God forbid—descend into the pits of perdition? Had Dolores actually seen the hoary deeps of hell?

If we can believe the spiritualists, it seems reasonable to believe so. Frederic W. H. Myers, under the aegis of the British Society for Psychical Research, conducted advanced studes on the paranormal for thirty years prior to his death. Then, for thirty years afterward he supposedly sent back information from the afterworld, mostly through a medium named Geraldine Cummins of Cork, Ireland.

Myers, for what it is worth, divided the afterlife into seven major stages. Stage one is the "Earth Plane"; stage two is the condition of the individual immediately after death: the "Intermediate of the Plane of Hades." Stage three is the "Plane of Illusion," and stage four is the "Plane of Color" or the "World of Eidos." Stage five is the "Plane of Flame," or the "World of Helios," and stages six and seven are the "Plane of Light" and "Plane of Timelessness," advanced states of spiritual existence that can best be described as planes of spiritual perfection too glorious to be depicted with our limited vocabulary.

Although Myers did not conceive of the second state, the "Intermediate of the Plane of Hades," in the same way Fundamentalists conceive of hellfire and brimstone, he intimated that stage two did resemble the ancient concept of a hellish place or plane.

While Dolores envisioned the horrible scene and lay trembling, I did not take time to consider theological or parapsychological premises, but this much is certain: To her it was real, and her excursion to the hellish place was not unique. Many persons in regression have experienced the same or similar horror.

For example, a beautiful young farm wife came to my

study a few years ago and said, "I want to be regressed."

I had known Marjorie as a friend and hypnotic subject for quite some time, and, laughing, I said, "Why? You got a hangup stemming from some long-suppressed vice?"

"No," she explained, "nothing like that. I . . . well, there are times when I am certain I have lived before."

"Déjà vu?"

"Not really. It's just that, well, sometimes I feel that I am not me, times when I say things and do things that the real me would never say or do." Then, looking at me hopefully: "You do understand what I'm saying, don't you?"

Marjorie had voiced a common feeling, and I agreed to do what I could for her. But after putting her into a trance and regressing her, I was shocked by the radical, gruesome transformation that changed her from a delicate, dainty person into a hideous gargoyle. Even now I can hear the deep, coarse, male voice growling through bared teeth with bated breath as she lay on the couch, "You must remove the ahhhuuuh large pillow from under the head as the ahhhuuuh spine must be perfectly straight."

Quickly lifting Marjorie's head and removing the pillow, I inquired of the alien voice that railed asthmatically through exhaling breaths, "Who are you? What do you want?"

"I am not of this world. I ahhhuuuh am not of this body. I am an original soul. I am ahhhuuuh one who works with her, and helps her, and ahhhuuuh guides and directs her in spiritual matters. I choose not ahhhuuuh to be called by name. When I am given an identity, it will ahhhuuuh distract from the work we do together. I am one of the soul mates, who ahhhuuuh works in close communion with this soul on the earth plane."

I interrupted, insisting on an identity. "Tell me who you are, or at least tell me your real purpose for speaking through Marjorie."

The voice rasped, "I have never lived on the earth plane; I ahhhuuuh do not have an earthly identity. There are ahhhuuuh many souls who have stepped into the time zone of earth life. There are ahhhuuuh many like me who work with souls on the earth plane."

"If you have never lived in this life," I questioned disbelievingly, "is your frame of knowledge bounded by our time frame?"

"No. In time I will ahhhuuuh speak of great mysteries; I will bring others, ahhhuuuh others knowledge as the vibrations of this soul attune to us."

But Marjorie had no desire to attune to whoever or whatever spoke through her. When she later listened to the tape of the recorded growler who claimed to "have never lived on the earth plane," she wanted to hear no more from the spirit world.

It was not the growler who repelled her. Unlike most somnambulists (who are amnesic), Marjorie had a vivid recollection of her ugly experience. She said she felt herself going down, "whirling down, down and around as though being sucked into the yawning arms of hell through a huge funnel. And then," she added with a shiver, "all around me I saw thousands of people, creatures—some lamenting, some praying, and others laughing hysterically. Ohhhh!" She shuddered. "It was horrible, doubly so when I realized I was in hell!"

"And what, specifically, made you think you were in hell?"

"Well, on one side was a large, barren hill, no grass, no trees, nothing! And people were all over the place, creeping, crawling, and climbing—some lay and writhed in agony, and all were weeping and wailing! I never heard anything like it before. But worst of all, down in the valley another group was congregated in a huge cathedral, just sitting there lifeless in the pews, mouths agape and eyeless sockets staring vacantly, while ghoulish priests in garish robes busied themselves in kneeling, praying, anointing, and offering bouquets of dead roses to someone lying prostrate on a burnt altar."

"Marjorie, do you really believe that what you saw was real?"

"Oh, it was real all right! Why, I even felt my soul leave my body and float toward the ceiling before beginning that dizzy, whirling descent. And, yeah! I saw my body lying on the couch, but . . . Ohhhh, you don't believe me, do you? You think— But hey! Wait! I've got proof. Yeah, now I remember! You were leaning back in your chair, and you scraped a hickey on the back of your neck.

Look!" she exclaimed as she got up and ran behind me. "Look! It's true! I did see—see, your neck's bleeding. You scratched it raw!"

And so I had! Apparently Marjorie knew everything that had happened that day in the study, even though she had been in a deep trance with eyes closed. Whether Dolores, Marjorie, and others who have viewed the horrendous torment in the great beyond were merely hallucinating is a matter of conjecture, but this much is certain: There was nothing vague about the otherworldly voices that spoke through them!

There are those who will argue that entranced persons merely manifested their own secondary (dissociated) personalities, but even if it were true, nothing in the reasoning of psychology tells us how Dolores managed to speak German, an unknown and unlearned language.

Dolores had ceased weeping and pleading for God's mercy during her regression.

"Dolores, are you still with the nameless, faceless creatures?"

"No, in the distance there is a huge portal, white and shiny, and . . . and it's opening. Ohhhh, there's a young girl in the doorway, waving."

"Do you know the girl?"

"Yes, I've seen her before . . . in the meadow." Dolores began to weep, softly demurring, "No! No, I can't . . . I won't go with you."

"Go where, Dolores? What's happening?"

"It's Gretchen, and she insists that I come to her, that . . . that I go with her. But I can't go. I just can't!"

Curious as to what Gretchen wanted, I asked, "Why can't you go with her?"

She paled. "If I go, I can't come back!"

"How can that be, Dolores? Surely you don't believe that she has the power of life and death over you?"

"No, not death," she tried to explain, "not the way you think of death. But if I go, I'll never see you and the children again, not . . . not in this life."

Since Dolores could not explain how she would exist from that time on if she went with Gretchen, and because she showed signs of nervousness, I decided to bring her out of the trance.

"Relax, Dolores. I'm going to bring you back! I'm going to awaken you in just a few minutes. Relax!"

"Ohhhhhhhh, no! They're coming after me!" she screamed. "Get me out of here! Help me, please!"

I ended the regression on that urgent note, knowing more than ever that there is so very much about the mind, the soul, and the life in the world to come that we do not know. Clearly, to me, it is the height of foolishness for learned persons to blithely turn their backs on the undiscovered worlds that can be explored through the subconscious. And to pontificate or attempt to explain and rationalize with psychological jargon without having plumbed the depth of these and other stories is to admit that we would rather sound pious and brilliant than know the truth.

One of my ecclesiastical superiors once asked, "Carroll, what happens if you actually prove reincarnation through your experiments and investigations?"

I said, "The pursuit of religion is to know the truth. So if reincarnation be the truth, would you have me walk away from it and deny it?"

"No," he replied with a nervous laugh, "I guess not."

CHAPTER III

Whence the Voices?

In addition to my duties as pastor of the Union Plains
United Methodist Church in Greenbush and teacher of
psychology and American history at Lynchburg-Clay High
School, my practice as a hypnotist took me to all parts of
southwestern Ohio for lectures, demonstrations, counseling sessions, and hypnotherapy. The hypnotherapy followed
counseling sessions with people who were unable to come
to my study, but the use of hypnosis was for business
and professional women's clubs, Future Farmers of
America summer camps, state Four-H camps, church organizations, high-school assemblies, and similar groups.

While hypnotism had a high priority in my life, I must
emphasize that the ministry in God's church is my life,
but apart from the ministry, hypnotherapy brought me
the greatest satisfaction. To be able to help someone in
need does more to uplift the soul (and the ego) than
anything else I know of. Just to see the lame walk, the
deaf hear, and the almost strutting walk of someone who
has just been relieved of a migraine headache or a terrible fear or phobia is worth more than all the money in the
world, and never have I accepted payment for counseling
and hypnotherapy. (I did accept expenses for lectures and
demonstrations.)

People from all walks of life came to my study for
help with every conceivable type of problem, but if I were
to select one particular group of people which set the joy
bells ringing in my heart when they were helped, it would
be the many young married women who sought hypnotherapy because of their inability to conceive and bear
children. Mary Anne Randall of Ashley, Virginia, is a
good case in point.

Normally a petite lady, Mary had ballooned during

the eight years of her marriage to a hefty one hundred sixty pounds. Ostensibly she sought hypnotherapy for the sole purpose of losing weight, but during the precounseling sessions, when I sought to find a cause for her obsession for food, she voiced her frustration over her inability to become pregnant. "Having a baby," she said wistfully, "is the greatest desire of my life!" I then suggested that if her husband, Don, felt as strongly about the matter as she did, "Bring him with you to your next session."

Both Mary and Don had undergone complete medical examinations and had taken every test known to medical science. No cause for their inability to conceive could be found. Still, their eight years of marriage had been fruitless, and worse yet, they were convinced that they would never have any children of their own. In fact, Don said when I met him at Mary's next session, "I think this trip is a complete waste of time, but if you really think you can perform a miracle, then I'm ready to let you try."

A miracle worker I am not! I possess no supernatural powers, and I am not a healer.

As I made ready to hypnotize Mary, I told Don he had nothing to do but sit and listen as I counseled his wife. But later I glanced at Don and saw that he too had been hypnotized, so I counseled both of them while they were in a deep trance. And, hallelujah! a few weeks later Mary phoned from Ashley and shouted excitedly, "Reverend Jay, I'm pregnant! I'm pregnant!" Today, thank God, they are the proud parents of little Alice Sandra, a beautiful child, whom I was privileged to baptize and dedicate to the Lord shortly after her birth.

What was the secret of my success with Mary and Don? There is none, really. There was probably very little difference between the things I said to them and what they had been told by their doctor. However, this may have made the difference: Most people in hypnosis will assimilate and respond to suggestions much more readily than people in the waking state.

For the most part my work in hypnosis was therapeutic, but there came a day when I became disturbed about the way many hypnotists used hypnosis as merely a trapping of the occult. Too, it seemed that many authors were either hypnotists themselves or used hypnotists in an attempt to prove that reincarnation could indeed be proven as fact through the use of hypnosis. I had my doubts. In fact, because of the shallowness of the evidence presented in most books, I determined to start regressing individuals as a means of producing evidence that hypnosis could not be used for such a purpose.

Subjects wanting to be regressed were plentiful, and I was able to record several excellent cases. Most of the stories of prior lives told by people in hypnosis could in no way be construed as reflecting previous lives that they had lived in an earlier time; the contradictions were too plentiful and too obvious. Yet some of the stories not only had a ring of truth to them, they withstood refutation in subsequent investigations. A good example is the case of Augie Luft/Eletha Helene Moore.

Augie Luft was an attractive eighteen-year-old high-school senior whom I regressed in my psychology class at Lynchburg-Clay High School. With the approval of school officials, I probably became the first teacher in a secondary school anywhere in the world to practice hypnosis in the classroom. I hypnotized many students and teachers almost every week, but the best subject for regression was Augie.

Augie was a somnambulist, and in several regressions, while lying on a table before my psychology class, she recalled a supposed prior life from the deep recesses of her subconscious. Although she told the same story several times over several weeks, she never contradicted either herself or the chronology of events, despite the fact that I deliberately tried to confuse her. I was not trying to find a flaw in her story merely as a means of embarrassing her. Rather, it was imperative that I not go off investigating the case if I could determine beforehand that the story had no basis in fact.

In the regressed state Augie called herself Eletha Helene Moore, but opted for the name Elly, because "that's what everyone calls me."

Elly supposedly was born on March 18, 1903, and died following an automobile accident on the old Pennsylvania Turnpike between Lancaster, Pennsylvania, and Philadelphia on March 19, 1915, while riding to Philadelphia with

37

her uncle George, her father's brother, who was also supposedly killed in the accident.

Elly was the daughter of Joseph and Ann Moore, who lived about "a fifteen-minute ride from Harriston, Pennsylvania." She had no brothers or sisters. Her only playmate was a first cousin named Arnie, the son of Theodore Moore and his first wife, Hellen (or Ellen). The only other relative known to Elly was her uncle George Moore. Close neighbors were Mr. and Mrs. Luke Johnson, whose children "were all growed up and moved away."

The Moores, according to Elly, "shopped at Brown's Grocery in Harriston, where Mr. Simmons preached at the Methodist church." Elly also knew a Mrs. Anderson and a Mrs. Smith, whom "all the children called an old witch 'cause they believed she killed and boiled her husband in a big kettle in the back yard."

Elly often spoke of going to Blainsburg with her parents, "about an hour ride by buggy," where "we shopped at Dawson's Grocery and Hinkle's Five and Ten Cent Store." Additionally, she saw signs in Blainsburg advertising "The Blain Press" and "Mr. R. W. Leeds, Attorney at Law." Mr. Gray was the pastor of the Blainsburg Methodist Church. Mr. Parks was the town policeman. A Mr. Townlinson, Towmlinson, or Tomlinson—"something like that," she said—was the mayor.

Buried in the church cemetery at Blainsburg, Elly told the class, as she read the following on tombstones were, "James Allen Ruskin, 1818–1864"; "Ellen Kleper, 1889–1904"; T. S. Wallace, 1864–1898"; "Elias Thompson" (no dates). Elly also said that she once attended church at Marysville, "but it burned and is not there now."

Although Augie had never lived in Pennsylvania or even visited the state, she was certain that as Elly she had lived near Harriston (which she always pronounced "Harristown"). One day, after failing to locate Harristown on the map, I asked Elly to look for a letter which had been sent to her father so she could read aloud the address on the envelope. After searching for several minutes, she read, "Mr. Joseph Lee Moore, Route 1, Harristown, Pa." When I asked her to spell the town's name, she spelled, "H-a-r-r-i-s-t-o-n." When I pointed out that she had spelled "Harriston" and not "Harristown," she replied, "Yes, I know, but we always call it Harristown." And, strange as it may seem, when I investigated the case a few months later and asked a resident of Harriston, "Is this place actually named Harriston?" she replied, "Yes, but we always call it Harristown."

The intrigue had only begun. Although there are no Moores living in Harriston now, I soon located an elderly lady living in the area with the exact same name as Elly, and I phoned her for an appointment to discuss the Moore family tree. Very pleasant and obliging, she agreed to help me all she could. Then she asked, "Just why are you interested in the Moore family?"

I informed her that I was hoping to learn something about an Elly Moore who died in an automobile accident in 1915.

"No!" she quickly said. "I won't be able to talk to you. I'm . . . I'm not feeling at all well." When I suggested that I come back in a day or two when she was feeling better, she replied bluntly, "No! I have nothing more to say to you, today or any other day!"

Apparently I had stuck a sore spot, because at no time did she ever say that she did not know the Elly of whom I spoke; and because her willingness to talk evaporated the moment Elly's name was mentioned, I could only wonder whether there had been an Elly at one time whose memory was too painful to bear.

Unable to learn anything about Elly in Harriston or the surrounding area, I went to Harrisburg to check the death certificates of all persons named Moore who died in or near Philadelphia in 1915. Some very interesting facts were uncovered.

Elly had claimed that she and her uncle were in an automobile accident on March 19, 1915, the day after her birthday. Supposedly they were going to Philadelphia when the accident occurred, and Elly tearfully relived the tragic moment of being thrown from the car. Lying mortally wounded in a ditch, before losing consciousness she described in detail the horrible spectacle of her uncle being burned to death in the flaming car.

Probably the most convincing evidence produced by Elly about the authenticity of her previous existence was not anything she said; rather, as she supposedly relived the accident, Augie's neck and chest (she wore a low-cut dress that day) turned a purplish-blue from blood congestion generated by the trauma of remembering her final moments. So great was the terror and the presence of death in the classroom in that moment that many students buried their heads in their arms on their desks and wept. Some said they thought they were going to faint.

With the aid of Mrs. Margret Coldren, I examined death certificates at the Department of Health and Vital Statistics in Harrisburg. We soon learned that an Eletha Moore, aged 19, had died on February 19, 1915. For a moment we concluded that Elly had supplied us with a record of incontrovertible evidence for reincarnation, but a second examination of the certificate showed that we would have to overlook a few simple facts to make that claim hold up. The Eletha Moore who died on February 19, 1915, was a nineteen-year-old black girl who died in childbirth, while our Elly claimed to have been a twelve-year-old blue-eyed blond. One could reason that the black girl was actually Elly by disregarding Elly's self-description and postulating that she had indeed been black and pregnant; that in an effort to conceal her out-of-wedlock pregnancy, a cause for terrible shame and disgrace in those days, she deliberately lied about her race and cause of death.

Was that possible? Assuming that Elly was a reincarnated entity in Augie, could she deliberately misrepresent? Well, why not? I have known several people in regression tell about living a prior life which embarrassed them when they came out of the trance, and when they were next regressed they changed some things in their story to make it less embarrassing in the waking state.

This brings up an interesting point: Many hypnotists insist that people have absolutely no control of anything they might say or do while in hypnosis, but it has been my experience that they will not do anything in hypnosis that is contrary to their moral character. If people can refrain from doing anything that violates their moral code while in a trance, then obviously they have some measure of restraint and control over all their actions in hypnosis.

Other authorities will claim that they have known hypnotized subjects who did commit acts which were definitely contrary to their moral code. At first glance it would seem that I would have to agree with them, since I too have had hypnotized subjects say and do things that appeared to be in violation of what I knew about their moral character, but basically, when hypnotized people act in such a manner they are merely fulfilling sublimated or repressed desires. The rationale for such people is: I am in a trance and for once in my life I can do as I please; if my actions are odd, vulgar, or self-debasing in any way, I can always use the excuse that I did not know what I was doing—I was helpless, in a trance and at the mercy of the hypnotist.

These conclusions are based not on any immoral acts or things said by former subjects in hypnosis; rather, as in the case of Elly: If I were to leave the room while she was in a trance, regardless of how deep, she would immediately come out of it. And although Dolores and other subjects would remain in a trance no matter how many times I left the room, it is obvious that Augie had some awareness in the trance state, since her conscious mind always assumed control immediately when she was left alone by the hypnotist.

We also need to question whether someone in hypnotic regression can tell a deliberate falsehood. Again, why not? A liar is a liar, a liar, a liar! Going to the ultimate, are we to believe that even in death the sudden transition from this life to an "afterlife" in the "other world" automatically transforms a deceased person from a liar into an infallible saint? It is doubtful! The Bible teaches in Matthew 16:19, "Whatsoever thou shalt bind on earth shall be bound in heaven: and whatsoever thou shalt loose on earth shall be loosed in heaven," implying, at least in one sense, that a person who holds on to the habit of lying in this life will maintain the habit and ability to fulfill it in the life to come. The same thing applies to hypnosis: A hypnotized person can prevaricate as readily in hypnosis as in the waking state.

Possibly it may be thought that by such reasoning I am trying to convince myself that Elly did live more than half a century ago despite all the evidence to the contrary. No, I believe that honesty and impartiality should be the basic tenets of every investigation, so it is imperative to consider all possibilities, even if that means we are saying that Elly may have been a pregnant black girl instead of a blue-eyed, blond accident victim. While it may be true that this supposition differs from Elly's description of herself, I point out that the eminent scientist and investigator Dr. Ian Stevenson applied a substitute theory when evidence in an investigation indicated that the facts accorded with an entity other than the one who supposedly spoke from the other world.

In 1973 Dr. Stevenson reported in the *Journal of the American Society for Psychical Research* that he began an investigation after Jacques Brossy of St. Étienne, France, reported that he had received a message from a discarnate personality named Robert Mary, formerly of Villers-sur-Mer, through Mme. B. Bricout, a Paris medium.

Robert Mary claimed to have been killed in World War I, and a notary of Villers-sur-Mer later confirmed that an Auguste Charles Robert Julien Marie (not Mary) had indeed died at the Battle of the Marne on September 17, 1914. But when Dr. Stevenson had completed his investigation of this case, the facts seemed to indicate that the entity who spoke through Mme. Bricout was Louis Ferdinand Marie, Robert's brother, rather than Robert himself. Dr. Stevenson stated his conclusions: "I believe it a serious fallacy to expect that a communication from a discarnate mind will come through with the accuracy of, say, a telephone message. If we wish to use a physical analogy, it seems to me that some of the garbled telegrams I have received provide a better example. One can say the sender of such telegrams had some influence on its leaving and on its destination, but very poor control over its actual content."

For our purpose it is necessary to go a step further, into the investigation of death certificates. In addition to looking for a death certificate for an Eletha Helene Moore, we also looked for and found a death certificate for George Moore who died in Norristown, Pennsylvania, on March 27, 1915, only eight days dollowing the accident in which Elly said she and her uncle were killed. Norristown is less than ten miles from the route Elly and her uncle would have taken on their trip to Philadelphia.

It seems reasonable to assume that Elly might not have actually seen her uncle die, since she told of seeing him in the blazing automobile as she lost consciousness. Possibly Uncle George was able to extricate himself from the wreck; maybe someone happened by the scene of the accident and pulled him from the burning car and took him to the hospital in Norristown. The death certificate reveals that he died from a cerebral hemorrhage and apoplexy, traumatic conditions which might have occurred as a direct result of the accident.

Unable to find names or dates that coincided exactly with Elly's story, we made a search of all death certificates for the years 1910–20, because it is believed by most learned investigators that dates given by discarnate personalities are sometimes totally inaccurate. That may be true in this case, because we did find a death certificate which showed that a George Moore died in Philadelphia of a skull fracture on May 14, 1911, following an automobile accident—but that Mr. Moore was black. So we wonder: Was he Elly's uncle, assuming she too was black? Obviously, unless further evidence is uncovered we will never know.

Because we could not locate a death certificate for a little blue-eyed, blond Eletha Helene Moore, it seems important to speculate about what could have happened to Elly following the accident, especially since there were two George Moores who could have been the uncle she referred to. Not many young girls in those days carried such personal identification as a Social Security card or an I.D. bracelet, and it seems logical to assume she may have died as an unknown person. As Elly said, "they carried me unconscious to a hospital, but I don't know where it was," and she might have been buried as an unclaimed body in one of the many towns near the old Pennsylvania Turnpike between Lancaster and Philadelphia—a possibility that Elly indicated in her heart-rending exclamation at the moment of her death, "Ohhhh, Mommy didn't come!" Possibly Mommy didn't come to her bedside because she did not know Elly had been in an accident, because of a lack of identification and poor communication facilities in those days.

Summarizing the Elly case, the following led us to seriously consider Elly might have been describing a prior life: 1) Elly called Harriston "Harristown," an obscure variation not likely to be known by anyone who had not lived there, visited there, lived as a nearby resident, or had relatives in the community; 2) she gave a fairly accurate description of the community; 3) there are several Moores living within a three-mile range of Harriston, and Elly said she lived a fifteen-minute buggy ride from there; 4) living nearby was a woman named Eletha Helene Moore, who was old enough to have been Elly's mother and who refused to answer any questions about an Elly who might have died in 1915—possibly she may have shut the memory of Elly from her life, not knowing that she had been killed, but thinking she might merely have run away from home; 5) we found the death certificate of a George Moore who died only a week after Elly and her uncle supposedly had their accident, possibly not far from Norristown; and 6) the death certificate of the black George Moore actually listed the cause of death as "automobile accident," the cause of Elly's death.

Most people who witness a regression find their emotions conflicting with reason, especially if they are hesitant about accepting the theory of reincarnation. Most people in regression tell their story of the supposed prior life as though reliving it right at that moment; the rise in blood pressure is real, respiratory problems are real, sweating, shaking, weeping, laughing, fear, pain, pleasure —all are real or at least seemingly so. This is true even for those persons who have absolutely no acting ability. Some do appear to be emoting, but by and large they tell the story exactly as it comes from their subconscious.

Augie convinced me that there was more, much, much more to regression than I had thought possible, and soon I had much additional evidence. Even before I had ended my investigation of the Elly case, Dolores relived in regression the account of a former life as Loreen Tuttle, a life supposedly lived in the rural hamlet of Springfield, Indiana, prior to her supposed incarnation as Gretchen.

Dolores had never been to Indiana, let alone lived in Springfield. To this day she has never been west of Ohio, yet while in a hypnotic trance she uncannily described

Springfield, a community of only ten or so houses located several miles from any major highway.

When Loreen emerged from Dolores's subconscious, I wanted to locate proof that Loreen had actually lived, so I challenged, "How do I know that you are alive, that you live in Springfield? You see, Loreen, I can hear you but I cannot see you, so how do I know that you are not merely a figment of Dolores's imagination?"

"All you have to do," she replied in a sickly, weak voice, "is come to Springfield and see for yourself." Then she added the instructions, "If you will just stand in the crossroads in the center of town you will see St. Paul's Methodist Church and the Springfield School on the corner to your left. Then, if you walk down the road past the church and school for about a hundred yards and look to your right, you will see a small grove of trees. In the grove is a small cemetery, and my brother, Johnnie, is buried there."

When I went to Springfield, which is located in Posey County in southwestern Indiana, and stood in the crossroads as she had instructed, I saw no sign of a church or a school. Near the site where the church was supposed to be were the remains of an old building, but it did not appear to have been a church. Believing my trip to have been futile, I left Springfield, intending to go home after inquiring of several local residents if they knew of any Tuttles living in the area then or in the past. No one had ever heard of the Tuttles, and I did not find any evidence of them at the courthouse in Mount Vernon, the county seat.

My search was less than thorough, since the county clerk was away for the Thanksgiving holiday and there was no one else present to help me research the birth and death certificates. Still, something kept telling me I should not leave too quickly. After all, Loreen had known about Springfield, a tiny hamlet several miles from a major highway, and she had been correct about the crossroads. Maybe there was more in Springfield than met the eye.

I sought help from a Methodist minister who had lived in that area most of his life and who then lived on the road from Mount Vernon to Springfield. "Yes," he said, "there had been a Methodist church in Springfield, and yes, it had sat on the corner at the crossroads, but it burned to the ground in 1920."

That bit of information intrigued me no end, because Dolores was not born until 1922 and she had never been to Indiana, yet, lying in a trance several hundred miles away, she told me about attending services in that very church, a church that had been destroyed by fire two years before she was born. How did she do it? Was it really true that reincarnation was fact and not fancy? It was unlikely that Dolores could have known about the church even if she had visited Springfield at one time or another, because there was no visible sign of a church. I concluded that it really was Loreen with whom I talked!

Quickly I thanked the minister and returned to the crossroads in Springfield, where I proceeded to step off one hundred yards, as instructed by Loreen. And, oh, yes, the old remnant of a building that remained had been the old Springfield High School.

"Ninety-eight, ninety-nine, one hundred," I counted, and looked to my right as I was led down the road. Sure enough, there was a grove of trees a short distance up the bank in the field. From the road it was impossible to tell if it contained a cemetery. Climbing the fence and wading through knee-high weeds, I made my way forward with great ambivalence. I was almost certain that I would find Johnnie's tomb, which would be a tremendous step forward in proving the theory of reincarnation, or at least whether reincarnation could be established as a fact through hypnosis.

I had gone to Springfield in search of evidence. Deep in my heart was a sublimated desire not to find proof, even though I was filled with a strange excitement. One thing was clear to me: If I had not been deluding myself, if indeed I sought to know the truth, I would soon know, because the cemetery was where Loreen had said it would be. Hurriedly I looked for the tombstone that she said marked Johnnie's grave, but none bore his name, nor was there one for any other person named Tuttle.

Had Loreen been so right about everything else, yet wrong on that one score?

It had been a wet, rainy day, and as I started to leave

the cemetery after making a second, more methodical search, I tripped over a clump of moss-laden grass. I pulled it loose, and lo and behold, it looked as though I had unearthed a buried tombstone. Finding a stick and digging furiously, I soon lifted an old, old tombstone from its grave beneath the grass. It was not Johnnie's.

But I had seen enough. The crossroads, the church, the school, the cemetery, and the town itself indicated that Dolores/Loreen had given me firsthand information about Springfield. Even though I had not located Johnnie's grave, it was logical that if one tombstone had toppled to be covered beneath the sod, the same thing could have happened to Johnnie's tombstone. A more thorough search would be in order at a more opportune time.

I was now convinced that Loreen had given me pertinent information, which further eroded my doubts about being able to disprove the theory that reincarnation could be proven through hypnosis.

It also convinced me that if Loreen could actually speak through Dolores, then Gretchen could speak through her too, even in a foreign language, even a language that Dolores had never learned. And although there is presently no way that we can know of a certainty how a reincarnated entity can speak through a living person—how an incorporeal entity such as Gretchen can incarnate and assume control of Dolores's voice mechanism and cause her to speak a language contrary to all her learning—the fact remains that it can be done, and has been done!

Some will insist there is no mystery, that it is merely one of hypnotism's strange facets, which gives a person in hypnosis the ability to do strange and wonderful things. It is true that people in the trance state can do things they had not thought they could do, but entranced persons are not given new abilities; new things done in hypnosis are merely the manifestation of latent talents—the ability was always present but was not previously used. But this does not apply to the speaking of languages. Normal newborn infants are equipped with the ability to speak more than one language. They can and will imitate any language spoken in their presence over a period of time. But without the presence of some paranormal influence an infant cannot naturally speak an unlearned language. Neither can a person in hypnosis.

Dr. Ian Stevenson states in his book *Xenoglossy* that "the ability to speak a foreign language is a skill, that skills cannot be acquired without practice, cannot be transmitted either normally or paranormally." This, then, says that a person speaking a foreign language for the first time, without having studied the language or practiced pronouncing it, of necessity must be either the living incarnation of a former being or under the influence of another personality who had previously learned the language. People can receive messages telepathically, but even recipients of such messages, while they may mouth the words well enough to be understood, cannot speak the words with correct clarity and inflection. More important, they cannot engage in the give-and-take of a conversation or interrogation if totally dependent on messages received telepathically.

Certainly I did not believe in reincarnation, nor had I previously given serious thought to the possibility of Dolores being the reincarnation of either Loreen or Gretchen, but now—believe me, there was much food for thought.

To even think that reincarnation was an actuality was painful. It was contrary to everything I had ever believed. Worse yet, as a minister of the gospel in the Christian Church I could envision trouble of tremendous proportion with my parishioners, my superiors, and the public in general. God knows that I was not a crusader. I had no desire to plow new fields for the sake of personal glory. I wanted only to help maintain the status quo of Christian thought, which totally denied the existence of reincarnation. I had tried to live in accordance with God's Word, and Jesus had said, "If ye continue in my word, then are ye my disciples; and ye shall know the truth, and the truth shall make you free" (St. John 8:31, 32).

But really, now—what was the truth? For me, there was but one way to find out: hypnotize and regress Dolores; and, if need be, submit our lives to a grueling investigation.

Returning home form Springfield, I told Dolores of my findings and conclusions. But when I suggested that she submit to further regressions so we could more fully investigate the Gretchen personality, she demurred. The mere thought of making our life an open book repelled her, and the thought that we might face open criticism and censure from church leaders frightened her terribly. Controversy was repugnant, especially to one so sensitive and desirous of living a private unobtrusive life.

But there was something about the Gretchen case that would not let us quit, and I continued to regress Dolores after we had spent a few days discussing all phases of the case and agreeing that we seemingly had no choice in the matter. It seemed to us that destiny had plotted our course. Why, we wondered, had fate brought us together in the first place? Was it fate that decreed we should meet as little more than children? What forces were in operation that brought us together almost thirty-five years earlier—her a somnambulist and me a future hypnotist, although I never dreamed at that time of becoming a hypnotist?

Frankly, I was the roughest, toughest kid in town. Each day was lived for playing ball or fighting. At night, though, it was a different story. I lay on my bed and dreamed of the day I would stand in the pulpit to proclaim God's Word, to minister to the sick, the poor, the needy. Was it, then, divine providence that we should meet and someday be called upon to bring forth Gretchen and the resulting investigation?

Dolores and I do not subscribe to the theory of predestination in matters of life and death, but we do believe that God's plans are often laid far in advance. Whether we fulfill those plans is up to us. We are creatures endowed with free will, and we can either submit our will to God's will— His plans for us—or we can pull up short and plot our own course independently of Him and His will. Dolores and I concluded after many long hours on our knees in seeking the Lord in prayer and in personal soul-searching that this was God's will for us.

We discussed the Gretchen and Loreen cases with hundreds of persons, but at that time we had not thought to bring in an outside investigator. Then one day, again providentially, I read in the March 1971 issue of *Psychic* magazine a statement by "the Amazing Kreskin" to the effect that "hypnosis, perhaps as you and I and everyone thinks of it, really doesn't exist." He went on to say, "I believe in this very deeply and have a standing offer of twenty thousand dollars to any physician, psychologist, or lay hypnotist who can show me that just one human being at any point is in a hypnotic trance."

I wrote to *Psychic,* challenged Kreskin, and waited for him to name the place and date when the test could be held. I waited in vain—Kreskin did not respond to my letter. I challenged him again on July 16 and August 26. Still he did not respond.

On the morning of October 15, 1971, I said to Dolores, "Let's drive into Cincinnati and go to television station WLW-TV. Something tells me that Kreskin will be on Bob Braun's *50–50 Club* program today." My ESP was in good order. Kreskin was indeed to be on the program. Unfortunately we were too late to see either him or Bob Braun in person before air time. But Richard C. Thrall, Manager of Television Programming, agreed to personally hand Kreskin a letter, which I had written, challenging him a fourth time. Mr. Thrall later wrote in a letter to me, "I presented your letter to Kreskin and he acknowledged on the air that he had received your challenges, but from the comments he made on the air, it did not appear that he intended to honor the challenges you had accepted which he made in a magazine publication."

Kreskin finally answered my letters on November 23, 1971, and expressed that business commitments and a backlog of television mail had prevented him from catching up on correspondence. By that time it made little difference to me: I was again in the hospital with another heart attack, obviously unable to challenge anyone.

When Kreskin learned of my condition, he sent word expressing sincere concern for my well-being and added that in all good conscience he could not at that time permit me to undergo the stress of defending my challenge in a public forum. I appreciated his kindness.

I have since concluded that it would be senseless to challenge anyone on hypnosis. Hypnosis is an art and a science, but it cannot be measured scientifically. Certainly it can be demonstrated and can appear to be fact to anyone watching an entranced subject respond to a hypnotist's commands; and it is accepted as an absolute fact by all who have experienced its marvelous curative powers.

Although Kreskin is entitled to believe as he wants, I am of the opinion that as a stage hypnotist he did not have the time to practice and develop the art to its full potential. Stage hypnotists must, by the nature of their profession and because of time limitations, select for stage roles those people most susceptible to suggestion and hope that they will automatically respond to simple suggestions and perform crowd-pleasing antics. Serious practitioners are never in a hurry, nor do they perform for the spectator. Hypnotism was never intended to be used as a stage-show gimmick.

My correspondence with Kreskin was rewarding. James Grayson Bolin, owner and editor of *Psychic* magazine, forwarded a copy of my letter to Dr. Stevenson and he in turn contacted me and arranged to come to our home on September 2, 1971. He was accompanied by Welby Mason, an attorney and research assistant.

Dr. Stevenson is a tall, angular, slow-speaking scholar, now in his late fifties. And if anyone was qualified to investigate the Gretchen case, he was that person. A medical graduate of McGill University in Montreal, he worked for several years as a psychiatric researcher and author before becoming interested in reincarnation and accepting the chairmanship of the Department of Psychiatry and Neurology at the University of Virginia's School of Medicine. Today he is Carlson Professor of Psychiatry and head of the University's Division of Para-psychology. Also, he speaks German.

Following the usual amenities and a brief discussion of our life and the Gretchen case, I hypnotized Dolores. When the trance was sufficiently deep, I asked, "What is your name?"

Always slow to answer in the trance state, Dolores seemed unusually slow that evening. She had dreaded going under for such an eminent scientist. "Suppose Gretchen doesn't come," she had worried, "I'll be so embarrassed. Besides," she added as a reminder, "I've been against this all along!"

And that was true to a certain extent. Dolores had been reluctant to let Dr. Stevenson come to our home, even though we had already determined to see this thing through to its ultimate conclusion. "After all," I reasoned, "we may have wasted a lot of time and research on nothing—maybe

51

there is nothing to the Gretchen case—but we will never really know until after qualified authorities have examined the case from start to finish."

"Well, maybe so," she said. "Maybe if we let Dr. Stevenson question Gretchen just once he will quickly learn that I cannot actually speak German and we can then put an end to these regressions."

Again I asked the entranced Dolores, "What is your name?"

Wetting her lips and smiling slightly, she spoke in a little girl's voice: "Ich bin Gretchen."

"Gretchen, what is your last name?"

"Gottlieb."

"How old are you, Gretchen?"

"Neun."

Relieved that Dolores's nervousness had not prevented her from entering the somnambulist state, I looked to Dr. Stevenson and nodded. "Get ready to take over." To Dolores I said:

"Gretchen, you know that I cannot speak your language, that I must always question you in English, but tonight I have a friend here who can speak your language, and I want you to talk to him and answer all his questions."

Nervously Gretchen asked, "Wer ist das Freund? [Who is the friend?]"

Leaning forward, Dr. Stevenson requested, "Wiederholen Sie das. Sprechen Sie das noch mal [Repeat that. Say that again.]"

"Ist Freund? [Is friend?]"

"Ist Freund. Ja, ja, ich bin ein Freund. Wo wohnen Sie jetzt? [Is friend. Yes, yes, I am a friend. Where do you live now?]"

"Ich lebe in Eberswalde. [I live in Eberswalde.]"

"In Eberswalde. Ja, und ist das in der Nähe von einer anderen Stadt? [In Eberswalde. Yes, and is that near some other city?]"

"Darmstadt."

"Darmstadt. Und in welchem Land ist Darmstadt? [Darmstadt. And in what country is Darmstadt located?]"

"Deutschland. [Germany.]"

"Ja, und also wohen Sie in einer Strasse? [Yes, and so, do you live in a street?]"

For those first few moments of conversation between Dr. Stevenson and Gretchen I hung on every word, even though I could understand little of what was said. Then, looking at Welby Mason, I relaxed with a sigh of relief as he winked and nodded in the affirmative.

As Dr. Stevenson continued conversing with Gretchen, my ambivalent feelings returned. In a way I wanted this to be the real thing, because we had been forced to endure considerable ribbing and outright slander. But if Dolores was speaking true German, if she was telling of a life lived in the long-ago, wouldn't she be tossing a proof-positive case for reincarnation into my lap? How could I explain that? Would I be asked by my bishop to turn in my ministerial credentials? "Dear God, no!" I prayed. "Don't ever let that happen."

Softly Dr. Stevenson asked, "Und wie heisst Ihr Vater? [And what is your father's name?]"

"Hermann."

"Hermann. Ja, und was für einen Beruf hat er? [Hermann. Yes, and what is his occupation?]"

Showing signs of nervousness, Gretchen answered, "Mein Vater ist der Bürgermeister. Mehr sagen sehr ist schlecht, verboten! [My father is the mayor. More talking is very bad, forbidden!]"

"Nein," Dr. Stevenson countered, hoping to calm her, "es ist nicht verboten. Wer hat das verboten? [No, it is not forbidden. Who forbade it?]"

"Der Bundesrat [The Federal Council]," she whispered.

"Wer—"

"Der Bundesrat! Sie hören zu [The Federal Council! They are listening.]"

Gretchen was terrified of the Bundesrat. When referring to it, she ususally put a forefinger over pursed lips and spoke in a whisper.

Dr. Stevenson questioned Gretchen for more than an hour, and she answered every question, usually with a word or a short sentence. He was well pleased, exceptionally so, and stated unequivocally that if he was unable to find reasons for believing that Dolores had learned the language, this case would be of tremendous importance: a potential case of responsive xenoglossy—the ability to speak a foreign language without having learned that language. To his knowledge, there was only one other case of a person in hypnosis having that ability which had stood up under severe scientific scrutiny.

The ability to speak an unlearned language borders on the miraculous, but it seems to me that it would be even more improbable that a person could lie in a trance with eyes closed, receiving no visible clues (as in lip reading) to the meaning of a word or a sentence posed in a foreign language, yet understand the spoken words. This would seem not only improbable but impossible, especially when the person hearing the language had had absolutely no practice in listening to that language before.

I had always thought my Dolores was something special, but until that night with Dr. Stevenson I had had no idea just how special she really was.

CHAPTER IV

The Heavenly Portal

The rigors of my many and varied activities were taxing on my heart, forcing me to resign my teaching position and limit the number of personal appearances and counseling sessions I normally engaged in each week. But my family and I were happy just to serve the church and the few persons I treated therapeutically on a selective basis.

One lady who desperately needed help was Polly Martin. She and her husband, Desmond, had become very dear friends during the four years of our pastorate at Greenbush. Polly had been hospitalized for an ingrown toenail, a seemingly innocuous operation, but due to diabetes mellitus her toe would not heal, and her doctor informed her that under the circumstances he would have to amputate her foot at the ankle.

Polly was a woman of her own mind, and she insisted on being released from the hospital immediately. Two weeks later our youngest daughter, Mary Jo, went with a friend to visit Polly at her home in Williamsburg and returned home with tears in her eyes. "Daddy, I wish you would go see Polly; she looks terrible! She's lost so much weight, and, Daddy, she doesn't even comb her hair anymore."

When I saw Polly that afternoon I was shocked. She lay on an overstuffed sofa in the family room, a shadow of her former self, hair uncombed, sallow complexion surrounding sunken, black-rimmed eyes devoid of all luster.

Shortly after my arrival, Desmond assisted her in removing a towel they had used to bundle her foot, revealing the infected toe, which had become a rotted black mass of gangrenous tissue. Fighting to overcome the nausea that assailed me, I suggested that she return to her doctor immediately.

"No," she said forlornly, "he says there is nothing more to be done but amputate." She bristled defiantly. "Even if it means my life, I'll never agree to that!"

After visiting with them for an hour or so, I prayed with Polly before making my way to the door, hoping to get home in time to see the last three quarters of Superbowl V, but when I attempted to reach for the doorknob, my arm would not move—it was the same experience I had undergone with Dolores and Old Joe, an experience which forced me to consider very seriously that a supernatural force had imposed its will upon mine, preventing me from leaving the room. It was a crazy experience, and I stood flexing my fingers for quite some time, trying desperately to reach the doorknob, but it was no go. I returned to sit, talk, and pray with Polly and Desmond for another full hour, hoping I could leave this time without interference —at least I could watch the last half of the big game.

When I again approached the door, it was still no go: My hand would not move to the knob. For a moment I was slightly unnerved, possibly because after my first failure to leave my arm was perfectly normal as I sat and talked with Polly. A bit flustered and made more uneasy by the questioning eyes of Polly and Desmond, I determined to do what I had to do, so I walked over to Polly and announced, "Never before have I offered to hypnotize anyone unless they first sought my services, but, Polly, you need help, and unless you order me to get out and stay out, I'm going to help you. Now lie back and relax. That's it," I said encouragingly as she surprisingly responded without comment. "Completely relax, and in a few minutes you will be sound asleep, the pain will be gone, and you will rest comfortably."

As Polly accepted every suggestion without question, I continued to induce hypnosis, and a wonderful feeling of peace flooded my soul—the Holy Spirit was present in that room, and I knew the Lord was blessing my efforts. In becoming so engrossed ministering to Polly, I had completely forgotten Desmond, and when I looked up and saw his penetrating eyes holding me fast, a tinge of fear marred the serenity of that moment. Quickly forcing a smile and hoping he would raise no objections, I explained, hoping to appease him, "Polly's all right, Desmond. She's just asleep, nothing more, nothing less. And, she will remain asleep until ten or ten thirty tonight." To my discomfort, he showed no expression pro or con, and I quickly added, "Now, Desmond, after she awakens she will feel better, much, much better. There will be no aftereffects as all the effects of hypnosis will have dissipated."

Then, for the first time, Desmond's steady, penetrating eyes flashed from me to Polly, then back to me. "She'll be all right, Desmond," I continued, hoping for a flicker of confidence in that stone face that made me terribly uncomfortable. "Now, after she awakens, if you and Polly want, phone me and I will come back and put her into a trance again. It will only take a few seconds the next time, but to your benefit and her health, she will sleep soundly all night; she will have her first good night's sleep in ages."

After a short prayer, I went to the door, opened it, and proceeded homeward, thankful that Polly was resting comfortably and that I could watch the last quarter of the game I had waited all year to see.

At eleven o'clock that night Polly called. Dolores answered the phone, and I knew from the gleam in her eyes that Polly was rejoicing. Dolores said she had never heard anyone sound more happy. Polly thanked the Lord, the preacher, and Mary Jo. "Sleep!" she sang ecstatically. "I never knew it could be so sweet."

At eleven fifteen that night I returned to minister to Polly, and again the next night and the next, every night for the next two weeks, to rehypnotize her. I was pleased that she began to look her old self again: clean, coifed, and happy! She had good reason to be happy: The gangrenous mass of rotted tissue on her toe had been replaced by new, baby-pink flesh; only a scab remained in lieu of the missing toenail.

"Polly," I suggested, "tomorrow you must go back to your doctor."

"No!" she rebelled, in chorus with Desmond. "I won't go! I don't need him anymore!"

"But you do!" I countered. "I am not a physician, and you need to be under a doctor's care and supervision. In fact, Polly, I will no longer treat you if you don't—I will not treat anyone who is not under the watchful care of a qualified doctor."

When Desmond took Polly to the doctor the next day, the doctor unwrapped the toe and fell back in his chair, exclaiming, "No! I don't believe it! It's impossible!" Then, looking at Polly in wonderment: "What happened? What have you done?"

"Do you believe in prayer?" She smiled impishly.

"Yes, of course, but—" He stammered and sat looking at her toe, shaking his head. "There's no way! There's more to it than that. There's got to be!"

"Well," Polly ventured cautiously, "what do you think of hypnotism?"

"Fine!" He laughed. "It's great, really great if you can afford it."

"Oh, I can afford it," Polly replied, "my preacher does it without charge."

"Oh, no!" The doctor recoiled in shock and railed, "That's the work of the Devil!"

Of course anything can be used for good or evil, and I grant you that many charlatans have used hypnosis in a degrading way, but at the time the doctor thought it was good, even great, when he supposed that one of his colleagues had performed the service, presumably for a tremendous fee. If, as he intimated, they had submitted to an evil practice—evil only because they let me perform the service without charge—then so be it. To his credit, he may have thought they were dealing with a novice, which is never a good practice.

To make certain that the healing of Polly's toe and the overall improvement of her total health were not merely temporary, I urged her to undergo a complete physical examination by Dr. Sanford R. Courter in Cincinnati. After the examination Dr. Courter pronounced her in excellent health. "But, Doctor," Polly asked, "what about my diabetes?" He replied with raised eyebrows, surprised that she had raised the question, "What diabetes? Your blood sugar is completely within normal range."

Polly and Desmond were extremely happy, and I was satisfied to know that the Lord had given me a talent to be used in helping to relieve suffering, but two months later it was again necessary for me to go to Polly's home and administer hypnosis and induce analgesia, because Polly reinjured her foot by stumbling over a large stone in the twilight. When the treatment was completed, Polly and I returned to the family room. A neighbor had arrived to sit with Desmond, looking as though all the world's hate had consumed her. As soon as I entered the room, she began to rant and rave, charging me with being the devil's advocate and worse: with practicing witchcraft on Polly. Saddest of all, Polly and Desmond made no attempt to quiet her or to defend me against her ungodly tirade.

It was then that I realized that antagonism was beginning to grow against me and my use of hypnosis. With a heavy heart I responded, "I am sorry, terribly sorry, you feel the way you do. I have tried only to bring health and happiness to Polly, and if even that offends you, then there is nothing more I can say to you." I left their home that day crushed in spirit, never to return.

I had gone too far to turn back. My ministry in hypnosis had wonderfully benefited hundreds of needy people, and in my own heart there was a burning desire to render service to my fellow man through what I knew to be a God-given talent. And, yes, that included our use of regression and the investigation of reincarnation.

While a belief in reincarnation was incompatible with my religious thought, the mere fact that it was a religious belief of considerable antiquity made me realize that it was at least worthy of serious study. Too, I wondered how 300 million Buddhists and 250 million Hindus could be misled through all these centuries by a belief that had no substance; and, knowing that the theory of reincarnation was present in the minds of many Jewish people in Christ's time on earth, I wondered why He had not repudiated it by speaking out against it, if indeed it was such a terrible thing to believe in. Surely the Apostles knew that the belief was prevalent in their day. They even informed Christ that they were acquainted with certain people who strongly believed in it, as clearly indicated by their response to the question posed by Jesus, "Who do men say that the Son of man is?"

"Some say," they replied, "John the Baptist; some say Elijah: and others, Jeremiah, or one of the prophets . . ."

Think about their response for a minute. The Apostles knew that Moses and Elijah and all the prophets (save John the Baptist, who was then awaiting execution) had gone the way of all flesh many long years before, yet here they voiced the thought that many people believed: that Moses, Elijah, or one of the prophets had returned to life in the man who was known as Jesus. This poses the question: How could the Apostles have explained the presence of Moses et al. in Jesus if not by the theory of reincarnation?

Parenthetically, a word of explanation is needed about how reincarnation takes place. Basically, reincarnation implies the transmigration of the soul after death into the body of another person who is to be born into this world. For example, when God decided to come to earth as a human being, the Holy Spirit entered into the womb of the Virgin Mary and was born as Jesus Christ, who became God in the flesh. Only once did God come to earth in human form; hence we speak of His birth as the Incarnation. Just so, many believe that since the human soul is immortal and continues to live, whether in this life or the life to come, so the soul in spirit form, which has knowledge and will, in an effort to attain perfection (becoming better and better with each incarnation) selects the zygote of an impregnated female and is reborn (reincarnated) through her.

While the Apostles clearly stated that "some [others] say" that Jesus may have been a reincarnated entity, permit me to point out and strongly emphasize that although knowledge of the belief in reincarnation was (is) present in the Bible, Jesus did not teach it! Although several times given the opportunity, He did not repudiate it or deny it. Rather, He seems to have just let it slide by as a part of the ideas accepted by many to be true in those days. I shall have more to say on this particular facet of Jesus' thought in a subsequent chapter. For now, let me note that Ecclesiastes and Psalms both strongly hint that the idea was prevalent in Jewish thought long before the time of Christ.

Ecclesiastes 6:6 says, "Yea, though he live a thousand years twice told, yet hath he seen no good: do not all go to the same place?"

Psalm 126:6 says, "He that goeth forth and weepeth, bearing precious seed, shall doubtless come again with rejoicing, bringing his sheaves with him."

Even the renowned Jewish historian Josephus made reference to it as if it were common thought when he wrote in *De Bello Judaico* (2:8), "They say all souls are incorruptible, but that the souls of the good men are only removed into other bodies."

What did Jesus mean in Matthew 11:14 when He spoke of John the Baptist and said of him as he sat in prison awaiting death by Herod's orders, ". . . if you will receive it, this is Elias which was for to come." And hadn't the Old Testament prophet Malachi concluded the whole of that Testament by proclaiming, "Behold, I will send you Elijah the prophet before the coming of the great and dreadful day of the Lord"?

Then, in Mark 9:11, the Apostles asked Jesus, "Why say the scribes that Elias must first come?" (The same question is asked in Matthew 17:10.) Jesus answered in Mark 9:13 and Matthew 17:12, 13, ". . . I say unto you that Elias is come already, and they knew him not, but have done unto him whatsoever they listed . . . Then the disciples understood that he spoke unto them of John the Baptist." One would be hard put to find clearer language in which the questions could be phrased; the same can be said for the straightforward answer that Jesus gave, clearly indicating that John the Baptist was the reincarnation of Elijah.

One more Biblical reference, please. In John 9:2, we read that a man born blind was brought to Jesus with the question "Master, who did sin, this man or his parents, that he was born blind?" The idea of reincarnation is very clear in that question, for if, as the Apostles believed, the man was being punished for sin committed, then the sin would have to have been committed in an earlier life, before he was born into this world. Jesus made it clear in His answer that neither the man nor his parents had sinned; still, His answer did not negate the fact that the Apostles asked several questions which indicated that the theory of reincarnation was much on the minds of the people in those days.

Further, it must be noted that reincarnation was accepted by early church fathers, such as Origen (in *De Principiis* and *Contra Celsus*), and some say that this is true even of St. Augustine in his *Confessions*, but this is doubtful.

Back to my heartache after being called the devil's advocate by Polly's neighbor. Despite the growing antagonism and scattered persecution, Dolores and I continued with the regressions and Gretchen became more and more a part of our lives. Although we frequently discussed her and spoke of her as a person—we were comfortable with her—Dr. Stevenson had suggested very strongly that Dolores not listen to any of the tapes or read the transcripts or translations. "Refrain from even discussing the case in Dolores's presence," he insisted.

This, of course, proved not an easy thing to do, and it posed problems and created strain between her and me on more than one occasion. The whole situation was unfair to Dolores; I honestly believe there are few women in the world who would have been so tolerant, patient, and kind under similar impositions.

Dolores and I were thankful that in the thirty years of our marriage we had kept no secrets from each other, else Gretchen's story might never have come to the fore. Complete trust and perfect rapport are essential ingredients for effective hypnosis. For example, although Dolores has absolutely no recollection of anything she says or does in hypnosis, she readily agreed that I should probe her subconscious without restraint. I could question her about sex, religion, friends, relatives, personal habits and desires —nothing was sacred or off limits, even though I often kidded her about "prying out secrets" and she always shouted, "You wouldn't dare!"

This does not mean we never experienced problems over information gleaned from her in regression. Dolores is a very human and very sensitive person, and there were times when her curiosity impelled her to insist that I tell her some of the information imparted by Gretchen, but after a day or two of piqued pride she would smile and agree that it was best for her not to know the details of the Gretchen story until the investigation was completed.

There were other problems, deep, traumatic, almost tragic problems. For example, one time I had hypnotized but not regressed Dolores while attempting to perform a new experiment. Possibly I should pause here and state that because most scientists have shied away from knowing the whole truth and nothing but the truth about hypnosis, especially in the area of regression, grave dangers are latent in the wrong use of hypnosis, even though hypnotism per se is completely harmless in the hands of competent practitioners. On this night I had permitted Dolores's spirit to run free after she was in the somnambulistic state. That is, I did not attempt to elicit information or guide her thinking. Shortly after the session began, Dolores found herself (soul/spirit/self) once again standing before a huge portal in the heavens, a vision she had experienced many times, hearing Gretchen on the other side of the huge open door calling plaintively, "Come! Come go with me. I need you!"

But Dolores would not go, and when she showed signs of terrible fear I intervened and told her, "I will bring you out of the trance; then after a five-minute interval, you will enter a posthypnotic trance. You will then go to the dining room, sit at the table, and write on a piece of paper which I place before you. You will know the reasons for Gretchen's insistence that you join her in that strange other world, and you will write those reasons down."

The suggestions worked perfectly, to a point. While Dolores reentered the trance and went to the table to sit down and write, she began to sleepily inscribe in German, "My dear friend, hang on despite your troubles. The situation is very dangerous with your wife. I may be able to help. It is not possible to talk more. There is no turning back. One day I will return."

While she began to write sleepily, the lethargy soon disappeared. She began to write faster. Her breathing became so labored that it could be heard all over the house. The more she wrote, the faster she wrote. The faster she wrote, the harder she breathed. Suddenly she dropped the pencil and collapsed on the table.

It was a terrible experience for both of us. For the first time in my twenty years' experience with hypnosis it appeared that I might not be able to bring her out of the trance. I had heard of amateurs not knowing what to do under similar circumstances, forced to call in psychiatrists, who then hospitalized the subjects. But all my learning told me that there was no cause for alarm—experience was on my side. Indeed, in a few moments I was able to awaken Dolores, tired but able to relate all the minute details of her horrible experience.

The following, I believe, is what happened. When Dolores sat down to write, she had become Gretchen, or apparently Gretchen's spirit had entered into her body in order to assume control and write the letter to me. She knew I was suffering from great physical afflictions due to the deteriorating condition of my heart. She also knew that certain people were trying to cause trouble for us because of our work with hypnosis. Too, Dolores was under a terrible strain psychologically, what with worrying about my health, rearing the children, and living with a subliminal fear that if she was not the reincarnated Gretchen, then she surely must be possessed by Gretchen's spirit. Both possibilities were repugnant to her.

Worst of all, I did not realize that if Dolores saw Gretchen and remembered the circumstances surrounding their meeting, she would suffer serious posthypnotic trauma. In ignorance I had told her just before bringing her out of the trance that she would remember everything that had happened that night. Normally, as I said earlier, she could remember nothing from her trance state. But I was performing an experiment, so the suggestion "You will remember everything" was necessary.

Hindsight makes us all wiser, or it should, and I have always regretted letting her remember that night. But then, I cannot honestly say that the results of that night were all bad. Since very few of my more-learned brethren in academic and scientific circles have experimented in regression, or at least have not made known the results of any investigations, Dolores and I will not count that night as a loss if our experience deters less-experienced hypnotists from engaging in hypnotic practices they do not thoroughly understand.

As a result of that night, though, we suffered moments of sheer torture, because Gretchen did return, not once but many times. She first came not many days after Dolores's horrible experience, while I was away for a ministerial meeting. When I returned home in the afternoon, both Dolores and the house were a mess. She was still wearing her nightgown and bathrobe. Her hair was disheveled. Her dilated eyes stared blankly ahead. The furniture was in disarray and upset. Breakfast dishes were unwashed and scattered all over the cabinets and on the floor, some of them broken. The refrigerator door was wide open. The beds were unmade, and drapes on one side of the living-room window hung askew. Flabbergasted, I demanded, "What in the world happened here?"

Dolores showed no sign that she heard me. She didn't even recognize me. Cautiously, patiently, I led her to the living-room couch and induced hypnosis. Gently I asked, "Dolores, do you know me?

"Do . . . Do . . . Doloreusss," she drawled haltingly. "Nein, ich bin Gretchen."

Quickly I assumed that in some unknown way Dolores had lapsed into hypnosis and spontaneously regressed—unless, of course, Gretchen had finally come and fully possessed her. But no! I could not accept that! Surely in some way I had inadvertently touched her on the forehead with three fingers that morning and thus administered a posthypnotic suggestion. Incidentally, a good suggestion for all hypnotists is in order: Never go to sleep with a hypnotic subject (Now you know that you shouldn't sleep with her anyway unless she is your wife) unless you can figure out a way to keep from administering posthypnotic suggestions in your sleep. Twice Dolores had awakened to find me sleepily groping for her forehead and was able to awaken me before she lapsed into a trance.

Whether I hypnotized Dolores that morning, I'll never know for certain. In any event, I used hypnosis to get her back on the right track that day. As I often did after working with her in hypnosis, I suggested that instead of waking up from the trance, she would sleep soundly for an hour before awakening—I needed the time to wash the dishes and straighten up the house. Just after I made the last bed and just before the children came home from school, Dolores walked into the bedroom, brushing her hair and apologizing. "I don't understand it," she said sheepishly, "I've never slept this late before." Then jokingly she dismissed the whole thing. "You must have drugged my coffee last night."

The worst was yet to come. A week later Joe Vasquez, an old friend from Spelter, West Virginia, was visiting us, and after Joe and the children had gone to bed Dolores became very argumentative for no apparent reason. Finally, after a half-hour of tearing apart everything I said, she flounced off to the bedroom. Thoroughly perplexed, because this attitude was so totally foreign to her gentle nature, I soon followed, hoping to find out what was troubling her. She would have nothing to do with me. We argued for an hour about nothing, really, until she jumped up and ran to the bathroom, shouting, "I've had it! I'm going to put an end to this nonsense right now!"

"Good!" I thought. "When she comes back, maybe we'll get some rest." But she didn't come back, and I began to get anxious, and wondered with a shudder, "Has she gotten into my tranquilizers?" Desperately I prayed, "O God, no! Surely those fifty-milligram Thorazines are too much for her." Running to the bathroom, I couldn't get in—she had locked the door!

"Dolores," I called softly, not wanting to awaken Joe and the children, "unlock this door and let me in."

"Go away!" she ordered. "Besides, there's nothing you can do—it's too late."

"What do you mean?" I demanded loudly, scared. "Did you get into my medicine?"

She didn't answer.

"Well, did you? Answer me, do you hear me, answer!"

"Yes," she finally yelled, almost hatefully, "and there's nothing you can do about it!"

The commotion awoke everyone, and Joe and the children swarmed around me at the door. "Get back," I cautioned them, "I'm going to break the door down!" And I did.

"Joe, you stay with the children," I called while jumping into a pair of pants and hustling Dolores off to the hospital in Georgetown.

En route to the hospital, after being stopped for speeding by a Mount Orab policeman—he promised not to give me a ticket or say anything to anyone after I hurriedly explained my predicament—Dolores finally told me that there had been only six or seven Thorazines in the bottle. "I couldn't find anymore," she added, "or I would have taken them, too!"

At the hospital a nurse examined Dolores and listened to my story before calling a doctor, who told her to send us home and "let her sleep it off."

On the way home we rode in silence until Dolores began mumbling, "Ich kann nicht sprechen. Nien! Es ist verboten!"

"Oh, no!" I moaned in distress, realizing that Dolores had lapsed into a hypnotic trance. "Not that again! Dolores, relax!" I urged, reaching out to touch her on the forehead in order to induce hypnosis.

"Du musst jetzt weggehen!" she screamed, and began to fight with a vengeance.

Stopping the car after being all over the road and almost being hit head-on by an oncoming car, I finally reached her forehead after pinning her arms and pleaded, "Relax! Please, Gretchen, I am not trying to hurt you. Don't you understand? I want to help you! That's better," I said encouragingly as Dolores began to slump in the seat. "Relax, honey. It will soon be all over. Relax, let yourself go . . . sleep . . . sleep."

Dolores was sound asleep when we got home, but to this day I cannot understand how such a tiny person could resist the effect of the Thorazines so long. It must have been an hour after she took them before I managed to force her into the trance state. Even then it was quite some time before they took full effect, but I was grateful for that at the time, because it afforded me the opportunity of questioning her.

"Dolores," I asked tenderly as she lay with her head in my lap, "can you tell me what happened to you tonight?"

"I didn't want to do it," she responded defensively.

"Do what? Are you referring to the medicine—"

"She made me do it after you went to the meeting . . . I got up from bed, but when I looked into the mirror to brush my hair, I saw her, and . . . then, ohhhhh, she was standing beside me, smiling. 'Come,' she said, and then she . . . she touched me on the forehead the way you do . . ."

"You say she came to you after I went to the meeting, but that was a week ago."

"I know," she said, "but the same thing happened last night. I went to the bathroom just after the children went to bed, and there she was, waiting for me."

I could get no more from Dolores that night. The drug had taken effect, and she began to ramble incoherently. I let her sleep, a sleep that lasted eighteen hours.

CHAPTER V

A Brief Journey into Gloryland

While we were preparing for Dr. Stevenson's second visit to our home, in October, the condition of my heart deteriorated rapidly, and it was highly questionable whether I would live long enough to see the investigation of the Gretchen case completed. Three times in the preceding years our doctors had suggested to Dolores that she call my family in—death was imminent. Thank God, I managed to rally each time and was able to live a fairly normal life.

In the early years of my life athletics had been my forte: Football, basketball, and baseball in high school and brief tryouts in baseball with the old Columbus Red Birds of the American Association under Burt Shotten and Johnnie Neun of the Akron Yankees (before a year at Marshall University in 1939) preceded my marriage to Dolores, in 1940. Afterward I played semipro baseball for the Willow Beachers in my old home town, Clarksburg, West Virginia. Following World War II I umpired professional baseball in the Blue Ridge League of Virginia and North Carolina, and after entering the ministry and returning to college to complete my education in 1955, at age thirty-three, I refereed college basketball and coached football, basketball, and baseball at the high-school level until my first heart attack, in 1964.

The rigors and discipline of active participation in sports served me well. Always a fighter and a hard loser, I simply would not give up and quit just because I had a heart no better than a dime-store resuscitator. Still, with my strength spent, I almost despaired of ever seeing another ball game. Yet the will to live was still there. I hung on to life with all the faith I could muster, and, praise to His holy name, I've made it safely thus far.

When I began feeling better, one beautiful early-fall day the desire to get out and move around began to stir, and I drove to Batavia, some fifteen to twenty miles away, to shop at a supermarket. As I began the trip home, I became so tired and weak that I hardly had strength enough to pilot the car; it will always be a mystery to me how I managed to make it home. I have no memory of anything from the time I left Batavia until after parking the car in our basement garage; not until I found myself standing at the foot of the basement stairs did I know where I was. Even then it was necessary for me to pause for several minutes and grope for enough strength to make it up into the house.

I couldn't make it! Oh, I managed to make it most of the way up, but as I struggled to pull myself upward with the aid of the handrail, groceries began spilling out of the shopping bag, alerting Dolores that I was home and in trouble. Running to help me, she found me lying about three steps from the top and immediately began lifting, pulling, and tugging me like a sack of potatoes up into the kitchen, where she was forced to let me lie on the floor while she ran to the telephone to call for an ambulance. But I wanted no part of that deal—the hospital was not for me—so I called her back. "I can't go to the hospital! Dr. Stevenson will be here in a few days, and I've got to finish the investigation."

Worried sick about me, Dolores insisted that I forget the investigation. "Forget everything! It's not worth your life! You've got to go to the hospital!" she pleaded while putting nitroglycerin under my tongue (we always carried it with us). But I petitioned her, "Please wait until we see what the nitroglycerin does!" Dr. Courter had insructed me to take the nitroglycerin at the first sign of pain, and if chest pains did not stop within a minute or two, to wait another ten minutes and take some more. Then, if there was no relief from pain, I was to call an ambulance immediately.

Dolores continued to weep and fuss over my stubbornness while getting a cool cloth to wipe away the perspiration that covered me like a hot shower. She sat on the floor with my head in her lap, scolding me for tempting fate. "If that is what you want," she relented temporarily, "I'll wait ten minutes, but not a minute more!"

At the end of the allotted time the pain had subsided. It had not ended completely, and I fibbed to Dolores, "I'm all right. See," I said, sitting up. "Just help me to bed." I was too weak to get up, so my good wife dragged me by the shoulders from the kitchen through the dining room, down the hallway, and into the bedroom, where it took a mighty struggle to get me into bed. I stayed there for the next few days.

I must have made life miserable for Dolores. In the preceding seven years I had been hospitalized seven times with seven serious heart attacks; in between there were several flare-ups that required many days of bed rest. God bless her! With never a complaint, she waited on me hand and foot, night and day.

In spite of my foolishness and weakness, I did not neglect my church or my family, nor did they neglect me. No man ever had a more loving and devoted wife and children—I was babied and doctored so well that there was only one time (when I was not in the hospital) that I did not preach in the Sunday services at Union Plains. In return, through a strong will and the love of God, I attended to the needs of my family. I wouldn't even let the grass in my yard get out of hand; a day or two before Dr. Stevenson arrived, I was on my riding mower, manicuring the lawn.

Dr. Stevenson brought with him Dr. Erika Klaus, a native born professor of anthropology at a nearby university. They arrived at about 9:30 A.M. on October 5 and spent the whole day interviewing Gretchen while Dolores lay in her usual trance.

Again Dolores was extremely nervous, as she always was when entering a trance in the presence of strangers. She always felt, "I must be some kind of an oddity, made only to be put on display so I can speak in a language I don't even know."

Dr. Klaus was only the second native German to question Gretchen, and the first German academic to converse with her. As usual, Dolores wondered what would happen if Gretchen did not come through and talk to her questioners. Although I still could not subscribe to a belief in reincarnation, the fact that Dolores always spoke of Gretchen as a person, and that she insisted it was Gretchen who spoke through her, not she herself who was speaking, reinforced my belief that Gretchen was indeed a real personality, not merely Dolores's own dissociated self. Regardless of Dolores's apprehension I was therefore certain that Gretchen would emerge and speak in her own native tongue.

After Dolores had settled down on the couch and entered the somnambulistic state I introduced Dr. Stevenson and Dr. Klaus to Gretchen—in English, of course. It made no difference to Gretchen whether she was addressed in English or German. She would always answer, always in German.

(Incidentally, she cannot understand any other language. For example, while I was questioning Gretchen before a large audience at Blue Ridge Community College, Austin Anderson, professor of biology at Blue Ridge, a linguist who speaks German, French, and Danish, asked me while questioning Gretchen in German if he could digress momentarily. Although I did not know what he planned to do, I agreed. I did not know that Mr. Anderson could speak French and Danish, but when Gretchen ceased responding to his questions except to say, "Ich verstehe nicht [I do not understand]," I assumed he had switched to another language. He confirmed my assumption when Gretchen again began responding to his questions and he announced to the audience, "I have spoken to her in German, French, and Danish, and I am convinced that she cannot understand any language other than English and German.")

Gretchen was always afraid of strangers and until she was convinced that everyone present was her friend, she would not speak to anyone other than me, whom she knew only as "Gut Freund." Everyone else she assumed was a member of the Bundesrat. The Bundesrat was the Federal Council of the federated states in the North German Confederation and its successor, the (second) German Empire. In the 1870s a severe struggle occurred between the secular authority of the Prussian government under Chancellor Bismarck and the Roman Catholic Church. That quarrel, known as the Kulturkampf, entailed much hardship and persecution for the Roman Catholics, and Gretchen was terribly afraid that a member of the Bundesrat might be present and listening to what she would say. Gretchen was a Catholic, and she feared for her life.

When Dr. Stevenson and Dr. Klaus began questioning Gretchen, she asked fearfully, "Wer ist das? [Who is that?]" When I explained that they were our friends, she asked ungrammatically, "Ist gut Freund? [Is good friend?]"

Dr. Stevenson and Dr. Klaus alternately questioned Gretchen about where she lived and if she went to church. "Ja," Gretchen said, "Ich gehe in die Kirche. [Yes, I go in the church.]" In response to questions about food, she said she ate "Fleisch [meat], Schwein [pork], Rind [beef], Küchlein [chicken], Gemüse [vegetables], Kartoffel [potatoes], Kohl [cabbage], Obst [fruit]—der Apfel [apples]." About friends, she talked of playing with Mrs. Schilder's children, Karen, Kurt, Karl, and Erich. Mrs. Schilder was their housekeeper and cook. Gretchen also told them that she could neither read nor write ("nicht lese, nicht schreiben").

Although Gretchen answered Dr. Klaus's questions, she did not respond to her as readily as she had to other interrogators. Possibly there was a personality conflict. Still, when the regression was stopped for lunch, Dr. Klaus was exuberantly intrigued and insisted that Dolores and I write a book about "this strange phenomenon."

When Dolores returned to the couch in the afternoon, Gretchen insisted she had to go into the house because her father would "Sich ärgern [get angry]."

Stevenson: "Ja. Warum müssen Sie zum Hause gehen? Wir sind Ihre Freunde, wissen Sie? [Yes. Why do you have to go to your house? We are friends, don't you know?]"

Gretchen: "Sehr gefährlich. [Very dangerous.]"

Stevenson: "Was ist gefährlich? [What is dangerous?]"

Gretchen: "Sache sehr schlecht hier. [Things very bad here.]"

Stevenson: "Was für Sachen? [What sort of things?]"

Gretchen: "Die Kirche streitet; viel Völkerkampf . . . torpen. [The church fights; many civilians . . . dead.]"

Stevenson: "Torpen? [Dead?]" Dr. Stevenson at that time did not realize that Gretchen always used part of "Gestorben" for the word "dead."

Gretchen: "Ja. Sache sehr schlecht. [Yes. Things are very bad.]"

Stevenson: "Ja, Gretchen. Setzen Sie fort. [Yes, Gretchen. Go ahead.]"

Gretchen: "Der Bundesrat, Sie hören zu. [The Federal Council, they listen.]"

Stevenson: "Was soll so gefährlich sein? [What is supposed to be dangerous?]"

Suddenly showing signs of restless fear, Gretchen demanded, "Du mussen weggehen! [You must go away!]"

Stevenson: "Ich muss weggehen; warum? [I must go away; why?]"

Klaus: "Nicht weggehen. Kannst du erklären? [Not go away. Can you explain?]"

For quite some time Gretchen refused to speak; then she said warily, "Es tut mir leid; ich muss kehren, zurückkommen. [I am sorry. I have to go, come again.]"

Klaus: "Wann kommen Sie zurück? [When will you come back?]"

Gretchen, sighing heavily: "Sehr müde. [Very tired.]"

Gretchen had begun speaking in the morning at age nine, but I had moved her to age fourteen for the afternoon session. Now I attempted to get her to advance up to age sixteen, but she rebelled.

"Why don't you want to go to sixteen, Gretchen?"

Gretchen: "Sache sehr schlecht hier. [Things very bad here.]"

Klaus: "Schlecht! Was is schlecht? [Terrible! What is terrible?]"

Gretchen, weeping softly: "Gretchen im Gefängnis. [Gretchen in prison.]"

Stevenson: "Im Gefängnis! Können Sie uns das Gefängnis beschreiben? [In prison! Could you describe the prison for us?]"

Gretchen, opening her eyes and looking around, sadly: "Viele Völker torpen. [Many persons dead!]"

Klaus: "Gestorben? [Dead?]"

Gretchen: "Gestorben, ja. Im Kerker. [Dead, yes. In

prison.]" (Note that here Gretchen used a different word for "prison.")

I had hoped that Gretchen would elaborate on the cause for imprisonment, and I interjected, "Tell us more. Tell us everything you can!" after Dr. Stevenson had looked up and translated Gretchen's word for "prison" aloud. But Gretchen continued to weep and mumble, "Viel Völkerkampf . . . Viel tot. [Much civil struggle . . . many dead.]"

Then Dr. Stevenson changed the subject and inquired, "Wer ist der Papst? Wissen Sie den Namen des Papstes? [Who is Pope? Do you know what the Pope is called?]"

Gretchen relaxed and grew calm: "Papst Leo."

Stevenson: "Hat der Papst einen deutschen Vertreter? [Does the Pope have a representative in Germany?]"

Gretchen: "Gretchen versteht nicht Vertreter. Der Bundesrat . . . Du soll weggehen. [Gretchen does not understand 'representative.' The Federal Council . . . you should go away.]"

Gretchen was getting tired, "Sehr müde [Very tired]," she said, but there was so very much we needed to know, and I urged her, "Tell us what happened on the day of your death, Gretchen." But she was so tired and distraught that she merely mumbled, "Ich . . . in . . . Kerker. [I . . . in . . . prison.]"

Stevenson: "Wiederholen Sie bitte. Was haben Sie gesagt, Gretchen? [Please repeat that. What did you say, Gretchen?]"

"Tot [Dead]," she moaned.

Again I urged her to elaborate, but she grew more and more reluctant to talk. It may have been that Dolores was physically weary—she had endured a very long day of questioning—but it was also possible that Gretchen simply did not want to again relive the moment of her death. The majority of persons whom I have regressed who suffered a violent death in the supposed prior life have avoided going through that experience a second time.

Showing more and more signs of strain and stress, Gretchen spoke briefly of her father: "Mein Vater torpen . . . Verrat . . . reiten das Pferd . . . [My father died . . . betrayal . . . ride the horse . . .]"

Stevenson: "Reiten das Pferd? Ja, und dann? [Ride the horse? Yes, and then what?]"

Gretchen: "Der Mann—"

Stevenson, interrupting: "Gretchen . . . reiten? [Gretchen . . . ride?]"

Gretchen, with great emotion: "Nein! Nein! Mein Vater . . . nicht . . . grauste mich! [No! No! My father . . . not . . . I am terrified!]"

"Gretchen," I entreated, "only one more question or two, please. Did you ever get out of prison?"

"Nein."

"Did they put you to death while you were in prison?"

Slowly, as if drifting away, Gretchen responded, "Schlafen. [Sleep.]"

Stevenson: "Schlafen? War das Ende? [Sleep? Was that the end?]"

Gretchen: "Auf Wiedersehen. [Good-bye.]"

It had been a terribly long day for both Dolores and me. Under normal hypnosis Dolores would always awaken rested and refreshed. but when regressed to the Gretchen state, she was usually exhausted upon awakening. And well she should have been, because she does not merely tell Gretchen's story. She lives it! It is as real to her as if she were actually back in the tragic moments of her abbreviated life. Because of the close rapport, I empathize and sympathize until I am emotionally drained. This is true not only of me, but of everyone who has seen Dolores regressed to the Gretchen state.

Dr. Klaus said in a statement relative to her part in the investigation, "Mrs. Jay responded only in German, and she did so as if she were a certain Gretchen Gottlieb of Eberswalde, now long deceased." Douglas Kiker of NBC-TV, when he first saw Dolores in a trance, went weak in the knees and exclaimed, "Oh, my God! She's dead!"

Lest anyone think that only those who believe in reincarnation were allowed to question Dolores/Gretchen, it is not true. Of all those involved in the investigation, only Dr. Stevenson expressed an interest in reincarnation. Dr. Klaus definitely did not, nor did others who were to assist in the investigation.

After that session with Dr. Stevenson and Dr. Klaus,

Dolores and I were more convinced than ever that elements of the supernatural were playing a tremendous role in our lives, and we fervently hoped that he would come up with a few quick answers. But Dr. Stevenson is a conscientious scholar, a man not given to hasty decisions. He had just completed a case comparable to the Gretchen case, the Jenson case; he had spent twelve long years on that one case alone.

One thing was certain: Dolores and I could not wait twelve years for an answer. In the Jenson case, the husband also was the subject's hypnotist, but he died before Dr. Stevenson wrote his official report, and at the time of Dr. Stevenson's second visit to our home it seemed foolish for anyone to even think that I would live another twelve years. As it happened, I went to see Dr. Courter a few days after Dr. Stevenson's visit, because I had become so weak that I could not walk from one room to another without leaning against the walls for support.

Dr. Courter had done a wonderful job of treating me —only his expertise had kept me alive—but even he could only go so far. He informed me that I should enter the hospital for an arteriogram, a test to determine the cause of my many heart attacks.

"Is the test dangerous, Doctor?"

"Well, in your case, yes," he answered forthrightly. "With your medical record, anything and everything has an element of risk."

"And what happens if I do not submit to the test?"

With a shrug, he hedged. "Who knows? Obviously you are not going to get any better. You could last a week, a month—a few months at the most."

Dolores and I went home feeling low, mighty low. Even though we had known for a long time that my condition was precarious, not until then did I accept that the end was rapidly approaching. There were a few times when I lay down at night thinking I might not awaken in the morning, but as time went on and the good Lord blessed me with the joy of living, my fears of death were reduced to nothing more than an occasional thought.

Conversation was sparse on that drive home. The whole weight of the world was on Dolores. She fought bravely to maintain a good front, and I truly empathized with her. To me, death was a way of life, a transition from a mortal struggle for existence to an eternity of happy security and contentment with the Lord. Still, I did not relish leaving my wife and children behind, nor could I feel easy about the burden which Dolores faced. Vonda was only thirteen, Mary Jo twelve, and Jesse eleven. Punky was twenty-three and married, and she would get along fine, but Dolores would have to get a job, and the children would have to manage the best they could without a father. It was not a pleasant thought. Too, Dolores would have to face the results of the Gretchen case alone; that was bad, really bad.

We were trapped. Opposition to our investigation of reincarnation was growing. Many professing Christians who knew of our exploration into the world of the unknown would not believe that it revolved around the sincere hope that we could invalidate the use of hypnosis in proving true the theory of reincarnation; they accused us of embracing reincarnation merely as a means of making money. On the other side of the fence, the occultists lambasted us because we refused to become one with them. Each new day revealed new evidence of animosity. We couldn't seem to win for losing. The position in which I had put Dolores and the children was detestable. Night and day I prayed that God would intervene, that He would not take me away and force my family to face ostracism and persecution alone.

Dolores and I had concluded on the way home from the doctor that we should gather the children together and discuss whether I should undergo the test. So after dinner we all sat before the fireplace and I told them what the doctor had said. They wanted to know, "What kind of a test?"

"Well," I attempted to explain, "a doctor would insert a long catheter into the femoral artery, where the leg joins the body at the groin, and then work it up into my heart, where dyes could be injected. X-rays would then be taken and, hopefully, the doctors could determine the cause of all my heart attacks."

When we had finished discussing the procedure and possible results, including the odds that I might not live through the test, the children were unanimous in their belief that I should not have the test.

"After all," they said, "you may live a long time without the test, but if you take the test, it might kill you. We'd rather have you the way you are than not have you at all." The next day I called Dr. Courter and told him that we had decided against the test.

Now each day became a struggle just to survive. Ninety percent of my time was spent in bed, and every evening when the children came home from school they came to my room to spend some time with me and tell me all that had happened that day. Then the girls would go to be with their mother, but Jess remained at my side. Except to go to the bathroom, he seldom left the room. We whiled away the time playing rummy, setback, and dominoes. One night I noticed that Jess was putting on weight, childish fat that came from inactivity. "Jess," I began to explain reluctantly—I liked having him with me—"I love having you with me, but this is no good for you, so starting tomorrow I want you to go out and play after coming home from school. I want you to do all the things you used to do."

"But, Dad," he protested, "I'd rather be with you!"

"I know, Jess. But, well—look, I'm going to be all right. I'm going to get well, just you wait and see. And when I do, we'll do things together just like we used to."

"But suppose you don't," he challenged fearfully, "suppose something happens to you when I'm not here to help you!"

"Now, don't you worry, son! Nothing's going to happen. Hey! Where's your faith? Don't we still live by the faith expressed in Romans 8:28, 'We know that all things work together for good to them that love God, to them who are called according to his purpose'? Good is going to happen, Jess—believe me, God will see us through!"

The next day saw Jess dropping in several times during the evening just to see how I was getting along. Gradually, as time wore on he began to act as a normal boy of eleven should. One night he and the girls were watching television and they began to laugh. It was the wild, high-pitched, hysterical laugh common to kids their age. But that evening I felt miserable—my nerves were frayed—

and I yelled, "Hey, kids! Lower it just a little, please!"
Immediately they turned off the television, and Jess muttered disconsolately, "Ah, shucks! You can't even laugh around here anymore!" Cut to the quick by the well-deserved jab, I suddenly realized just how unfair my illness was to Dolores and the children. I called Dolores and said, "Tomorrow you phone Dr. Courter and schedule the arteriogram. I'd rather be dead than see you and the children living like this."

On November 18, 1971, I entered Christ's Hospital in Cincinnati. The next day I was prepped and taken to the X-ray lab at seven A.M. By ten o'clock, when the test should have been completed, the doctors were only halfway through, and I felt a sharp, stabbing pain at the top center of my heart. "Hold it, Doctor!" I called, hardly able to breathe. "That thing has pierced the wall of my heart."

"No," Dr. Courter replied softly, compassionately. "No, it couldn't do that." Then: "How do you feel?"

"It hurts, but," I added, while wondering why no one moved, "can you stop for a minute and let me go to the bathroom?"

"Let it go," he said, still frozen in position, looking to the right rear of me. "Let it go on the table!"

"Oh, I couldn't do that!" I argued, repulsed at the thought.

"We'll clean it up," he said. "Let it go—you shouldn't strain like that!"

I looked around, puzzled that nobody moved. They looked like frozen statues: a doctor holding the catheter in place, the X-ray technician clutching in midair an X-ray plate he had just gotten from the machine, the nurses and assistants in gruesome stances, all looking with unblinking eyes at the monitor. Suddenly I realized that the urge to go to the bathroom had passed. I felt good, wonderful! For the first time in years I was without pain or labored breath; and, thank God! there was Mom! Oh, I was so happy! I hadn't seen her since her funeral, just after last Thanksgiving. And—

It can't be! Dad! Is that really you, Dad? Gee, how long has it been—ten years? fifteen? Twenty. Yeah, almost twenty! Oh, it's so good to be with you again!

Strangely, I couldn't understand all the commotion below me. When I last looked while lying there on the table, Dr. Courter and everyone else were frozen in position, but now—

Look at them! They're running around like crazy. What are they doing to that poor guy on the table, hitting him on the chest and side with things that look like flatirons, making his body bounce like a rubber mattress?

Gee, it's nice up here, high above everyone—just like floating. It's . . . it's almost like the time when I was a little boy with my brother Bill and some other guys on a raft in the old West Fork River near Grandma's, and they jumped off and upset it with me on it. And Bill, I felt sorry for him. He was so scared—he didn't stop to think that I couldn't swim. But, gee—the foamy, soft water and the bright lights, they . . . they were all around me . . . and I was floating downstream. Oh, I wished Bill hadn't grabbed me and pulled me out of the water. I liked it down there at the bottom of that cool, cushiony river.

But that was a long time ago, and—say, that guy down there on the table, he looks familiar! Funny-looking, though. Hey! Well whatta you know, that's me! But it can't be! I'm up here, and—There's Dr. Courter. He's working so hard; why does he look so worried?

That light, that bright light off in the distance, what is it? Oh, it's growing—it's getting bigger and brighter. But no, it's not a light, not really. It's love, peace, joy, happiness. It. . . It . . . but it's not an it, it's Him! Mom, Dad, wait! Don't go—don't go . . . Oh, hi, G. H.

G. H. West! Why, you were just a kid, maybe thirty-five years ago, when you ran into the side of that car in front of our home. But, well—I gotta go, G. H. Oh, I hate to go back. If only—if only the peaceful, happy serenity could last forever—I want that!

And the brightness of Him! The light that is brighter than a thousand suns, yet so easy to look at, to love and adore. No glare—a pulsing, vibrating essence of . . . of life. That's it! The light, the life that came into the world that we might have light and life. Amen! Amen! Hallelujah!

But I must go back now. Yes, back to my body on the table. What's that? Did I hear someone say "It's been almost five minutes"? No, it couldn't be. Surely I've not been up here more than a second or two. But, no matter, old body, here I come. Oh, my aching body! Look at them massaging, one on each arm and each leg, rubbing like crazy. And now they're covering me with everything they can lay their hands on: blankets, sheets, smocks. I think I'll open my eyes, and—

"Doctor, what are you doing leaning over my shoulder like that?"

"I've got to give you a shot of digitalis. There, feel better?"

Well, no, I didn't feel better, but at least it was all over and I had made it through, or so I thought. No, the test was not completed, and it never will be—my heart was too far gone to withstand the strain of the dyes.

CHAPTER VI

Christmas, A Beautiful Interlude

Vaguely I remember Dr. Courter telling me in the X-ray lab "Because of complications I must send you to the Coronary Intensive Care Unit," but I remember nothing more until being wheeled off the elevator at the ICU, where I caught a fleeting glimpse of Dolores and Punky standing some distance down the hall, looking very sad, talking to Dr. Courter.

Dolores later told me that Dr. Courter had reluctantly informed her there in the hallway, "I am sorry, but under the circumstances there is very little chance your husband will live; however, should he make it, you must realize that he may never walk or talk again."

My heart had fibrillated in the X-ray lab, and to all intents and purposes, I had died. There was the possibility that during the almost five minutes when I was out of this world brain damage due to lack of oxygen might have been incurred. At the time, Dr. Courter had no way of knowing the extent of damage, if any.

When Dolores saw them take me off the elevator, she asked Dr. Courter if it was possible for her to be with me for a moment. He agreed that it would be all right. Together, she, Punky, and Dr. Courter came to where I lay. Dolores put a hand on mine and exclaimed, "He's so cold!"

Dr. Courter looked at her and smiled reassuringly. "If you think he is cold now, you should have felt him a moment ago."

For the next two days I lay in a semi-coma, and I have no recollection of anything until Saturday evening. From six A.M. Thursday until nine A.M. Saturday Dolores never left the hospital. Although only Dolores and Punky were permitted to visit me in Intensive Care, and only for brief periods, Dr. Courter made arrangements for Dolores to sit with me Thursday and Friday nights, because the possibility of my leaving the unit alive was practically nil.

Then the fun began. Sometime early Saturday morning, when Dolores was getting a cool washcloth to wipe perspiration from my brow and dampen my parched lips, a nurse came into the room and ordered her out, screaming, "Don't you know that no one is allowed in here except during visiting hours!" Dolores tried to explain her presence, but the nurse, who had been off duty Thursday night, did not know that Dr. Courter had given Dolores permission to be there, would not listen, and proceeded to force her out into the lounge.

For the remainder of that night Dolores lay on a couch in the lounge. When our son-in-law, Larry, brought Punky to the hospital on Saturday morning, he tried to talk Dolores into going home for some rest, but she refused to leave. He finally took her by the arm and forced her to the car and home for rest.

Although I was in a coma, somehow I knew that Dolores had been treated roughly and rudely by a nurse. Unable to comprehend what the commotion was all about, I was under the impression that someone was deliberately trying to harm her and the children.

Nothing made sense to me, possibly because before I entered the hospital for the arteriogram I had put such a high priority on the Gretchen case! I had worked so hard on it that I was completely exhausted. Apart from my family and church, it was number one in my life, and I was determined to proceed with the investigation regardless of any and all opposition. And the opposition was beginning to mount, though I really wasn't conscious of it at the time.

A few weeks earlier, in October, my District Superintendent, the Reverend George Myers, phoned me in anger because he had driven to the church earlier that evening for a Local Conference and found no one there. I was stunned by his actions: The parsonage was located right beside the church, but rather than come to me for an explanation, he got into this car and drove the 65 miles back to his office in Hamilton to phone me. When I inquired why he hadn't come to the parsonage, he refused to answer, preferring to rant and rave.

Every church or charge in United Methodism is obligated to hold a special meeting (Local Conference) each year and lay plans for the following year, the date being set by the District Superintendent. At no time in 1971 did I receive a letter from the Reverend Myers notifying me of the date of our Local Conference, though I am certain he had set a date. Either his letter had gotten lost in the mail or his secretary missed sending one to us. No matter, Mr. Myers had only recently been appointed District Superintendent, and probably did not stop to think there might have been some mix-up or that I might have had some valid excuse.

I was piqued because District Superintendents are required by church discipline to visit each parish during the conference year to oversee and assist all ministers under their supervision in any way they can; but even though I had been seriously ill, not once had the Reverend Myers contacted my wife or me by phone or in person. I wouldn't have known the man had I met him on the street. Even when I went to the hospital there was no get-well card or word of encouragement from him.

Mr. Myers was the least of my worries. But because of my condition, I was worried about a man of horrible visage who was trying to hurt Dolores and the children. I had no idea how, but the hallucination seemed so real that I was determined to protect them at all costs. That Saturday night in a hospital bed it made no difference how. I kicked the standard holding the glucose bottles until they shattered on the floor, and stripped myself of the urethral catheter, electrodes to heart monitor, and several venicaths, then got up and walked barefoot on the broken glass, to destroy everything in the room, even the room itself.

In my confused state, Dolores and the children seemed in danger of being destroyed by that man, and I had to stop him, whoever he was. I could not find anything to use for a weapon. Then I saw the oxygen jet sticking out from the wall. I thought it was a natural-gas pipe. I ripped it from the wall and aimed it at the nonexistent man, certain that the deadly fumes would stop him.

Although the carnage took place in the Intensive Care Unit at Christ Hospital in Cincinnati, in my confused mental state I envisioned the action taking place in my mother's old-fashioned kitchen, as it was forty years ago in our home back in Nutter Fort, West Virginia, where we used natural gas for cooking and heating. But the locale of my hallucination is unimportant. That man was all that counted. I would stop him if it was the last thing I ever did!

My rampage ended suddenly when the smallest nurse on the floor bravely stepped forth and entered my room, even though every available guard, custodian, and orderly in the hospital had been summoned to subdue me. When she finally reached me, to everyone's amazement I merely put an arm around her and pleaded, "Honey, help me, please!" I was later told that when anyone spoke to me that night, even while I was destroying everything in sight, I would reply courteously, "Yes, ma'am, no ma'am" to everything said to me. When my rampage had ended, I had shattered thousands of dollars' worth of expensive equipment, windows, doors, and walls.

Five days later I awoke for the first time following what is now laughingly referred to as "Jay's Raid," and saw a nurse's aide with her back to me, cleaning something from the floor. "Ma'am," I called out, "is it six in the morning or six in the evening?" With a shriek she jumped up and ran from the room, screaming, "Oh, my God! He's alive! He's alive!" I then lapsed back into a coma. When I again opened my eyes, Dr. Courter and another doctor and nurses were entering the room hurriedly.

"Hi, fellow," Dr. Courter greeted me brightly, "glad to see you made it back!"

After checking me over, Dr. Courter stood at the foot of the bed and held his forefinger and thumb a quarter of an inch apart and said, "Preacher, do you know that for the past five days you have been just that far from death?" I hadn't known, but it made no difference to me —a quarter of an inch was as good as a mile.

For the next several weeks I lay in the hospital, often dreaming of the man who I thought was intent on hurting Dolores and the kids. Always I awoke wet with sweat. Little did I realize that within a few short months I would meet that man face to face. For the moment I wanted only to get out of the hospital and go home to be with my wife and children. Each day when Dr. Smith came in to examine me (Dr. Courter was on vacation) I asked, "When are you going to let me go home?" I thought I could go home any time, because before I entered the hospital Dr. Courter had told me I would be there only a couple of days for the test, and I couldn't understand why they wouldn't let me go home. For the first few days Dr. Smith always answered, "Maybe soon." But one day he exploded and said, "Dammit, fellow, don't you know you've had a heart attack!"

I was shocked, not by his language or attitude, but by the sickening realization that I had suffered my eighth heart attack. Not until then did I realize why I didn't have the strength to brush my teeth.

A couple weeks before Christmas Dr. Courter came to my room at about nine A.M. and told me, "We're going to let you go home soon, but you must be very careful never to get angry, never let yourself get excited, and never stick your head out the door to get a breath of cold air. If you do, it may be your last!"

"What happens when spring comes?" I queried hopefully.

"Don't worry about it," he replied with a tone of professional finality, "you probably won't be here then."

"You're sending me home to die, then," I said, with the hopeless feeling that there was nothing else he could say.

Reluctantly and sympathetically, he nodded. "I'm afraid that's about the size of it."

When we had first discussed my undergoing the arteriogram, Dr. Courter had said that if they could locate the cause of my trouble, possibly they could operate—a prospect I had not entertained joyfully. Now I was ready and willing to go all the way, do anything that held the promise of my living just a while longer.

"What about surgery, Doctor? You said that—"

"Yes, I know," he interrupted, "but sorry—an operation is out of the question."

When pressed for an explanation, he said that the X-rays revealed that three of the four main arteries were completely useless due to arteriosclerosis. The only operation which might help me was a heart bypass, a relatively new type of surgery that required the removal of the afflicted arteries and their replacement with veins from my legs. "However," he added, "I'm afraid your arteries are so far gone that there is not enough healthy tissue left to which the new inserts could be attached."

I slumped dejectedly—that was that! I had reached the end of the line. Believe me, that was a long, long day, and I dreaded the moment when Dolores would arrive for her daily visit. She was the one who had fought the good fight: hoping, praying, and encouraging me not to give up. How could I tell her that although we had won many, many battles, we had lost the war.

Thankfully, at five o'clock that evening Dr. John Flegge walked casually into my room and leaned against the wall just inside the door. Still dressed in his green surgical uniform, he raised a hand. "Hi, Preacher. How's it going?"

"Not so good," I responded, discouraged. Then, "Hey!" I challenged. "They tell me you are the world's greatest heart surgeon—so why won't you operate on me?"

Soberly, looking me straight in the eye, he said, almost tauntingly, "Hell, man, you're gonna die!"

"Yeah!" I shot back angrily. "I am going to die, but at least let me die fighting!"

"Not on my table you won't," he countered, in what appeared to be a deliberate ruse to aggravate me.

"Look, Doctor," I continued to plead, "you've got to give me a chance! You know I've got a strong constitution and an even stronger will to live. Look at what I did to that room upstairs! You remember . . ."

Beginning to laugh, he put up a hand and walked to the bed. "Yeah, Preacher, I know. I've just been teasing—the Board decided last Saturday that if you go home, behave yourself, and gain some weight and strength, we'll operate!"

"But," I choked, hesitant to believe the wonderful news, "Dr. Courter said this morning that—"

Dr. Flegge said, "Dr. Courter was on vacation and he doesn't know yet—I haven't seen him to tell him of our decision."

Oh, happy day! I knew then that the good Lord had spared my life once again, and no matter what, I would have that operation. I would live!

Christmas that year was most glorious. The children had their father back, which no one had ever thought possible. Dr. Courter's fears had not come true: I did live! I did walk and talk! True, I was just a shell of my old self—from a hundred eighty pounds to a skinny bag of bones—but I was alive, and that was all that mattered.

Christmas Eve, the tree was decorated more beautifully than I had ever thought possible; maybe it just looked more beautiful to me. The Christmas carols from the record player were music from heaven to my ears. The floor under the tree was loaded with Christmas presents for the children, thanks to Grandma and Grandpa Skidmore and all our relatives and friends, who made certain that Santa Claus came to our home. It was good to be alive, so wonderfully good!

Probably the most precious moment of my life came when Vonda, Mary Jo, and Jesse brought me my Bible. "Daddy," Vonda said, with a light in her eyes that outshone the brightest star on the tree, "every year at Christmas you've read us the Christmas story, so can you, will you, will you read to us about the baby Jesus, about the angels, and . . . will you read to us—please, Daddy? We've all prayed that He would let you come home just so you could read to us again."

And I read, with unashamed tears in my eyes and joy bells ringing in my soul. Jesse, Mary Jo, Vonda, Punky, Larry, and Dolores gathered around me before the fireplace, and together we saw in the flickering flames all the glorious things that happened on that first Christmas night, so long ago.

My open-heart surgery was scheduled for February 22, 1972, giving me two months to prepare and gather all loose ends. As soon as the holidays were ended, I busied myself in getting all the Gretchen material together and sending it to Dr. Stevenson in Charlottesville. Regardless of what happened to me, I wanted to be certain that the investigation would be completed. As for Gretchen, I could not regress Dolores—I was heavily sedated, and it was impossible for me to concentrate effectively. Besides, as I lay so close to death in the hospital, Dolores had several terrible dreams involving Gretchen and life in the other world which caused her to suffer much emotional trauma. Dolores did not tell me about the dreams at the time, because she did not want to say or do anything that might disturb me and impede my recovery. But because of dreams she refused to even consider the possibility of letting me regress her.

Still, there were times when I tried. One night, not really realizing how medicated I was, I insisted that Dolores let me hypnotize and regress her. Thinking to humor me, she had me sit in a chair beside the bed and she lay down, pretending to be in a trance. When I went through the motions of putting her under, she pretended to be speaking in German, babbling nonsense syllables, thinking I would not know the difference.

Well, I had listened to Gretchen long enough to know what German sounded like, and I knew that Dolores wasn't speaking German. Because of my fuzzy mind, I did think that possibly another personality had emerged, probably speaking a foreign language I had never heard before. Not taking any chances, I set up the tape recorder, hoping to record that new language for posterity. Sadly, when the session ended and I attempted to play back the tape, there was no sound—I had forgotten to press the record button. Several months later, when I wanted to regress Dolores again and search for the new-found personality, she confessed that there was no new personality. "I did not even enter a trance that night," she added, hoping I would not be angry or upset.

From that experience I learned that for the first time in her life Dolores had attempted to learn a few German words. Evidently I had been persistent in insisting that she submit to regression, so to appease me she decided that, rather than let me put her in a trance, she would memorize a few German words and pretend to be Gretchen the next time I asked her to let me hypnotize her. Accordingly, while shopping at Beechmont Hall near Cincinnati, she bought a small, cheap German dictionary. When she attempted to study it, she learned to her dismay that she couldn't make head or tail of the German words; a day or two later she threw the dictionary in the trash basket.

Many people pretending intellectual sophistication (while denouncing anything and everything they cannot understand or explain with trite answers) have proclaimed that Dolores's purchase of the dictionary is tacit admission that she learned the language. That simply is not true! Sadly, Dolores and I have found that honesty is not always the best policy when trying to explain to skeptics how the supernatural has affected our lives. Common sense would indicate to any rational person that there was absolutely no reason why Dolores should have even mentioned buying the dictionary apart from her inherent honesty. After all, it is a proven fact that she had spoken German while in a trance for more than two years before buying the dictionary.

My strongest reason for believing that Dolores is an honest woman lies simply in the fact that for the third of a century she has been my wife I have had no reason to believe that she ever lied to me. Remember, too, that Dolores had given me free rein to probe her subconscious; there is not one facet of her life that is not known to me. In hypnosis it is possible to determine when a person is not telling the truth. For example, many persons have come to me for help in quitting smoking. The case of Harold Miles is comparable to many such cases.

I had hypnotized Harold and given him the usual instructions to relieve his craving for cigarettes, subsequently reinforcing the suggestions (instructions) to enable him to accomplish his goal without being forced into a tremendous battle between craving and willpower. The staying power of hypnotic suggestions is of longer or shorter duration, depending upon the person, and after hypnosis Harold could go for a day or two without smoking, but by the third day his willpower and the power of suggestion had so diminished that he would succomb to his craving for a cigarette and light up.

One day when Harold came to my study, the odor of smoke clearly discernible, I asked how he was getting along and he said, "Good! Great! I haven't had a cigarette since I last saw you." Obviously he was lying, so after putting him into a trance and reinforcing previous instructions, I added the posthypnotic suggestion: "Should you smoke between now and the time I see you at your next session, your right knee will feel painfully sore and you will walk with a limp. However, you will not even suspect that your smoking has caused your conscience to invoke a psychosomatic pain in your knee, but rather, you will ascribe the pain to rheumatism." Sure enough, three days later Harold walked into my study with a pronounced limp, complaining that the foul weather had caused his rheumatism to "act up." He was pretty sheepish when I told him the cause of his "attack."

In hypnosis Dolores has been put to that test, as well as most other tests known to science. One test that is most effective is the psychosomatic reflex. I have used it on Dolores many times. While she was in a deep trance I would tell her that every time she answered a question truthfully her right forefinger would automatically rise. To make the test functional I would ask her several innocuous questions, like "Are you Dolores Jay?", "Is your husband a minister?", "Do you have four children?", and "Were you born in Clarksburg, West Virginia?", to establish the subconscious habit of getting her to raise her right forefinger when the answer was "yes."

Then it was necessary to establish a false response to questions such as "Are you six feet tall?", "Are all your children boys?", "Do you have red hair?" When the pattern was set, both true and false questions were asked until the yes/no response in concert with the raised forefinger was automatic.

In the many times I used this test on Dolores and others, it has never failed; I would literally stake my life on any answers supplied by Dolores through its use. Her answer to the question "Did you ever learn to speak German?" has always been a definite "No!"

The proof of her honesty naturally was not dependent upon my say-so. Any time anyone would suggest by word or implication that she had learned the language, Dolores would state that she was willing to undergo any type of test or examination to prove that she had not. Then, on May 29, 1971, I wrote Dan Tehan, sheriff of Hamilton County (Cincinnati), and requested that Dolores and I be given lie detector tests by his polygraph operators at the Hamilton County Communications Center. A few days later Sheriff Tehan phoned me and asked laughingly, "Are you sure you want that test?" When I assured him that I did, he wondered what would happen if I learned things about my wife I really didn't want to know; and "Are you sure your wife won't leave you when she learns the truth about you?"

After convincing him that we had no secrets, he agreed to let us take the test providing we signed a waiver absolving him and everyone connected with the Communications Center from all responsibility. Detective Philip Andres and Chief Deputy Harry Culler were assigned to administer the test. But when Dolores and I arrived at the Center a few days later, Detective Andres apologized to us: "I'm sorry, but someone higher up decided it best not to give you the test."

We were crushed. Although we knew that polygraph tests were not normally admitted in courts of law, we felt that if we took the test voluntarily most people would accept the conclusions of the polygraph operator. Personally, just knowing that my extremely sensitive wife was willing to take the test was enough for me, and I now know that even if we had taken a thousand tests, many skeptics would choose to ignore all the evidence and still cry fraud.

The day did come when Dr. Stevenson made arrangements for Dolores to be given a polygraph test, by Richard O. Arther, president of Scientific Lie Detection, Inc., of New York. During the test Dolores was asked, "Before May 1970, in your ordinary state of consciousness, did you ever know how to speak German?"

"No."

"Before May 1970, did you spend time with anyone who spoke German?"

"No."

"Before May 1970, did anyone talk German with you?"

"No."

"Did anyone ever teach you to speak German?"

"No."

"Before May 1970, while in your ordinary state of consciousness, did anyone ever say a complete sentence to you in German?"

"No."

"Before being hypnotized in 1970, did you ever hear yourself say a complete sentence in German?"

"No."

When the test was completed, Mr. Arther said to me in the presence of Dr. Stevenson, "Mr. Jay, your wife is a very brave woman, a very sensitive woman, and a very honest woman." Shucks, I knew all that before she took the test!

Even a positive polygraph report did not convince us that the Gretchen personality could adequately be explained by reincarnation; there were just too many strange facets to the case, which led me to look more and more into every phase of the paranormal. As a consequence, I accepted a few invitations to lecture before occult groups, an experience that I deem an exercise in futility, or at the least a short course in the bizarre.

I can never forget looking at my daughters during the Christmas holidays and shuddering at some of the revolting (to me) beliefs being disseminated in those groups. What have my daughters to do with the occult? Nothing! Absolutely nothing! I had merely posed a question about their fate in the theory of reincarnation following one of the meetings at which I had lectured on hypnosis. Several members of the audience that night invited me to a restaurant for dinner. They hoped to convince me that the fruit of their doctrine, "as ye sow, so shall ye reap," did not apply to punishment or reward in this life or the afterlife, but to a future life on this earth.

The leader of the group had dogmatically insisted during the meeting that there was no such thing as sin or evil in this world. "All the bad things that happen in this life," he proclaimed with an air of authority, "were acts of retribution for bad things done in a prior life: the working out of karma." I could not accept such a doctrine, so I asked as we dined, "Do you expect me to believe that if any one of my daughters was struck down and ravaged, even killed by a sadistic maniac, that I could not classify such an act as evil? As sin committed by a deranged pervert?"

"That's right!" he snapped, with what appeared to me a

wicked smile. "Your daughter would merely be getting what she gave to someone in a former life. According to the law of karma, the attack on her would be just what she deserved."

"Oh, c'mon now!" I rebutted in shocked amazement. "I have one daughter twenty-three, one thirteen, and one twelve, and I have tried to rear them as good, Christian girls. If what you say is true, then all of my parental duties are in vain. They will either be good because they are atoning for misdeeds in their past lives, or they will receive punishment in one way or another as retribution for those same misdeeds."

"That's right, Preacher!" he almost chortled, shaking a finger at me. "Even you chose to become a minister of the Gospel in this life simply because you were a hellion in the last life. You see"—he smiled in pleasure at his hoary exhortation—"your conscience from your former life compels you to atone in this life. Unfortunately, because of your ignorance and fear, you merely pretend to be a goody-goody in the hopes of appeasing some God who you think lolls around somewhere in space, but man!"—he shook his head as if pitying me—"you've got it all wrong! There is no God out there to watch over you, condemn you, or to applaud your pious actions in this life. God is within you—you are God! Don't you see, fellow, you and you alone determine your own fate. Likewise, if anything that you call bad or evil should happen to your daughters in this life, it would happen to them because they did that same bad thing to someone in their former life! 'As you sow, so shall you reap.' That's the law of karma: the working out of cause and effect. Even your Bible supports that bit of teaching."

Such reasoning was not his alone. It has persisted from the ancient Eastern religions to the present, being watered down with time and telling until now it is accepted as the panacea of salvation for all who want to have their cake and eat it too. Ruth Montgomery is one of many authors who have quickened the rapid spread of the belief that neither God nor society has the right to judge and condemn our individual acts as good or evil: "Our souls are their own judge of good and evil," and she adds, "God loves us all equally, and through His mercy we will be granted as many lifetimes as we choose in which to atone for our waywardness . . . we are our own judge and jury. . . ."

Such a rationale is to me ludicrous and revolting. True, it is recorded in the book of Galatians (6:7), ". . . whatsoever a man soweth, that shall he also reap." But foolishness of all foolishness, are we to swallow a doctrine based on a single passage of Scripture which, if taken literally and alone, demands that the concepts of love, justice, mercy, and the salvation offered to us in Christ Jesus be marked off as illusionary concepts? Surely only the most gullible will accept any preaching or teaching predicated on a single text.

If the whole of our lives is to be patterned after epigrammatic texts, then it automatically follows that one text is as good as another. And if that be true, let us begin living our lives in accordance with Biblical one-liners, such as "Let the dead bury their dead" (Luke 9:60)—a neat trick if they can do it; or "Let your loins be girded about, and your lights burning" (Luke 12:35). Lights? What lights? Surely if I am to take that passage of Scripture out of context, I can only conclude that nature shortchanged me, since I have been unable to locate a bulb or a light switch anywhere within me.

The man also said that there was no God; that I was God or a god. C'mon now, how could any mere mortal be God? If words are to have any meaning whatsoever, they must be designated as symbols which convey concepts, or are used to link several symbols (words) to convey a mental image of a thought or object. As such, the word "God" is a combination of letters molded into a symbol which has been used from the earliest times to inform us that there is a Supreme Being, Infinite Mind, Power, Creator, and Love who is omniscient, omnipotent, and omnipresent. So again I ask, how could anyone be so presumptuous as to claim to be God when no one can ever pretend to be all-knowing, possessor of all strength and power, always everywhere present at one and the same time? I cannot make a blade of grass, an oak tree, or even my own offspring—I can only assist my wife in the latter through a divine process instituted by a divine Creator. I can make a loaf of bread, but I cannot create the substances that go into the bread. (Yes, I can plant the seeds that will culminate in flour, but create a seed? Not in a thousand years!)

As a consequence of my visit with the occultists something happened to me: The kindly thoughts about reincarnation which had slowly filtered into my mind were punctured by a doctrine I believed was too blithely accepted and too simplistically espoused by a group which hung as a fringe to the real parapsychological organizations attempting to make a valid study of the paranormal.

Every group or organization has its fair share of nuts, even the Church, so when I was extended another invitation to lecture to another group which I knew to be occultic, I accepted, admitting that I could not condemn all people of like mind because I disagreed with the inane teachings of just one group. Too, I seriously hoped to find someone who could provide a more sensible explanation of the doctrine of reincarnation. I had read widely on the subject, but I felt a need to understand it as it was taught and believed at the grass-roots level.

There was no teaching of the doctrine per se that night, but I did learn something of the weird naïveté that dominates such groups when a young, heavy-set woman corralled me. "Aren't you from Virginia?"

"Yes, I lived there a few years ago."

"Have you ever heard of a place called Elkton?"

Surprising her, I replied, "Yes, I served a church there in the early sixties."

"Well, then," she went on enthusiastically, "you're just the man I want. Is there a Spotswood Avenue in Elkton?"

When I said yes, she exploded excitedly, "Oh, my God! This is it!"

Amused, I asked, "It is what?"

"In Elkton," she asked, short of breath with excitement, "is there a stop light at the corner of Main Street and Spotswood?"

"Well, yes and no," I replied, and explained that Spotswood was Main Street, but there was a stop light (street light) at the corner of Spotswood and Route 340, which many people think of as Main Street.

"That's it! That's it!" She danced exuberantly. "That's where I lived in my last life!"

97

Encouraged to explain, she elaborated. "A few months ago I dreamed that I was driving through Elkton and I saw a sign saying Spotswood Avenue on the corner of Main Street at the stop light. And . . ." She paused before adding what she deemed the clincher for proof of reincarnation. "I was driving a red 1968 Pontiac, but I have never been to Elkton in this life, nor have I ever driven a Pontiac!"

"So?" I began to question her reasoning.

"Don't you see," she pleaded for understanding, "I had to have driven through Elkton in a former life since I have never been there in this life, nor have I ever driven a Pontiac!"

"Not really," I responded honestly. "I don't see how you could have lived in another life and driven a 1968 Pontiac in that life when that model came on the market just four years ago."

"Oh!" She flinched. "I never thought of that. But no!" She brightened momentarily and glared haughtily. "You people who don't believe in reincarnation are all alike. You always pick out some tiny flaw and use it as an excuse for not believing. But not me! I believe! I believe!"

She did, just as if she had good sense.

CHAPTER VII

Life's Injustice—God's Justice

As the date for my open-heart surgery drew near, Dolores took me to the lab at Christ Hospital for a blood test; typing was necessary to insure that an adequate supply could be gathered and on hand for the operation. While at the hospital we stopped to see my surgeon, Dr. John Flegge. He wanted to make certain that we thoroughly understood all the rules and procedures for such an operation.

Just knowing that I was to receive the operation lent tremendous encouragement to Dolores. Certain I would overcome my heart problems, she was in high spirits, but when Dr. Flegge found the opportunity to talk to her in strictest confidence while I was busy elsewhere in the hospital, he admonished, "You shouldn't let yourself get too high emotionally."

"Why not?" she questioned, surprised. "The fact that you are going to operate is the greatest news I've had in ages!"

"Yes," he agreed, "right now it is good news to you, and I have very high hopes that it will be even better when this is all over, but let's be realistic: The chances of your husband's being alive and in good health after the operation are about one in ten. If you expect too much and anything goes wrong, the disappointment could be devastating."

Completely subdued, Dolores and I rode most of the long way home in silence. "But, hon," I blurted out encouragingly just before pulling into our driveway, "God has been good to us! After all, He did let me come back from the dead for two glorious months of love and adventure with you and the children. Besides, I cannot believe that my time has come for me to leave this old world! I cannot believe that God would ordain that you and I bring

Gretchen into this world and then take me away before giving us a chance to uncover the cause of her emergence."

In my heart I knew that God was with us, that all we had done was in accordance with His will. Still, maybe subconsciously I was not so confident as I appeared. The Sunday before the operation I had expressed a vague uneasiness when I petitioned the congregation in the morning service to pray for us: "If God wills that I live through this operation, I will never be afraid of anything again."

"So, buck up, hon!" I added as I put my arm around her and walked into the house. "As far as I am concerned, the worst is over!"

There was still much work for me to do. I had promised Dr. Stevenson that I would send him every bit of information I had on Gretchen, and I busied myself listening to tapes, reading everything I had written about Gretchen, and added postscripts which I thought might be important.

While for the most part I experienced peace of mind, one thing bothered me. Many people had intimated that my dependence on God and my attempt to unite religion and science in the use of hypnosis was sacrilegious. "God and hypnosis will not mix!" they said. Apparently their logic was born of the premise that if I had God, I did not need hypnosis, and if I used hypnosis, I did not need God.

To me, as I said before, hypnosis is an art and a science, and all science is an orderly extension of God's creativity. He created all the elements present in the universe and then gave the learned of this world the ability to ferret out and use those elements in a constructive form that we have labeled "science," a process of building on what God made. As a consequence, my appreciation of God as Maker and Creator is enhanced beyond measure.

I still fail to understand how anyone except an absolute Darwinian cannot reconcile religion and science. I like to think of myself as a progressive evolutionist: God created, supplied the seed (germ cell), the absolute prerequisite in the initial process of evolution; and, yea, in the germ cell of every creation is the magnificent wonder and glory of God wherein He formulated and placed within the very first cell of self-contained ability to evolve step by step from the initial cell into a final product a trillion times removed from its lowly beginning. Humbly I bow in awe of

God's omniscience, which permitted Him to go one step further and give to us finite mortals the ability to discover and utilize the uncountable possibilities which He incorporated into the genesis of every phylum.

Consider the neonate. How anyone can look at a newborn baby and not marvel at God's omniscience is more than I shall ever understand. Just think: Nine months before the neonate is born, the copulation of two individuals from diverse backgrounds causes the issuance of millions of spermatozoa from the male, one of which unites with an ovum from the female to form a zygote (a fertilized egg), which becomes a new creation inherent with every characteristic possessed by the mating parties and all their ancestors.

If we examine just one of the millions of characteristics inherent in the person who evolves from the zygote, we learn that there is a built-in mechanism in the memory bank of the brain which records everything a person will ever see, hear, smell, taste, touch, or think. To the glory of God and the enlightenment of the whole human race, under certain conditions, such as psychotherapy, hypnotherapy, dreams, and the utilization of truth serums (sodium pentothal and others), every experience in life can be recalled, including the personal thoughts an individual had at the moment of birth. Many scientists are even of the confirmed opinion that an individual can recall many things which happened long before birth.

I believe this is true, because I have tested the premise many times and found it verifiable. One day as I was preparing to regress Dolores to the Gretchen state, I wondered what would happen if I stopped the regression at the moment of her birth into this world. So I asked, "Dolores, can you tell me what is happening to you right at this moment?"

To my surprise, she answered in an infantile voice, "My name is not Dolores."

"Oh, then what is your name?"

"It's Baby—just Baby!"

"Well, Baby, can you tell me where you are? What you are doing, and who is with you?"

"I'm in the bedroom—in bed. And Mother is here beside me." Then, rolling her head with the loose, almost uncontrollable motion of a newborn baby, she said, "There's Mrs. Smith, and . . . and Dr. Arnett."

"Dr. Arnett? And what is he doing there?"

"He's washing his hands in a bowl; he just brought me out."

"He brought you out! Out from where?"

"From my home in Mother."

At the time I did not put too much credence in her report. To my knowledge, Dr. C. L. Post had been the Skidmores' doctor since the day of their marriage. Having been reared in the same vicinity, I was puzzled because I had never heard of a Dr. Arnett.

Later, while visiting her parents, Mr. and Mrs. Boyd Skidmore, I asked Mrs. Skidmore the name of the doctor who delivered Dolores. Without hesitating, she said, "Dr. Post."

"Are you sure it was Dr. Post?"

"Yes." She laughed. "I would never have considered getting another doctor." But a few moments later she turned to me and said, "Ked, I was wrong. I just remembered that Dr. Post was out of town that day and we had to call in another doctor. A Dr. . . . Dr. . . . Oh, Boyd," she called to her husband, "who was the doctor with me when Dolores was born?"

At first Boyd also thought it was Dr. Post, but when Mrs. Skidmore reminded him that Dr. Post was out of town that day, he said, "Yes, I remember, but . . ." He reflected. "It was . . . uh . . . uh . . . ahhhh, Dr. Arnold! That's it, Dr. Arnold."

The name given by Boyd was similar to that given me by Dolores in regression, and I simply assumed that Dolores had been mistaken. After all, she was just a tiny baby. But, "No!" Mr. Skidmore interrupted my thoughts. "It wasn't Dr. Arnold. Something like that, though."

Dolores and I had moved to the living room and were conversing with Ken and Helen Colvin, Dolores's brother-in-law and sister, when Mrs. Skidmore rushed into the room breathlessly.

"Dr. Arnett! That's his name, Dr. Arnett."

Until that moment I had told no one of my experiment with Dolores. Even then I did not tell the complete story, waiting to make certain that Boyd concurred with his wife's memory. Mr. and Mrs. Skidmore could not recall ever having talked about Dr. Arnett in Dolores's presence, at least not since she was an infant. It is conceivable that Dolores had heard the name as an infant and not remembered it until hypnotically regressed forty-eight years later. However, in subsequent regressions when I took Dolores back through the years of her life to the day of her birth, not once did she recall knowing a Dr. Arnett, or even hearing his name.

Why anyone would entertain serious doubts about a person's ability to remember the moment of their birth is beyond me. At birth, a neonate has been alive for at least nine months, in a normal gestation, and it has all the inborn faculties it will ever possess. All innate functions are controlled by the brain. Since we know that the brain is active at the moment of birth, because, like the rest of us, a neonate cannot move a muscle anywhere in its body without first sending messages from the brain to the muscles, we can assume that that which is true of the physical function is also true of all mental activity. Based on obvious facts, this is more than assumption. We have all heard the wailing cry of a newborn baby—at least most of us older folks have. It tells us that the neonate is endowed with the emotions of fear and anger. If they are present, so is love. We should also realize that the brain, the repository for the memory bank, is the most highly developed organ in the body, weighing at birth almost one tenth the body weight, in contrast to a mere three pounds in the adult.

Again, why marvel at memories that begin only at birth? Even the prenatal fetus has a fully formed brain and can think, can it not? If you say no, then what sets it to thinking? Does the obstetrician activate its cognitive powers by inserting a special key in its navel and commanding, "O.K., pal, you're on! Do your thing and begin thinking"? Seriously, if a baby is born prematurely at seven months, five months, or even earlier, all component parts are present and begin to function immediately, because the brain is active, signifying that a new life has begun.

A schoolteacher friend told me when in regression that her neck hurt while she was in the fetal position in her mother's womb after her mother had fallen and jarred her position "a little out of kilter." Another person told of being angry and kicking her mother for sitting too long in a position that almost caused her to suffocate . . .

Regardless of what anyone thought about my devotion to God and the use of hypnosis, there was no way I could bring myself to chuck the investigation. Just listening to the childish voice of Gretchen made me consider seriously the possibility that reincarnation might indeed be an actuality in spite of my total disagreement with those in the occult.

I thought: I had suffered eight heart attacks and lived to tell the story while all around me people, some much younger and stronger than I, were falling over dead after just one heart attack. It didn't make sense! Was it fore-ordained before birth that each person would live just so long and no longer? The question made me search for an answer, even if it might possibly be found in reincarnation.

One concept of reincarnation says that everything is preordained (predestined), even length of life. Many people steeped in reincarnation believe that even when we buy a suit of clothes, we may select the color of the suit, but the suit label was predetermined. They further believe that because the life we now live is predicated on the sum total of past lives we have lived, we have free will only to choose whether we will be happy or unhappy, sick or well, rich or poor. In other words, we have the prerogative of determining only our attitudes in this life. Everything else is preordained.

Reincarnation as we hear it espoused today has been Westernized considerably. Initially reincarnation was one of two main religious thoughts inherent in prehistoric Hinduism. The other was caste, a doctrine not espoused much in Western society.

The doctrine of reincarnation assumes that a person's destiny is not confined to a single earth life but is worked out in many incarnations. Originally this included the concept of transmigration and involved an entity in 8,400,000 life spans. Early believers in reincarnation went from one shape to another in a succession of existences stretching from the far past into the distant future; a person moved up or down the scale of evolution toward perfection in accordance with just deserts, based on the assumption "As you sow, so shall you reap." In other words, a person who acted well and developed spiritually would be reborn into a better position in life in the next incarnation. Someone whose actions deteriorated would become an animal, or even a plant.

The ancient Greek writer Herodotus tells us that the Egyptians were the first to teach that the soul is immortal; that at the death of the body the soul enters into some other living thing, then coming to birth; that after passing through all creatures of land, sea, and air the soul once again enters a human body at birth. (This process supposedly takes three thousand years to be completed.) In today's Western civilization, not many people subscribe to the theory of transmigration, concentrating almost exclusively on the evolution of the human soul in human existence.

The reincarnationist, in effect, makes his own world, and the law which governs the inexorable working out of cause and effect is called karma, literally meaning "works" or "action." The goal of every reincarnationist is to be released from the power of karma, evolving to reach a oneness with God upon reaching nirvana, the Buddhist's conception of heavenly peace. Some have described nirvana as a perfect happiness one reaches by completely absorbing oneself into the supreme universal spirit, or as the Hindu idea of freedom of the soul; or reunion with the world soul, which is attained by the suppression of individual existence.

Being Christian, I could not argue with the evolution of the soul since we too have hope for sanctification (in this life) and ultimate existence with God the Father. But, convinced that my salvation in Jesus Christ was absolute, belief in the evolution of the soul in the life to come was not necessary. What then was there about reincarnation that made it attractive?

Well, if Christians believe in the survival of the soul in the afterlife, they also believe that God is a God of love, a God of mercy, compassion, and, above all, He is just! No matter how much injustice we see existing all around us, we believe with the Apostle Paul that in the end "All things work together for good to them that love God, to them that are called according to His purpose" (Romans 8:28).

But not everyone can accept Paul's premise. You see, if we look at the world without rose-colored glasses, seeing the world as it is, we soon learn that life for some people seems terribly unjust. Consider all the people born into this world destined to an existence of misery and woe, such as those born with defects which keep them shackled to beds of affliction, wheelchairs, or mental institutions, preventing them from knowing true joy and happiness common to most of us.

I remember Nellie Roth, born blind and afflicted with spastic paralysis. Her home was a hovel of abject poverty, and her father was a drunken sot, too lazy to work. Often, without provocation, he beat his wife and children unmercifully, including the helpless Nellie. The poor girl was trapped in a living hell! She couldn't go to school, romp in the playground, or marry and have a family of her own. Her dresses were hand-me-down rags, and her only toy was a patched-up doll from the Salvation Army. Her life, at best, was a constant struggle for mere existence. Mercifully, she died at a comparatively young age.

Then there was Betty Froman, who lived just a few blocks away. Born into breathtaking luxury, her every whim was catered to by loving parents and "Nanny," a black maid and personal attendant.

Betty was extremely healthy and was educated at an exclusive finishing school for girls before she married a wealthy, handsome young man, who gave her two lovely, healthy children. Her life, lived to a ripe old age, was one of joy and many riches.

How do we explain life's inequities? Can we glibly gloss over the matter with the pious affirmation that our heavenly Father is a God of love, a just God, who will make everything right in heaven? If so, does this say that because Nellie suffered terribly in this life she will automatically be rewarded in the life to come? That her atonement was made through suffering, and her karmic debts were paid in full?

106

Conversely, like the Dives (Luke 16:24) in the New Testament who had everything in this life and found himself in hell when life on this earth was done, was Betty automatically damned and made to suffer because she, too, had everything in this life? Such an assumption would seem to be the only logical conclusion if justice alone were to be served. But really now, where is the justice in that?

Nellie had suffered through no fault of her own, and I would be the first to extend sympathy and say that she deserved merciful justice, but why should Betty suffer simply because she enjoyed the good things in life? Would it make Nellie happy to know that Betty was in torment? Does Betty's suffering or Nellie's reward compensate for Nellie's suffering in this life?

What about suffering, anyway? Does God capriciously demand that some must suffer, that one out of every ten persons be born blind, deaf, or maimed? Or do we attribute our circumstances in life to luck? If so, can anyone then say that God or life deals fairly with us? If luck is not to blame, then is all distress attributed to God's will?

The reincarnationists say "No!" Their position is: Life is determined by the premise, "As ye sow, so shall ye reap." In this sense, reincarnation does seem attractive, especially when we know that if we live the good life in this life, things will be better for us in our next incarnation.

But then, I remember the many times in this life when I tried to the best of my ability to live a good life, and then, bloooeeeee! Everything went wrong, sometimes causing me immeasurable anguish.

"Why?" I cried. "Why me, God?"

When I got no answer, I searched for an answer. Sometimes I rationalized, "The Devil did it to me!" If my troubles were caused by a slight mistake, I alibied, "The Devil made me do it!" Sometimes I even went so far as to lay the blame on my ancestors. The Old Testament notes in many places that "The iniquity of the fathers shall be visited upon their children to the third and fourth generation."

Any one of the preceding provided me an excuse, or at least absolved me of blame. Reincarnationists, however, need not examine reasons because they accept the cosmos of cause and effect: "As ye sowed [in a prior life], so ye reaped."

For me, facing the prospect of one-chance-in-a-hundred of living beyond February 22, 1972, I could readily understand the logic of this argument for reincarnation; maybe I had sinned in a prior life and must now pay my debt. Yet I could not reject my belief that it was much safer for me to face the coming days with the solid belief that I need not look toward the possibility of another life in this world because I had accepted in my heart, mind, and soul the promise of Jesus, "Come unto me all you that do labor and are heavy laden, and I will give you rest"; "Come ye blessed of my Father, inherit the kingdom prepared for you from the foundation of the world."

In reality, death per se held no fear for me. I had tasted life after death and it was good—very, very good! But I cannot honestly say that I enjoyed the prospect of leaving my wife, children, brothers, sister and friends. Neither did I relish leaving Dolores to face the Gretchen investigation alone. There was too much we did not know about Gretchen; so much yet to be done. Would anyone, I wondered, be able to satisfactorily explain whence Gretchen came?

Was it possible that reincarnation did not enter into the picture? Was it possible that Gretchen was a spiritual entity who somehow managed to speak through Dolores, even making herself manifest in a vivid apparitional form? I knew that Dolores had actually seen Gretchen, that she had talked with her and that Gretchen had spoken through Dolores, but wherein lay the truth? Was it possible that the Roman Catholic concept of purgatory was an actuality? If so, it could explain much about Gretchen.

Suppose Gretchen had actually lived in this life as a Roman Catholic, as she said she did. Then suppose that Gretchen had died when the "scraggly group of men came up over the bank" and fought with her and her uncle, beating her to death with sticks and stones, Suppose further that she died there in the forest without ever having been baptized into the faith—she said she attended the Roman Catholic church, the only church in Eberswalde, but she did not say that she actually belonged to the church or been baptized into the faith. If that be true, it is entirely possible, in accordance with the teachings of the Roman Catholic Church, that she abided either in limbo, because she had not been baptized, or in purgatory, because she had not fully made amends for sins committed in this life.

Bishop Fulton J. Sheen says that "Limbo is a place of confinement . . . on the fringe of Hell where unbaptized infants are kept . . . where neither the joy of heaven nor misery prevails." He further states that "Purgatory is a state . . . in which persons who die in the friendship of God but without having fully made amends for their failings must atone for them by suffering before being admitted into heaven. Catholics," he stresses, "believe that these sufferings are lessened by the offering of prayers and masses."

Clearly Gretchen could have been in purgatory. She had died with her uncle in the forest. It is entirely possible, even probable, that the bodies of both herself and her uncle were quickly buried on the spot by her murderers, to keep down any possible trouble with the church. She would not have received final Catholic rites, and it is possible that the local priests assumed that Gretchen had merely left town. After all, it would have been the sensible thing to do, since her father, the mayor, had already been put to death. With the priests ignorant of her death, no prayers would have been offered to lessen her suffering or hasten her entrance into heaven.

Even if we assumed that Gretchen was left to suffer in purgatory, how could we really believe that she spoke to (and through) Dolores? How could we account for her manifestation in our home as a visible entity without resorting to a belief in stories that we once labeled ghost stories? Do ghosts really exist?

A mother once brought her young son to me for hypnotherapy because of enuresis. The boy was eleven years old, but only in the past two years had he been afflicted with the problem. In hypnotherapy he told of going to the bathroom one night and seeing a ghost, which would be enough to make anyone wet the bed, but I was inclined to believe that a tree in the yard between the house and a street light had cast a shadow on the bathroom wall. In any event, the therapy worked, and the boy no longer sleeps in a water bed because of his fears.

This is not to say that ghosts do not invade this world we normally reserve for the living. Dr. Norman Vincent Peale told of seeing his father walk down a church aisle many years after he had died. I too saw my father's face several years after he had died. Since there is no way such appearances into this world can be verified, we can only believe what we see, hear, and read, trusting that the stories are true, especially since many of the stories are told by men of honesty and integrity. Even Billy Graham relates a comparable story in one of his books, about a Dr. S. W. Mitchell, a celebrated Philadelphia neurologist, who had gone to bed and was suddenly awakened by a knock on his door. Getting up and opening the door, he found a litle girl standing there, poorly dressed and deeply upset. She told Dr. Mitchell that her mother was seriously ill and asked if he would go with her to see her mother. When Dr. Mitchell subsequently saw the sick woman, he complimented her on her daughter's intelligence and persistence.

"But, Doctor," the woman replied, "my daughter died a month ago."

Billy Graham referred to the little girl as "an angel who may have appeared as a little girl on behalf of the sick woman." I like that, but really, is there any difference between Billy Graham's story told for religious purposes and those told at Halloween for fun? True, he did not say that the little girl had come back, only that an angel appeared as the little girl; still, the apparition was not of this world, so even though the designation may seem gross, the truth is that in other situations she would have been described as a ghost.

Technically, then, we could assume that the purposes for which a departed person returns designates the title of the returnee at the time of the appearance; or does the name of the person telling the story determine whether the apparition is to be labeled "ghost" or "angel"?

What about people living today who may have been ghosts at one time (a distinct possibility if you believe in reincarnation)? Can they come back and ultimately become angels? A good case in point is that of Vada Hill-man, who came to me one day because she was considerably overweight. Vada was a high-school senior, terribly self-conscious about her appearance and intrigued by the stories she had heard about regression. She wondered, "Can you help me lose weight and simultaneously take me back in time to when I lived in another life?"

In regression Vada turned out to be Susann Calley of Petersburg, Kentucky. Supposedly born in 1790, she married Bill Calley in 1808, but had lived with him for only a short time when he was killed in a coal-mine slide. Vada described herself as tall and skinny, with "yellow hair." After Bill's death she continued to live in a shack on "Bill's farm" until, at age thirty-eight, she was burned to death when a group of neighbors sealed the doors and windows of her shack and set fire to it because "They hated me! They called me a witch, and . . . damn their rutted souls, I hate them, too!"

During the reenactment of her death she fought and raged and screamed in pain and fear until wilting and sobbing pitiably, "The pain didn't hurt no more and I just stayed there. I hated them and I wanted to hurt them . . . . hurt them the way they hurt me, and . . . and I haunted them!"

"After your death," I asked, "where did you go?"

"Nowhere," she whined plaintively. "I just stayed there haunting them, tormenting them, hoping when they saw me they'd die of fright!"

Whether Susann actually manifested as a ghost I do not know, but one thing is certain: She wanted to! I am equally certain that many other spirits have made themselves known to the living both before and after Susann's bizarre wish. The story is told about noted author Mary Roberts Rinehart going to bed with her husband in an apartment in Washington, D.C., and shortly thereafter being startled when someone or something ran through their bedroom. Turning on the lights, they saw nothing. The next morning, their maid brought them coffee while they were still asleep, saying that someone had rung the signal bell used to notify her that they were ready for coffee.

Other strange phenomena baffled them. Their alarm

clock was often found lying in the center of the bedroom floor, and they could not keep their bedroom door locked. Often there was knocking on the door, or the door was opened when no human was present. On other occasions heavy furniture was moved, leaving scratches on the floor. Flowerpots that normally were kept on the front porch were found sitting in the center of their living-room floor. Although Mrs. Rinehart said that she did not believe in ghosts, she did concede that possibly a poltergeist (noisy spirit) was at work in their home.

Can spirits come back to haunt, to tease, or to seek help? If Vada actually hung around to haunt her tormentors and executioners, as she said she did, we might all consider being a little nicer to the next ghost we meet. You see, it might just turn out to be your future mother-in-law, if indeed reincarnation is fact.

Was Gretchen an earthbound entity making herself known to the world through Dolores? It is possible, even probable!

CHAPTER VIII

Kicked Out of Church

Hospitalized eight times in eight years for heart attacks, I spent a minimum of twenty-one days in bed in the hospital each time, and sometimes more, but due to the modern miracle of science and the incomparable skill of Dr. John Flegge, my open-heart surgery required that I be in the hospital only ten days.

Thankful to be home again, even though I was still very weak, I was extremely happy in the knowledge that life for me was a whole new ball game. Contrary to original plans, I went into the pulpit on the second Sunday following my release from the hospital. I had hoped to take a few weeks to recuperate, but it had been three months since I had attended any church service, and when several parishioners asked if I would "just come and administer the communion rites," I agreed, although still too weak to walk without leaning on my wife for support. Thankfully, between then and now, four and a half years later, I have not missed a Sunday in the pulpit because of heart problems.

On the Monday following my second Sunday back in the pulpit, Dolores roused me from an afternoon nap with the announcement, "Reverend Myers is here to see you."

"Well, well, well!" I mused, surprised at his coming. "At long last my ecclesiastical supervisor finally found time to see one of his laborers out on the farm." In the eight months that he had reigned and ruled as District Superintendent, I had heard from him only once: the phone call about Local Conference. Not once did he visit me in the hospital; not once did we hear of his inquiring about my condition.

Was I bitter? No, not really—just disappointed that

such a high-ranking official in the church could have so little Christian concern for one of his subordinates.

Slowly I ambled to the living room, and—"Oh, no!" I reeled in shock, almost fainting at the sight of the man sitting in the overstuffed chair. Although I had never laid eyes on the man before, I knew him well—too well: He resembled the grim-visaged ogre who had haunted me in my hallucination that night in the hospital. "Has he come at long last to fulfill the dastardly mission I envisioned?" I wondered. "No," I quickly reasoned, "this mild-appearing, timid-looking man would never harm anyone."

I soon learned that my hallucination and devastating rampage were more than the frenzied actions of a drugged and dying patient. He had indeed come to run me out of Greenbush. "Reverend Jay," he intoned bluntly and with grave finality, "I want you and all of your family out of the parsonage by June fifteenth!"

"Huh?" I grunted idiotically. Then I reflected hazily as if it were only a dream. What is this? What was he saying? No common courtesy! No "How are you?" No "Glad to see you." No "Glad you made it through the operation." I didn't understand; the full import of his words simply did not register. Maybe . . . yes, possibly he was embarrassed about making a change in pastoral assignments? Maybe he didn't like telling me that he was going to send me to another church? Oh, he shouldn't have been so nervous—moving is a way of life for most Methodist ministers. Surely he knew that, since he himself had just recently moved up from the ranks.

"Where are you sending me?" I inquired, as any itinerant minister would, hoping to learn the location of my next church and put the man at ease at the same time.

But he was not merely nervous. He was mad, vindictively so. "Nowhere!" he boomed brusquely. "I'm not sending you to another church! I just want you out of the parsonage by June fifteenth!"

I was stunned. So the Lord had come to me in my sickness and forewarned me—the man was, as it seemed at the time, trying to destroy us! After eighteen years, eighteen good years as a parish minister, now this? To be kicked out, just like that! He had to be joshing! The church was my life. Didn't he know that without it I would die? Sure, other things were important: The Gretchen case was important, and yes, I was glad just to be alive, and I should be grateful—but without the church? There was no way I could go on living and not proclaim the good news about God and His love in Jesus Christ.

Didn't he know that even though I had already been proclaimed totally disabled by the Veterans Administration and the Department of Health, Education and Welfare (Social Security) I was going to renounce my pensions as soon as I was able to? I had a duty to God, an obligation that I intended to fulfill by working in His vineyard rather than sitting back and just drawing a pension for the remainder of my days. Why, I would rather be the janitor of a small rural church than the president of the world's largest corporation.

"Why?" I demanded. "Am I being defrocked because of my activities in hypnosis?"

"No," he said, staring uneasily at his feet, unable to look at me. "You are not being defrocked; you are not being asked to relinquish your credentials. I just want you out!"

"Then why?" I demanded to know as Dolores began to weep and plead with me to remain calm: "Please, Ked, don't! Don't let him upset you! Don't let him undo all the good the doctors have done! Please, you're just beginning to live again! You've got a whole life ahead of you—and God has been good to us, oh, so very good! So please . . ."

She was right—God had been good to us. For better or for worse, he had given us a long and fruitful life together; and in that moment I looked at Dolores and saw a saintly woman with heart and soul being wrenched out by the roots. "It isn't fair," I moaned despairingly, "for her to suffer like this. She has labored long and hard for the Lord as co-pastor without pay."

Dolores had suffered more than most parsonage wives, because . . . well, it's not easy for me to admit being a maverick. But the truth is, I was! No, not because I wanted to be. I dreaded being different. Yet I had to be true to me and my calling. You see, deep within me beat a strange, rhythmic tom-tom that called me to plow the fields and swim in deep, mysterious waters. Dolores knew that, although I had heard and answered God's call, I would never be stereotyped in my role as minister: My meat had to be that I submit my will to His will; that I follow the roads laid out for me by He who called me; that I employ my talents, whatever they might be, wherever and whenever the need arose.

No, Dolores had not had an easy time of it, even before I entered the ministry. In those days I would have died before letting her or anyone else know that to be God's servant was my most precious and secret dream. "Might makes right!" and "Only the rough and the tough will survive" were my creeds. Even worse, God forgive me, I didn't merely mouth my philosophy: I proved it with my fists if anyone dared disagree with me. Why Dolores ever put up with me, I'll never know; a lesser woman would have turned and walked away, especially when I went from job to job, dissatisfied, disgruntled, angry, and contrary—rebelling, unbeknown to her, against the insistent divine petition that I serve Him. God bless her, she stayed and she suffered through it all in silence, waiting, hoping, praying, and believing in me when I believed in nothing, having faith in me when I thought faith was only the name of a distinguished author or a piano that was plunked off-key in the choir loft.

Even after I submitted my will to His will and became active in His Church, she suffered hardships, albeit in peace and happiness, simply because service to the Lord was more important to her than personal rewards of monetary gains. For example, at our first Annual Conference, in 1954, when I received my first pastoral assignment, Bishop David T. Gregory huddled with us in the little chapel at Waynesboro, Virginia, and said, "Carroll, both Mount Clinton and Mount Horeb want you as their pastor. I will assign you to whichever church you choose, but before you make a decision, permit me to point out that Mount Clinton will pay you the sum of two thousand four hundred eighty-two dollars a year compared to Mount Horeb's sixteen hundred fifty dollars."

Well, shucks, obviously it was no contest—the answer was simple. "Hon," I began pointing out to my little wife, standing so tall with shining eyes brimming the reflection of the Lord's love, "Mountain Clinton pays eight hundred dollars more than Mount Horeb, a third more in annual salary, so—"

"But we didn't go into the ministry for money," she interrupted reproachfully, "we were called into His service and, well, I believe the Lord wants us at Mount Horeb; we're needed there!"

What a woman! I was going back to college, and she knew that we had not saved one red cent for tuition, books, or gasoline; that that eight hundred dollars would have covered all my expenses; that Punky had been confined to bed for the past eight months with rheumatic fever, and obviously we would need money for doctors and medicine; that my old '49 Studebaker was on its last legs; that we needed clothes, groceries, and—well, you name it, we needed it! She knew all that, and yet . . .

I didn't argue with her. I could see in her eyes that she was remembering the words of Jesus: "Take no thought for your life, what ye shall eat, or what ye shall drink; nor yet your body, what ye shall put on. Is not life more than meat, and the body raiment? Consider the lilies of the field, how they grow; they toil not, neither do they spin: And yet I say unto you that even Solomon in all his glory was not arrayed like one of these. Wherefore, if God so clothe the grass of the field, which is today, and tomorrow is cast into the oven, shall he not much more clothe you, O ye of little faith?"

That Dolores! She made me ashamed of being concerned only with money as she stood in her sister's hand-me-down dress and told Bishop Gregory, "If we go to Mount Horeb, the Lord will take care of us. He will provide!" And He did! Amen.

Then there was the time, four years later, when I intended going to seminary until sidetracked by Dr. Floyd L. Fulk, my District Superintendent, who urged me to forget seminary and go to Cherryvale in Staunton, where I would receive the fabulous sum of $4,500 per year. Holy gee! It was unbelievable! I'd never seen that much money before, let alone dreamed of getting that much just for serving the Lord. So after four wonderful years at Mount Horeb, we went to Cherryvale. Dolores and I saw that large raise in salary as an opportunity to better serve the

Lord by providing shelter for homeless children, and we quickly made plans to fulfill a dream of long standing: to found an orphanage. We did not intend to merely herd children into an abandoned old mansion; we would build cottages where only six or seven boys and girls would live under one roof with house parents, a comparatively new concept in those days.

Well, the Lord blessed us in our labors at Cherryvale. That first year we took in sixty new members, almost doubling the total membership of that comparatively new church, which had been floundering when we arrived. With the help of friends, we soon began to build our orphanage on forty-five acres of rolling countryside.

Before starting construction, we discussed every aspect of the orphanage with our District Superintendent and all the local ministers. Everyone with whom we talked led us to believe that we would get complete cooperation. Sadly, we learned the politics of religion the hard way —after we had begun taking children into our home (our Mary Jo was the first to come, a little girl of five months), borrowing money to build, breaking ground, and slaving like serfs for almost a year to get the orphange going.

The roof caved in on us when the Conference Council of Administration decreed behind closed doors, without giving us a hearing, that we were to cease and desist from establishing a home for children. Their reason? Who knows? One excuse is as good as another when you want to put the clamps on someone. They had reasons, I am certain, yet I feel they could have found a far better one than that expressed by one member of the Council, who made clear to me his pretension at being a member of the human race when he snidely remarked, "For the life of me I cannot see why you or anyone else would ever want to take a bunch of snot-nosed kids into your home to raise."

Naturally, when the Council voiced its objection many of our supporters withdrew their financial aid, making it impossible for us to continue. Discouraged, disillusioned, and heartbroken, I put the tools away, gave up building the orphanage, and resigned as pastor of Cherryvale. Deeply in debt and broken in spirit, unable to fathom the slanderous slurs and vicious hostility engendered by a few former friends and neighbors, we began to question our calling—maybe God didn't want us as His servants after all. In the meantime, still needing to eat and pay rent, I began a second career as schoolteacher and coach.

For eight months we remained outside the denomination, which at that time was the Evangelical United Brethren (it had not yet merged with the Methodist Church), but never were we outside God's love. It was then that I truly learned that while we may turn and walk away from God, He is never far from us. One day Dr. Fulk came to us and pleaded with us to return to the fold. After Dolores and I had spent several days on our knees in prayer and consultation with the Lord, we returned to the active ministry while I continued with my new career as teacher and coach.

The next few years were hard on Dolores, extremely hard, but she never once failed me as I taught, coached, preached, and matriculated at Shippensburg State College to work on my Master's in guidance and counseling. The same could be said of her when I later enrolled at the University of Alabama, where I had been awarded a doctoral fellowship in guidance and counseling and psychology. Now there was this, the most degrading shame of all: to be callously kicked out of house, home, and church! It was almost too much to bear.

Thank God, all was not lost. Even before my operation we had felt the Spirit moving, urging us to go home— back to Virginia—and we had made tentative plans to that end. Because ministers in the Virginia Conference would not assume the pastorate of their newly assigned churches until the first of July, we were in a bind, with no place to live or store our furniture. Thinking it conceivable that the Reverend Myers might possibly have a few ounces of compassion left in him, I asked, "Will you extend that date until July one?"

"No!" he thundered. "June fifteenth and not a day later!" Then, as easily as a chameleon changes color, he sauntered to the door, turned with hat in hand, and mouthed with a solicitude that sickened me, "Brother Jay, if ever I can do anything for you, please call on me, will you?"

"Yeah, sure!" I thought uncharitably. "I'm less than two weeks out of the hospital, hardly able to walk, and you are kicking me out into the street like cleaning day dirt! Asking you for help would be like asking a hungry cannibal to please salt me heavily before eating."

For a few moments that day threatened to be a "long dark night of the soul." I had believed with heart, mind, and soul that the ministry was my life; that I was ordained by God and His Church to serve Him and His people. At that precise moment I was assailed by doubts. I wasn't so sure, and, like other mortals with little faith, I questioned God. "Why? Why did You let me live through all those heart attacks and surgery only to bring us to this shame and disgrace?"

Dolores, always a rock, "a shelter in a time of storm," comforted me. "Don't be angry and faithless, Ked. Pray for that man! He's the one who needs help! Please, don't question God; God had nothing to do with what happened here today. True, a mistake had been made, but a more experienced man would have realized that and set another date for a Local Conference, but that is all past now and there is nothing you can do unless you want to appeal to the bishop. Personally . . ." She paused to kneel before me and cup my hands in hers. "I want to start anew. Let bygones be bygones as you, I, and the children sit down and regroup in prayer. This much I know," she assured me with faith and confidence, "God called you into His ministry! He has a task for you, a job that no one else can or will do! Don't you see that?" she challenged, looking me straight in the eye. "God did let you live, even in the face of insurmountable odds! And I am not going to let you repay Him by turning your back on Him as if to say that your recovery was merely a matter of luck! Please!" she petitioned, with tears trickling her cheeks. "Look to God and seek His help, as you've always done in the past."

And pray I did, after cautiously descending the stairs to my study and closing the door to sit and meditate, being renewed in the faith, knowing that the Lord sat with me, talked with me, and counseled me. "Thank you, Jesus," I wept in sweet contrition, "whither Thou goest, I will go; where Thou lodgest, I will lodge: Thy people shall be my people, and Thy God my God."

It had been a long, long time since I last sat in that

chair, the same chair where I sat and heard Gretchen utter her first words. It felt good to be there—the stairs had been a no-no prior to the operation, but now I could begin moving about, doing things and rebuilding my strength.

One of the first things on the agenda was to resolve the question: What shall I do with Gretchen? I think my question was only natural. When trouble comes we always look for the cause, an excuse, so I wondered: Did God approve of my work, or did He, like some people of this world, really decree that my investigation into the paranormal was evil? If He did, why? Why did He give me the talent to bring forth from the subconscious such stories as Gretchen and Loreen related?

What about the others, the people of this world who proclaimed that hypnosis was evil, especially when it was employed to explore the subconscious to determine whether a person might have lived in another time and another place?

As for God, I was inclined to believe that He did not object. I had prayed over the matter much in the past few years and had received no negative answers. Besides, hadn't God created us—everything in us? And didn't the Scriptures state that "God saw everything He had made, and, behold, it was very good" (Genesis 1:31)? If He had constructed us so that our memories exceeded what we mortals consider normal limits, then again, why? Are we to believe that God did not know what He was doing? that He added unneeded facets to our mental abilities, or that He just got careless and forgot to cut off memory at birth? Even supposing that the stories we get from the subconscious are not memories, that they are what I call sub-fabulations (subconscious fables concocted through some strange quirk of the individual's personality), do they not have a purpose comparable to that of dreams? And should we not try to find that purpose?

Personally, I believe the good Lord in His omniscience knew what He was doing; that He intended us to explore that area of our make-up. True, LeCron and Bordeau said that "miracles cannot be performed; all hypnotic accomplishments are strictly in accordance with natural laws." That all sounds nice, but who set the limits of natural laws? Are not those laws more often than not set by our

121

own ignorance? The natural law in Columbus's day ended at the earth's horizon, where it was believed that the ocean suddenly dropped off into an endless abyss. When I was a boy the natural law said that we could never soar beyond the stratosphere; that about all that could be done for the mentally ill (crazy, we called them in those days) was to keep them locked up away from the rest of society.

Especially noteworthy is the objection by many persons in the medical world, especially psychiatrists, that hypnotic regression transcends natural law. Dr. F. L. Marcuse has written, "Regression has unfortunately lent itself to the manipulations of the quack in an ultra-sensationalistic fashion, and even more unfortunately to uncritical beliefs by physicians and dentists . . . a quasi belief in miracles makes one both mad and sad. Mad that there is no law protecting individuals . . . and sad that the veneer of scientific thought is so thin."

What are the facts? Well, facts do indicate that Dr. Marcuse is correct. Hypnotism has at times been wrongly used, and the veneer of scientific thought is thin, very, very thin, because our supposedly learned scientists have been much too slow in becoming truly scientific. Even now they are the very ones who earn a very substantial living off Freud's innovative willingness to go far afield. Worse yet, they were the very types who almost totally rejected him and his premises in the beginning. The *Encyclopedia of Human Behavior* states that "because of his views, he was the most unpopular member of the scientific community."

When Freud started out, psychology persisted in explaining mental life as a purposeless mechanism, but he undauntedly ventured to inquire everywhere in the psychic realm for the meaning of hidden secrets; he sought meaning especially where apparently it could never be expected, and he performed his greatest deeds in his study of hysterical symptoms, absurd obsessions, foolish dreams, and blunders of all sorts, opening the gate through which all modern psychologists enter the garden of modern mental-health science.

The trouble with many (if not all) psychiatrists is that they adhere to the methodological principle that a phenomenon whose cause is not actually observed is to be presumed to have arisen from causes of similar past phenomena. This is good scientific procedure, but only to a point; by this method most psychologists can observe similar causes and blithely ignore the dissimilarities between new phenomena and old; or they sometimes postulate ad hoc similarities which were never observed. Then, too, they sometimes go the other way and stretch to the breaking point some of those similarities which were observed.

If all scientists were so minded, if all adhered to applying the methodological principle, no as-yet-unknown laws of nature would ever be discovered; every new fact would be trimmed, bent, or stretched to fit the Procrustean bed of already discovered explanations. Anyone, regardless of academic stature or scientific bent, who insists that all personalities coming from a person's subconscious are merely dissociated portions of one total personality is saying the knowledge should be limited to the past. Such a person wants no part of the new and exciting discoveries that lie ahead.

Enough for now. Dolores had faith in me; more important, she believed that God had a job for me to do. So, I concluded, if this was my job, I would continue, come what may—after prayer. God always answers prayer!

The day after the Reverend Myers's untimely visit, two friends from the church, Odessa and Landra, came to the parsonage, hoping to bring some cheer into our lives. But it was a strained afternoon, and we were all ill at ease.

Eventually Landra ventured, hoping to break the ice, "Reverend Jay, we want you to know that the people of this church had nothing to do with Reverend Myers's actions. We love you and Dolores."

"Yes," Odessa added, "we tried to hold that man off." She shook her head in dismay. "He wouldn't listen to anyone!"

"Did you know," Landra asked, knowing full well that we didn't, "that on the night you went into the coma, Reverend Myers called a group of us to his office and threatened to get rid of you?"

"No, I hadn't known, Landra. But just what do you mean, he was out to get rid of us?"

"Well," Odessa answered, "he had made up his mind to dismiss you as our pastor that very night, then and there!

And, oh!" She shook her head in disgust. "He was so hateful and bitter and mean!"

"Mad!" Landra chimed. "Downright mad, because he blamed you for not holding the Local Conference. But we told him, no! You're a good man. We told him that we wanted you to continue as our pastor!"

"Not until we told him that you were in the hospital, maybe dying," Odessa added, weeping, "did he soften. Then——"

"Only then," interrupted a sniffling Landra, "did he say he would wait until you got out of the hospital to discuss the situation."

"That's right!" added Odessa. "And you know, he almost acted like he didn't really care what happened to you."

"Now, Odessa," Landra cautioned between sniffles, "you shouldn't say that about anyone—such a horrible thought!" Then, turning to me: "But, Reverend Jay, he really didn't give us a chance to . . . to . . ."

"Don't worry about it," I said comfortingly, touched by their concern, "I'm certain everything has turned out for the best. Remember: 'All things work together for good to them that love the Lord, and are called according to His purpose.' "

"Just one thing more, Reverend Jay," Landra added nervously, "and this has nothing to do with Reverend Myers." She grimaced. "Ohhhhh, I hate to even speak his name anymore, but . . . Well . . ." She paused, uncertain how to begin. "You remember the service you had with the lighted candles sitting on the pulpit? The one where you had us look at the candles while you preached, 'Believe that Christ is the light of the world,' and how you said that if only we believed——"

"That's right!" Odessa helped. "You said if only we believed!"

Well," Landra continued, after looking at Odessa as if to say "This is my story!", "Reverend Jay, you know that my daughter, Betty, was home that week, and she was there in church that day—and, ohhhhh, she believed! She really believed. Reverend Jay, you won't believe this, but it's true!" she exclaimed dramatically. "Betty was healed!"

"Oh my, yes!" the uncontrollable Odessa blurted. "She

had a—oh, my!" She blushed. "For a long, long time she'd
had a—well, she'd had a—"

"A female problem," Landra whispered, staring em-
barrassedly at Odessa, "but we didn't want to mention it
before because we were afraid you would be offended."

"Offended? Why should I be offended?"

"Well," both ladies started nervously, before Landra
summoned the courage to explain.

"Some people said that you used hypnotism that day.
But you didn't"—she raised questioning eyes—"did you?"

Of course I hadn't, but since few if any parishioners in
the congregation that day had any idea of how hypnosis
was induced, maybe they had a right to question our motives. Although we were never personally attacked by
members of that church because of our activities in hypnosis, I feel certain that some members might eventually
have raised a rumpus about it. Still, my family and I will
always be grateful for the good years we had at Union
Plains and Brownstown.

As for using hypnosis in the church, I can look the
world in the eye and honestly proclaim, "No! Never did I
dream of such a thing!" I cannot go so far as to say that
hypnosis was never employed in that or any other church;
worship services by their nature include the elements of
hypnosis. Every minister, teacher, coach, lecturer, actor is
a hypnotist of sorts, albeit unintentionally.

To truly understand this shocking statement, one needs
to have at least a basic understanding of hypnotism. So,
what is hypnotism?

A. Forel says that "while it is not merely sleep, the relationship between natural sleep and hypnotism is unmis-
takable"; Liebeault goes a step further by stating that
"hypnotism is distinguishable from natural sleep only in essence." Braid described it as "nervous and artificial sleep."
Pavlov declared that "hypnosis and sleep belong to the
same group; they are different manifestations of inhibitory
processes." To merely compare it to natural sleep is misleading, since a great difference between the two appears
when the brain waves (fluctuations in the electrical potential of the brain) of people in hypnosis and natural sleep
are monitored. We must examine a few more definitions.

Winn defines hypnosis as a "prestige-and-faith" relationship "in which the practitioner uses his position to influence the subject's autonomic nervous system in order to effect bodily inhibitions and excitations and to condition his mind accordingly." Rhodes defines hypnosis as a "condition in which a shift in the relative positions of the subjective and objective minds are consummated, bringing the subjective to the fore and having it controlled by either the hypnotist or the recessive objective." Weitzenhoffer says that "hypnosis is a condition or state of selective hypersuggestibility which is brought about in an individual through the use of certain psychological or physical manipulations of an individual by another person."

Winn's "prestige-and-faith" refers to the rapport between the person to be hypnotized and the hypnotist, an absolute necessity for effective hypnosis, while Rhodes teaches that every person has "two minds"—the conscious (objective) and subconscious (subjective)—and that it is the function of the hypnotist to awaken the subconscious and bring it to the fore while at the same time quieting the conscious and causing it to recede into the background in a state of quiescence. Finally, Weitzenhoffer says that hypnosis will be achieved when the hypnotist attracts the subject's total, noncritical attention through one of the following procedures: 1) fixation (or concentration) of attention, 2) monotony, 3) limitation of voluntary movement, 4) limitation of the field of consciousness, 5) inhibition, and 6) successive response to suggestions or their equivalents.

Please note that a hypnotist is not always needed. Many have been hypnotized through daydreaming, through the rhythmic beat of drums or other tranquilizing music. Many more have been hypnotized while driving an automobile or truck. I remember a cold winter day in 1950 when I drove a patient to Johns Hopkins Hospital in Baltimore from Clarksburg, West Virginia. On the return trip, in the early-morning hours, I suddenly awoke at the wheel while traveling in excess of ninety miles per hour on a straight stretch of road fronting Dawson's Camp on U.S. Route 50, at the foot of Cheat Mountain. How I got to the bottom of that mountain shall forever remain a mystery, since the western slope of Cheat Mountain is nothing but a three-mile ride of twisting, turning, descending curves. Surely

God must have been my co-driver that night. I have absolutely no recollection of traversing that portion of highway, but mine was hardly a unique experience.

An impressive amount of evidence has been accumulated in recent years to indicate that people become easily hypnotized while driving. Almost everyone has become sleepy while driving or riding in a car, and it is known that much of the sleepiness is caused by the monotonous hum of the motor and the whine of the wheels on the pavement. Too, when people drive for prolonged periods without interruption, looking at the endless ribbon of highway stretching out before them, their eyes soon drift to the center line and become transfixed, much as in a daydream. In such a hypnoidal state one soon enters a deep, sound sleep unless somehow snapped back to alertness. The number of people who can recount passing over certain portions of highway, even through whole cities, without recollection of the event is tremendous, and it is truly miraculous that the number of highway tragedies is not doubled every day.

As for ministers being hypnotists, I believe my logic will be understood when one considers the church setting: a quiet interior often darkened by stained glass or opaque windows, with subdued lighting, a hushed atmosphere, and the centrality of the altar, often brightly lighted with candles, which creates a point of fixation (many practitioners use eye fixation—looking at a specific object for trance induction). Add the choir and liturgy, all arranged for leading the congregation up to the day's main event: the minister and his sermon.

If the minister is well prepared and eloquent in delivery, he may soon have his audience sitting on the edge of their seats, spellbound, eyes unblinking and mouth agape. Even if the minister is as dry as burnt sand, the members of the congregation may turn to look at lighted candles or some other object and drift asleep, especially if there are no cute children to entertain them or distract and keep them awake. You see, there is no magic in hypnosis! It is an art and a science developed to lead people into a trance (sleep) state, and regardless of the paraphernalia used by the hypnotist or the subject's body position (sitting, standing, or lying down), two things the hypnotist must do: get the subject's attention and get the subject to relax. Once that has been done, nine out of ten people will succumb to hypnosis.

There is one other important ingredient: rapport. The more faith and trust the person has in the hypnotist, the better the results will be. And, pray tell me, where will one find more faith and trust than in a minister's captive audience sitting completely at ease in church? Any who doubt my premise should remember what I have just written when next seeing a sleeper in church. Or remember the many times you have fought sleep in the sanctuary and attributed the call of Morpheus to a hard week or the excesses of the night before.

Paul Malley's wife was always apologizing to me for his habit of sleeping in church until one day I overheard him trying to convince someone who did not attend church to come and listen to one of my sermons. I appreciated his compliments, but later when we were alone I ribbed him with a smile: "Paul, how can you urge another person to come and listen to my sermons when you always sleep through them?" He defended himself, laughing. "Believe it or not, Reverend, I hear every word in all your sermons."

When I raised the skeptical question, "How can you?" he answered, "I don't know, but I can prove it. Next Sunday, and every Sunday for so long as you want, I'll review your sermon immediately after the worship service before anyone has a chance to brief me." He did, never missing a point. When I tested him for hypnosis, it soon became apparent that when a minister began to preach, Paul entered a trance, just as if he were under the influence of a posthypnotic suggestion.

Paul was not the first to teach me that some persons became hypnotized in church. Many years ago I attended a Pentecostal type of service. There was much laughing, singing, praying, shouting, and loud preaching, conditions normally considered antithetic to the induction of hypnosis. During that service the minister suddenly stopped in the middle of his message, struck a dramatic pose, and pointed at a woman who sat spellbound, eyes riveted on him as he commanded, "Laugh!" Laugh she did, a wild, hysterical laugh that continued unabated for several minutes.

On an another occasion he struck the same pose and commanded the congregation, "Run to the altar and pour out your heart to God! Beg His forgiveness!" And run they did. For a moment it looked as though the church had been turned into a track meet. A dozen people leaped to their feet and scrambled to the altar, where they collapsed in pleading, begging prayer. Intrigued because I knew some of the people in that group, people who were good, quiet Christians, I inquired of them, "Were you led by the Holy Spirit to actually run and beg, to plead in agonized screams?" Several of them replied, almost remorsefully, "No! It seemed as though I had no control over my actions, like maybe the Devil himself made me do it." Although I would not attribute it to Satan, they had been made to do it! They had been hypnotized.

The preceding was not related in an attempt to inject levity, or to belittle anyone's religion. People have the right to worship as they please, according to their own religious tastes. I do not accuse that minister of deliberately hypnotizing people. It is doubtful that he had any idea hypnosis was involved. Apparently at some point in his ministry the man simply learned that when he saw a certain look on the faces of people in his congregation, they would obey any command given. And they would! Although not knowing how or why, he had employed the tricks of a stage hypnotist.

I repeat: Never have I used (nor will I ever use) hypnosis in a worship service. To use hypnosis in a worship service would be the height of foolishness; Christianity does not need it! There is more power present in the Church in the supernatural presence of God in Christ through the ministry of the Holy Spirit than can ever be generated by a thousand arts and sciences such as hypnosis. The long and glorious history of the Church testifies to that fact. It has weathered wars, revolutions, persecutions, schisms, and slander; and, as Christ proclaimed, even "the gates of hell shall not prevail against it."

While hypnosis can be used for fun, for good or evil,

by and large the use of hypnosis without therapy will do neither good nor harm. Like tranquilizers, its effectiveness is of short duration. No religious experience, such as I have related, will cause lasting, effective changes in a person's permanent thought processes. Many people in the hypnotic state may act out any command given by a hypnotist (unless it violates their personal moral code), even though they still have enough mental control left to know that what they are doing is inconsistent with their rational actions or desires.

For example, while I was visiting with a physician friend, he requested that I demonstrate my technique by hypnotizing his niece. She had volunteered to be a subject. Amy was a good subject, and I was able to perform several experiments with her for the benefit of the many who were present. Then, after about thirty minutes, I induced limb and body catalepsy and told her that no matter how hard she tried, she would not be able to get up and walk around. She tried, even to the point of opening her eyes and threatening through gritted teeth, "Damn you! If ever I get up from here, I'm going to knock your blankety-blank head off."

At the time she meant it. Aggravated because she knew everything that was happening, galled because everyone laughed at her antics, she became frustrated and angry because she had absolutely no defense against my commands. Once I had brought her out of the trance, I had no more control over her, mentally or physically.

The time was drawing near for us to leave Greenbush and the Union Plains Church, but there was one woman who appealed to my sympathy whom I simply could not refuse to help. Helen Cable, an attractive fifty-three-year-old lady, and her husband, Henry, had driven from their home near Columbus, believing I could help her walk again. She said she had been an invalid since the age of seventeen, when she underwent surgery on her right leg. Henry, a loving and doting husband, whispered out of the side of his mouth, "It's all in her head." Helen glared at him and said she thought hypnosis could help her since the doctors could find no clinical reasons for her disability.

Helen was a good subject for hypnosis, and just before I started trance induction she asked, "If you have time, would you regress me? I'd like to know who I was in another life." I agreed, and after hypnotherapy for her leg— I started to take her back in time.

"Oh, this is terrible!" she complained. "I'm freezing." She began to draw her arms tight against her chest as though shielding herself against the cold. "Yaaaaa," she suddenly slurred, and curled her lips in scorn, "those half-naked beasts, they're filthy . . . dirty filthy!"

Apparently Helen was reliving her life as a Sioux Indian in North Dakota in the nineteenth century, a life she abhorred. She despised the unsanitary conditions and the nearly raw, charred rabbit being eaten from a campfire spit.

When the regression ended, Helen got up and walked without a limp to a chair beside my desk. Henry looked at me and winked knowingly. When they left my study, she got up and walked pertly to their car, Henry tagging along carrying the walker. He later told me that Helen rode the one hundred miles home without a single complaint, for which he was most grateful, since she usually complained that his driving and the car motions jarred her leg so badly that the pain became unbearable.

"But the best was yet to come." He laughed. "At home she got out of the car, walked up the stairs, and into the house alone. As she crossed the living room, I called out, 'Hey, Babe, where's your walker?' And would you believe it!" He continued to laugh and shake his head. "She plopped into a chair and exclaimed, 'Oh, no! I left it at the preacher's!' Now," he moaned, "I don't know what to do! She hasn't walked a step since."

I am inclined to believe there was nothing physically wrong with Helen's legs, but I am not a doctor and I will not attempt to make a medical evaluation. In my own mind, since there appeared to be no leg atrophy and the muscle tone seemed good, I did wonder. Was she really an invalid? Or did she, when Henry was away from home, walk around the house as any normal, healthy woman would? I am sure Henry was inclined to wonder the same.

Helen was the last person I hypnotized before leaving Greenbush; I just didn't have time for anyone else, what with the hundred and one things to do before moving. I hated to leave that study, though, with its many precious memories of the hundreds of persons who had found strength and comfort in the Lord there; the many who had laid bare their heart and soul and had received help through therapy, counseling, and prayer.

Prayer! It was and is the strength of my life, even in hypnosis. Always I found it expedient to pray for all who lay in a trance; after the many had been helped, even healed, through hypnosis or the rest and relaxation brought on by hypnosis.

Even now I think of Vonda, so nervous and scared, a piano concert looming terribly large in her young life. She had said, almost in tears, "Daddy, I just know I'm going to flub it! I haven't had time to practice." So when my fatherly concern failed to pick her up, I suggested we go to the study for hypnosis.

As Vonda lay in the trance I gently instructed her to forget the concert. "Think of yourself at the keyboard, calm, relaxed, confident. Honey," I encouraged her, "remember that Jesus said, 'Lo, I am with you always.' And that's the truth, baby! He was not giving you merely a verse of Scripture to memorize: Jesus said what He meant, and meant what He said. Yes, see yourself playing the piano—you are an accomplished pianist! Your timing is perfect, and no—don't fret, you'll never miss a note. You needn't worry, honey, everything will be just fine. 'I am with you, Vonda'—that's His word to you right now! Remember that beautiful old hymn you've played for me so many times:

> I come to the garden alone,
> While the dew is still on the roses,
> And the voice I hear, falling on my ear,
> The Son of God discloses.
>
> And He walks with me, and He talks with me,
> And He tells me I am His own;
> And the joy we share as we tarry there,
> None other has ever known.

"Well, Vonda, when it comes time for the concert and it's your turn to perform, this is what I want you to do:

Put your right thumb and forefinger together, forming a circle—the symbol of perfection—and, honey, every time you do that, you will experience the feeling of peace and confidence which you are enjoying right now."

Sure enough, Vonda performed wonderfully at the concert. Afterward she laughed and said, "Daddy, I did just as you told me, and, oh! it was so wonderful! I was so scared and nervous just before I went on stage, but when I touched my fingers together it worked just like you said it would. Oh, it felt so good!"

CHAPTER IX

Back Home in Virginia

Three months after the Reverend Myer's traumatic visit to our home in Greenbush, we were back in Virginia, the land we fell in love with after moving there from West Virginia in 1954.

Our District Superintendent had given us a choice of three charges, but because we had served churches near Harrisonburg from 1954 until 1962, we decided to accept a charge of four churches near the Blue Ridge and Massanutten Mountains.

The charge was building a new parsonage, and until it was completed we were forced to live in a rented apartment in a small community a few miles from Elkton. Although we were happy to be home, subtle signs began to show up almost immediately after our arrival that we had made a wrong choice in going back to Elkton, but since only one or two people knew I was a hypnotist, we simply ignored them. For example, a month or so after we had moved into the apartment a neighbor lady asked if we had heard a child screaming the night before. "It sounded as though someone were beating it to death!" she said. But we heard nothing.

A few days later, though, I had gone to bed and lay there trying to get comfortable in the hot, humid night. Suddenly I heard a low moan. Unable to locate its source, I moved to the window at the foot of the bed to listen; even as I moved, the sound grew louder. At the open window there was no mistaking it: someone was in great agony, or so it sounded. Quickly I jumped up and ran for the door, stopping short when the moaning changed to a chorus of many voices blending in an otherworldly "Te dum . . . te dummm . . . te dummmmmmm . . ." like a hundred mantras in unison. Opening the door, I called for Dolores. By the time she entered the room and heard the chanting, the sounds had changed to a screaming, shrilling lament, comparable to the voices of hundreds of souls in torment.

"That can't be real!" Dolores whispered, a little frightened. "Surely someone is playing a prank."

"Yes," I agreed, "it has to be a prank," and backed out of the room to go outside and catch whoever was having fun at our expense. When I reached the living room, the wailing stopped. Returning to the bedroom to tell Dolores I could no longer hear the strange wailing, I faltered in my tracks: The noise in the bedroom was louder than ever, and it seemed to be coming through the open window. I told Dolores, "You stand here at the window and watch while I slip outside to the back porch and turn on the light. If anyone is out there, I will catch them."

When I got to the porch, I stood in the darkened shadows for a few seconds, surveying the area around the window, which was lighted by a street lamp, but I saw no one nor was there a sound to be heard. I flipped on the light switch, but saw nothing. Nor did I hear the sound of anyone fleeing the scene. When I walked to the window, Dolores informed me that the noise ceased the exact same second the light came on. Needless to say, we were all shaken up and slept very little that night.

The next morning we questioned the children, but they had not heard a sound; neither had our neighbors. However, there was one neighbor who lived across the street, a Mr. Hackley, whom we were unable to contact until he returned from work that evening.

"No," he said, "I didn't hear a thing. But," he asked with a strange glint in his eyes, "do you have a picture of Jesus hanging anywhere in your apartment?"

"Why, yes," I answered, "I do have a Sallman's head of Christ. Why? What has that to do with the horrible noises we heard last night?"

"You are worshipping an idol," he charged, "and it is my considered opinion that those sounds you heard were real. They were the voices of all who had heretofore believed in your Christ and had died, but now"—he gravely paused—"they have come from the dead to instruct you that you must renounce your heathenish belief in Him and join us."

"Join you?" I asked incredulously. "And just who are you?"

"I," he boasted, "am a member of God's Eternal Select, the possessors of absolute truth!"

"Do tell!" I laughed and walked away, thinking I'd better not mention wailing voices to anyone else lest I run into another messiah.

Finding no satisfactory answer to the weird wailing, I secretly began to wonder if maybe Gretchen had had something to do with it. Had she somehow managed to bring a host of her friends from the spirit world to renew her contacts with us, if indeed she was a spirit-world entity? I had not regressed Dolores in over eight months and so had not afforded Gretchen the opportunity to speak to us through her normal channel.

In my more sober moments I realized that such thinking was not consistent with the facts. Gretchen had never manifested in my presence, nor had she ever spoken (or made herself known to me) except through Dolores. She could have chosen a more direct route as a means of ending her frustration, but if she was merely trying to get my attention, why would she use such a bizarre method?

To this day Dolores and I have no idea what the weeping and wailing and gnashing of teeth of that night were all about. I did begin regressing Dolores again soon afterward, so if it was Gretchen, we negated her need to resort to such spine-tingling tactics. Yes, we had considered the possibility that someone had somehow piped the weird sounds into our apartment through the open window, but finally concluded that explanation was inadequate, because neither the children nor our neighbors had heard the hideous sounds even though their windows were open also.

That was only the beginning. I had no intention of keeping my activities in hypnosis a secret, and when some of the local people learned that I was a hypnotist, they immediately got up in arms and threatened to run us out of town. Foremost in the conspiracy was Hackley, who pronounced at every opportunity, "He's a devil and he's brought evil demons amongst us with his ungodly hypnosis." He soon found an ally in one of my parishioners, Ava Warson, who had formerly denounced all members of God's Eternal Select as workers in Satan's army. Ava had always been a leader of a fringe group of Christians who sought joy in denouncing anything and everything not consistent with their strange brand of Christianity. She had abhorred all members of God's Eternal Select, and reviled all ministers with college or seminary degrees as educated devils. She constantly denounced all women in slacks, fancy clothes, church dinners. Also on her list of hates were all women who wore make-up. Many people described her as being happy only in her own misery and in making life miserable for others.

Ava, a tall redhead, skinny as a rail, had no cause for rejecting us because of my use of hypnosis. There were four churches on the charge, and when I delivered my first sermon in each church, I fully informed the parishioners of my hypnosis activities. I insisted that anyone who objected to my use of hypnosis should please let me know then and there and I would move to another charge without hard feelings. Most members seemed well pleased, and many of them even went so far as to come to the parsonage, where they spent many hours discussing hypnosis. Many requested that I hypnotize and regress them.

I fully realize that many people fear hypnotism because of the way it has been exploited by stage hypnotists, occultists, and charlatans. I can sympathize with their fear. I fully realize that many people in the church have a right to look askance at hypnosis, but I must insist that it was a contradiction in terms for any member of that charge to object to my use of hypnosis, especially after I had asked everyone to come to me with any objections.

Moreover, in the United Methodist Church every minister is assigned to a church for only one year. During the course of each year a group within the church, known as the Pastor-Parish Relations Committee, receives reports, good and bad, from any and all church members. Any criticisms they might have are then passed on to the District Superintendent, who, in line with the Committee's recommendations, decides in conference with the bishop whether the minister should remain as pastor of that church or be moved to another at Annual Conference. If complaints against a minister are too grievous, he is asked to surrender his credentials and is no longer permitted to serve as a pastor in the United Methodist Church.

At the end of my first year on the Blue Ridge charge there was not one single complaint lodged against me, and the records will show that not one vote against my returning as pastor for another year was registered with the District Superintendent.

Despite Hackley's efforts to have me run out of town, we were happy in Elkton. Persons from all over Virginia, Maryland, and the District of Columbia came to our study for hypnotherapy and/or regression. I also lectured and conducted seminars far and wide. Then, on Thursday, February 24, 1974, the Harrisonburg *Daily News-Record* ran a story on Dolores and me under the banner headline HER IDENTITY CHANGES WHILE HYPNOTIZED. That marked the beginning of the end of our stay in Elkton.

Our predicament and the antics of our aroused antagonists would have been funny had they not been so tragic. The story appeared following one of my lectures for the Elkton Business and Professional Women's Club. I had enjoyed lecturing that night, and, thankfully, I had been cordially received, but when a few of my parishioners read about the lecture, they didn't like it one bit! They later rationalized that they didn't mind my hypnotizing and regressing people, but they didn't want the whole world to know about it. It seems they could tolerate my sinfulness, just as they enjoyed their own, so long as everything was kept secret from the people outside the community. But, shucks, I've tried to live a Christian life, and in my heart I had done nothing to be ashamed of—I had nothing to hide —and so far as I was concerned, those who got so upset should have known that sooner or later my activities in hypnosis and their ungodly actions would be revealed. As it is written in the Scriptures, "For nothing is secret that shall not be made manifest; neither anything hid that shall not be known abroad" (Luke 8:17). But they didn't know or they didn't care.

In any event, they declared war on me and my family by resorting to World War II tactics of subversion. They got on the telephone and called everyone this side of the grave. One ol' biddy, who must have gone down the numbers of the phone book without looking at the names, called me and asked if I knew that "evil man, Preacher Jay." When I acknowledged that I might, she said, "Well, it don't really matter whether you know him or not; it's just that if he don't quit being our preacher and leave town pronto, we're going to get rid of him even if we have to haul him out of town on a rail. Now"—she paused for breath—"what I want to know, are you willing to help us?"

"I might," I said, tongue in cheek, hoping to learn who "we" were and what they planned to do.

"Good!" she cackled. "Give me your name so if I need you I'll know how to get ahold of you."

"Would you still want to get ahold of me if I told you that I am Preacher Jay?" I laughed. But I shouldn't have. Whoooeeee, did she let me have it! I cannot repeat what she said, but I wouldn't be a bit surprised if the telephone wires were still smoking in Elkton.

Today I sometimes think I can understand their wrath, at least in part. But I didn't really know them at that time. Most are mountain folk, not too well educated, and clannish, which is to say that if everyone is not blood-related, they are at least related by the code of the hills. Most are really good people, some of the finest this world has ever known, but few if any are inclined to accept new-fangled ideas. As they say, "We don't want no truck with anything we don't understand."

While most are endowed with strong convictions about what they believe or disbelieve, they will tolerate anyone from the outside who does not force opinions on them. However, a few are blessed with a dog-eat-dog temperament, and while they are not ipso facto leaders of the clan, the majority will not cross them for fear of retaliation. To my misfortune, it was that group I seemed to offend the most.

Conceivably I could have spared myself their wrath had I not been led into a false sense of security by their holiness in the first year of my pastorate. Some of them prayed as if they had heaven in their hip pocket. And smile? They could flash a winsome countenance that would make cherubs look like monsters. Worse yet, the honey really dripped with "Brother Jay" this and "Brother Jay" that. I thought for sure I'd never have to leave earth to experience heaven. Alas, I soon learned that while I cannot pinpoint the exact location of heaven, I now know for a certainty if it's anywhere near that charge, I want no part of it.

Resigning my work there was out of the question. My family and I had gone there for the sole purpose of serving the Lord, and never did I discuss hypnosis from the pulpit after our first Sunday there. Our trouble really started not because of hypnosis but because that one woman, Hackley's accomplice, Ava Warson, wanted to be the big rooster. For years when she shouted, "Jump!" they had asked "How high?" on the way down. But for a while even she was one of our strongest supporters.

Although Ava was usually in church somewhere, going from one Pentecostal meeting to another, she very definitely lacked the qualities of mercy, justice, and forgiveness for anyone other than members of her own family. She had a husband who lived on the bottle and a houseful of children who were a constant source of trouble. While she was always condemning drinking, partying, and waywardness in other people, she would scour you with a double dose of hellfire and brimstone if you so much as suggested that either she or members of her family were less than perfect.

Ava and I began to walk different paths when I objected to her questioning the morals of a few high-school girls who wanted to join the church. Her objection: "They wear pants, paint their faces, and dance, and," she snarled with disgust, "the church ain't got no place for the likes of them!" I disagreed, and after failing to convince her that she should be more charitable in her thinking, I reminded her that all her daughters (who did not attend church) wore jeans and make-up and danced, so "Let those who are without sin cast the first stone." Ava merely pursed her lips and scorned, "You are the Devil's own son come to drive God clear out of His own church!" From that time on, she spent most of her time on the phone trying to line up opposition to me and my family.

She had some success: A few of the less-educated backed her and began threatening us with physical harm; others made life miserable for us by calling Dolores a witch and me a warlock. And, despite her hatred for us, she could always be counted on to be in church. She never missed a

Sunday service. After I preached my last sermon there, she even hugged me and told me she would miss me.

One night shortly after a parishioner called to warn us that Ava was trying to start a rebellion against us, a drunken woman began the first of many nuisance and sometimes vulgar calls. "Is youse the ah . . . ah . . . pre . . . preach . . . preacher hic . . . hip . . . hipatist?"

"Yes, I'm the preacher."

"Go . . . goooo . . . goods!" She laughed and cackled with great effort. "Kin . . . kin youse hippa . . . hippatize me an . . . make . . . makes me come . . . comes backs . . . as . . . as me own mothers!"

Although my family and I were determined not to turn tail and run, I must confess that we did fear for our lives. You see, their threats were not based on idle talk, as I will clearly show.

While none of my churches was located in Elkton, all the people for miles around claim Elkton as their home town, and, sadly, through no fault of its own, it has been erroneously saddled with a terrible reputation, engendered by the hell-raisers who come to town and cause trouble. Elkton's reputation helped feed our fear, but it would be terribly wrong for me to blame Elkton itself for our troubles.

Elkton is a good town, a town that honored our daughter, Vonda, as Miss Honorary Fire Chief, applauded our son's activity on the ball field and Mary Jo's participation in the band. Yet even the local residents will not deny that it has a reputation as a rough, tough town. And this, mind you, even though Elkton (with a population of only fifteen hundred) and the surrounding areas support no fewer than twenty-one churches. It is a hotbed of religious activity, very conservative or Fundamentalist.

Although the knifings, shootings, and fighting has declined in the past few years, Elkton gained notoriety through the influx of the Saturday-night crowds that came down out of the mountains to fight, shoot, and kill. In the many years I have known the people of Elkton and the surrounding towns, I have heard hundreds say with a fearful shake of the head, "I wouldn't go back into those mountains or up one of those hollows at night for all the money in the world."

As I previously stated, had not our situation been so serious, our life there could be described as hilariously funny. In fact, it was tragic. My experience with Fannie McCray is a good example. Fannie is a big woman—fat, five foot five and two hundred pounds of rippling blubber —whose right hand was severed at the wrist when she raised it to ward off a meat cleaver thrown at her by her husband. Fannie wanted to see me to discuss family problems. Her husband, she said, preferred to spend his weekends in bed with other women.

Fannie lived near New Market, but one day she hitchhiked to Elkton just to see me, and her first words were "Preacher, I hear you can help women lose weight and make them beautiful, so boy, please get busy on me and do the best you can."

"Well, Fannie." I smiled and replied honestly, "No matter what you have heard, I may be able to help you lose weight, if you really want to, but don't expect me to perform miracles!"

"That's good enough for me!" She laughed like a banshee, and bounced like a blimp when she flounced down on the couch. "Whoooeee! Preacher, this feels good! Get busy and make me beautiful so Don'll want me so bad he can taste it!"

That was a tall order. Moreover, to my embarrassment, it soon became obvious that losing weight was not Fannie's paramount concern. Judging by her actions, sex had to be her one consuming passion.

One day as she lay on the couch in the study preparatory to entering a trance, she asked me to examine a mole on her left cheek. "I've heard that you can make warts disappear with hypnosis," she began, "so see what you can do with this mole."

"Nothing, Fannie," I answered, leaning over for a closer look. "That is a mole, and you will have to see a doctor and have it removed."

"Oh, don't worry about that, baby!" She laughed and grabbed me by the arms, pulling me down on top of her. "Come to Momma and have some fun!"

What a revolting development that was! "Come to Momma," she had said. I assure you, had my Momma been like that, I would have disowned my father for hav-

142

ing had such poor taste in selecting such a mother for me.

Surely that afternoon my study was a sight to behold. With her fat lips all over me like a hog lapping slop, it was all I could do to keep from heaving the contents of my dinner. And laugh! She laughed and squealed and giggled between grunts until I really got sick. O Lord, I wondered, what did I ever do to deserve that?

Luckily I managed to break loose with only my pride bent and my esthetic senses insulted. But for a moment I wasn't so sure I had won the battle. She struggled up from the couch like a hamstrung rhino, nailing me with blue flame.

"Why you blankety-blank blue-nosed S.O.B., I've slept with better men than you'll ever be. You hear me, man! You ain't nothin' but a tinhorn preacher tryin' to make me look like a common whore. But you just wait, fella!" She shook a hammy fist in my face before grabbing her purse and waddling to the door like an elephant. "I'll get you and your whole damn family if it's the last thing I do. You hear me? You'll regret the day you crossed this old gal with your pretendin' to be something you ain't!"

Fannie was true to her word, going everywhere, corralling everyone, and working overtime to stir up trouble. And she waylaid me at every opportunity. Stopping me on the street one day, she shook a stubby finger in my face and screeched, "I'll get you for tempting me and trying to rape me, taking me to the very brink of hell. But you ain't gonna get away with it. Believe me, brother," she railed, "you ain't never gonna get out of this town alive." She glared, wiping spittle from her chin onto her forearm. "Yeah, we're gonna get you like we did that preacher a long time ago, if you don't die of a heart attack first, or chicken out and blow your brains to kingdom come." On and on she rattled, until I turned and walked away, more than a little shook up.

I had good reason to be. Clyde Morrow, a loyal church member, had previously cautioned me to be careful, explaining that some years earlier a former minister on the charge, the Reverend Paul Jackson, was driven to suicide by a bunch of rowdies. Apparently the Reverend Jackson had been ill and heavily sedated with medicine prescribed by his doctor; and because he was thoroughly disliked by a few members on the charge, they attempted to force him to resign. When he refused, the rumor was circulated that he was having sexual relations with one teenage daughter's girlfriend, a wholly unsubstantiated charge. Later, because of his medication, he was arrested as a drug addict. Unable to bear the shame and disgrace, he took a gun and ended his life.

Another friend, learning of the vicious attacks on me and my family, warned us, "When Dad was pastor of that charge, they would drive by the parsonage at night and fill it with buckshot."

Living in Elkton was a lonely experience. While our children had a multitude of friends, Dolores and I had absolutely no social life, even though we had many friends in and around town. For the most part, although all but our avowed enemies were friendly if we met them on the street or at church, they would not visit us at the parsonage for fear that the radicals might turn on them. Even the local ministers shied away, all but the Reverend Charles Kindred. That hurt more than anything else. I had talked with each of them personally, and not one of them had voiced an objection to my use of hypnosis. One was a former would-be hypnotist, who had given it up because he was not too successful in getting people to respond, but there was no fellowship between us.

I thought maybe things might be turning for the better after one of the ministers, Jacob Horton, and I conducted a funeral together. After the funeral Jacob said, "Carroll, I don't understand this ruckus about hypnotism, so if you don't mind, explain it to me. What is hypnotism, anyway?"

For two hours Jacob and I sat in my car by Naked Creek as I attempted to explain everything and answer all his questions. When I had finished, he thrust out his hand and said, "Shake, brother! I admire you for what you are doing—someone has to make this investigation of reincarnation—and while I don't know the first thing about hypnotism, if ever I can be of help to you, don't hesitate to call on me."

Wonderful! I thought. Here was a man I could depend on! Yet from that day on our troubles multiplied as members of his church began sending us a barrage of hate mail. We were to learn later that when a few of his parishioners informed him that they did not approve of our activities, he did an about-face and encouraged them to let Dolores and me know that they thought we were evil and that hypnotism was the "Devil's tool."

Serving that charge was quite an experience, but I wasn't about to let them drive us out of town. Even after a group of sixteen people filed a petition with my District Superintendent, I informed him, "If it is agreeable with you and the bishop, I'll stay on the charge for another year." It was agreeable, and we stayed.

To say that we should have moved may be a gross understatement. But then we would never have learned about the true fickleness and the total depravity of some people. Too, because we had to lean so heavily on the Lord for strength and courage, we were made stronger in every way. It was during that time that we fully learned that it is to the glory of God that His Church has survived and grown into the world's greatest institution despite those who would use it disreputably. There are many people in the world like Ava, who want desperately to be somebody important. Since the Church is for everybody, some of these people are bound to be found there, and well they should be, for if the Church is not for them, then where can they go to find a reason for being? Where is there a better place for people to suddenly meet the Lord and through His actions become important to themselves, God, and society? As for Fannie, she was crude and lewd, but she is to be pitied. Except for speculation, we can never know the root cause of her lust.

Once, while working with the state police from another state, I hypnotized a woman who the officers thought might have murdered her own son. While interrogating her under hypnosis, we were led to believe that she consorted with homosexuals, or at least was friendly with them. We pursued that line of questioning, considering the possibility that one of her friends or acquaintances might have attacked and killed her son. She admitted that her stepfather was a homosexual. Worse, she recounted in regression, with great hysterics, the time when her stepfather forced her to have sexual relations with him at the tender age of six. Oh God, forgive me! In that moment when I listened to the poor woman reliving her childhood, screaming, pleading, begging, "Don't! Don't do it! Please God, make him stop! Oh, God! Let me die . . . please, let me die!" I hated that man with a passion! Even the troopers, hardened to life's cruddiest, turned their backs to one another and to me, gritting teeth and clenching fists till the skin grated while they struggled with heads hunched between shoulders to stifle agonized tears.

Condemn Fannie? Not on your life! Maybe we're not all so bold, but how can we know the depth of her lust, having been spared such a hellish torment? Or how can I know the cravings of an alcoholic or addict when the fanged teeth of addiction never chewed my insides raw? How can I know the insidious hatred that boils and boils and screams the urge to kill, knowing that only the satisfaction of seeing another person die can quench that inner fire? How? O God, I must confess! I know! And forgive me, Lord! Forgive me, for as I sat there hearing Edna scream, for a moment, maybe only a fraction of a second, I knew in my heart that if I could have laid hands on that stepfather, I might have. Thank God, the moment of irrational desire to do violence never came to me when it could be vented uncontrolled.

Our fame (notoriety?) as a result of the Gretchen case brought all kinds of people to our study. One blond woman in her early thirties came down out of the hills and expressed a strong interest in hypnosis and the Gretchen case, but it soon became evident that she was all mixed up and that her marriage was falling apart. Hesitantly, with great trepidation, she summoned the courage to ask, "Will you try to help me?"

Marilyn was not overly intelligent, but she was fairly attractive and affected a pseudo-sophistication which she naïvely thought was all she needed to succeed in life, even though she had flunked out of college, lost several jobs through incompetence, and was quickly making a shambles of her marriage. Marty, her husband, she said, "was sexually frustrated."

No wonder! The poor woman was so confused about sex and religion that she would never take a shower and lather herself with her bare hands, because "That would be fondling myself, and the Bible says, 'Abstain from all appearances of evil!' Still," she added wistfully, "I really like for him to make love to me if he don't run his hands all over me. And that goes for all the others, too. I don't like that fooling around; I can't stand to be touched!" The others, she explained, "are all the guys who want me and sometimes get me if they promise just to make love and keep hands off."

Marilyn was to be pitied. Obviously love and sex were one and the same to her. Her promiscuousness was her way of expressing hatred for her mother. As a teenager she had been caught by her mother standing in front of a mirror fondling her breasts. "I just did it out of curiosity," she explained. As punishment, her mother dragged her in unholy righteousness to the kitchen stove and held her hands against hot coals, screaming, "No daughter of mine will ever become a harlot! I'll burn the fires of lust from you if it's the last thing I do!"

Marilyn responded well to hypnotherapy, at least for a while. She was a good subject, and made what seemed to be excellent progress until the day when she suddenly stood up from a chair in the precounseling session and dropped her coat to stand as naked as a peeled apple. "Preacher"—she leered enticingly—"today I graduate! You are going to lay with me and play with me! You've got to play with me—I want to experience every emotion I've ever read about."

"Hold it, girl! Whoaaaa!" I shouted, grabbing her coat and throwing it at her as I headed for the door. "Cover up or I call Dolores!"

She knew that the study door was never locked, that Dolores was free to come and go at any time, since I always made it clear to someone wanting to be hypnotized that the door was never locked and Dolores could walk in any time. Undaunted, Marilyn pleaded, "Do it to me once! Just this one time and I'll be all right!"

Sick at heart because I had failed, I started to open the door, but she quickly draped herself against it, threatening, "You can't do this to me! I'll tell Marty you tried to rape me. See!" she screamed, scratching herself horribly with both hands. "He'll see the scratch marks and the blood and I'll tell him you did that to me."

I knew that I was safe from her charges, since I recorded all sessions of hypnotherapy. Still, she told Marty that Dolores and I had made the tape just so we could frame her. To my good fortune, Marty said that he was aware of her "little peccadilloes" when he came to see me, at her request.

When I next saw Marilyn, a few weeks later in a supermarket in Harrisonburg, I was relieved when she came up to me, smiling, and began telling me that she and Marty had been converted. My happiness disappeared when she added that they had joined a group of charismatics. "We've been baptized by the Holy Spirit, Preacher! Praise God! And, Preacher," she continued, with a wild gleam in her eyes, "the Spirit has instructed us to pray for you. You're lost, Preacher! You know that, don't you? You're lost because you and your hypnotism are leading people straight to hell. But, oh, Preacher, I love you like a Christian should, and I want to save you!" She wailed in a weeping, pleading solicitation for God as she dropped to her knees. "God is able, Preacher! Praise God! Repent, Preacher, repent!" She grabbed my hand, attempting to pull me down with her. "Repent and He'll save your soul from the fiery torments of hell!"

Stricken momentarily with shock and embarrassment before breaking loose and fleeing the store under the startled eyes of the few shoppers present, I too began to pray: "Yes, Lord, do save me! Save me from ever again running into a nut like that!"

CHAPTER X

The Dead Do Live

It was a beautiful spring day in May, and Dolores and I looked forward with great expectations to Dr. Stevenson's visit to our home for a regression session that afternoon. We were especially thrilled to know that he would be accompanied by Dr. Otto Rohl, professor of German at a southern school for women. Dr. Rohl is a native-born German, and we were convinced that if a man of his stature confirmed that Gretchen's German was authentic, our time together would be most pleasurable.

In the two years we collaborated with Dr. Stevenson, a warm friendship developed. But he was more than a friend. Always a perfect gentleman, congenial and courteous, he was also a conscientious scientist, meticulous in the minutest detail. In truth, because of his studious penchant for observing strict rules of scientific procedure, Dolores and I put him in a most embarrassing position that day by inviting a few friends to be present for the regression session. When he and Dr. Rohl arrived and saw our friends sitting in the living room, Dolores and I were momentarily stunned when he inquired in great surprise about their presence. Our friends, the Reverend Charles Kindred, pastor of Elkton's First Baptist Church, his wife, Dee, and Carl Schumacher, owner and editor of the *Valley Banner,* were even more surprised than he, as was Punky, who had driven down from Hagerstown to spend a few days with us.

Even Dolores and I were momentarily at a loss for words, because we had invited our friends to attend the investigation, never dreaming that Dr. Stevenson would prefer that the session be conducted in complete secrecy. Quickly we regained our composure and assured him that we meant no harm, and that since all present were our

149

friends, they would not interfere. But Dr. Stevenson was reluctant to proceed under the circumstances and again suggested that they be asked to leave.

Somewhat shaken, Dolores protested, "Dr. Stevenson, I am sorry, but never will I ask my daughter to leave my home for any reason, nor would I ever dream of ordering dear friends to leave, especially after we extended them a special invitation to spend this afternoon with us."

A little more than disturbed, Dr. Stevenson said that under the circumstances he thought it best not to continue with the investigation that day.

"Then so be it!" I blustered angrily, unable to comprehend his reluctance to proceed as planned. "Frankly, Dr. Stevenson," I reasoned, "I see no reason why they should not be here, especially since they have pledged that under no circumstances would they ever reveal what transpires here today."

Admitting that possibly they wouldn't, he nonetheless reminded us that we should consider his position. In essence he said that since this was a scientific investigation and his colleagues would eventually have to pass judgment on all that happened that day, they would be highly skeptical of the results if they were to learn that outsiders were present. He again insisted that our guests be asked to leave.

Dolores appealed, on the verge of tears. "Surely your colleagues are not so insensitive as to deny us that right to invite whoever we want into our own home. Don't they realize," she challenged from our point of view, "that this investigation is as much ours as it is yours? Frankly, Dr. Stevenson"—she paused to dab her eyes and gain control of her emotions—"without Ked and me being willing to sacrifice our reputations, maybe even his career in the ministry, for the benefit of science, you would have absolutely no case at all!"

Seeming to understand our situation he agreed sympathetically, "But . . ."

"No! No buts." Dolores rebelled, openly weeping. "When the day comes that I have no voice in determining who can or cannot visit in our home, then that will be the day when I refuse to continue with this investigation!"

"That's right, Doctor!" I added in support. "Either you

accept us and our guests as we are or we call the whole thing off!"

Through it all Dr. Rohl stood aside, helplessly embarrassed. I later learned that Dr. Stevenson had assured him that no one other than Dolores and I would be present, else he would not have come, so naturally he felt deceived on walking into our home full of people. Too, Dr. Rohl was a novice in the world of the paranormal, and he was quick to associate our case with the occult, saying something to the effect that one could never be too careful about being linked with the occult.

"No, Dr. Rohl," I answered, hoping to allay his fears, "we have nothing to do with the occult. This is strictly a scientific investigation, and these people are our friends. They know and understand the situation, and we have nothing to be afraid of; neither do you."

Charles, Dee, and Carl were so terribly embarrassed that they got up to leave, apologizing for their unwanted presence. But I objected, "No! You stay!"

"Oh, please," Dolores wept and pleaded with them, mortified by the turn of events, "if you go . . . oh"— she turned to Dr. Stevenson—"it's not fair! From the day we first met you we have done everything possible to please you; we have responded to every request, and . . . oh, Dr. Stevenson," she added brokenly, "we haven't even had a life of our own these past two years simply because we have practically ordered our lives to fit the demands of science, but now this! Oh, how can you possibly insist that we make them leave?" she cried and ran from the room, completely distraught.

Momentarily flustered by her tearful outburst and exit, Dr. Stevenson looked at me, painfully apologetic, and expressed regret, indicating he was sorry about the misunderstanding. Then he paused reflectively to suggest that possibly he had been too hasty, that maybe Dr. Rohl and he should step outside for a moment or two and discuss the situation privately.

As he and Dr. Rohl retreated to the front lawn, I apologized to Charles, Dee, and Carl before hastening to the bedroom to comfort Dolores. For a moment I could only stand and grit my teeth as I looked at my Dolores lying on the bed weeping. "It really isn't fair!" I thought.

"Life in all its existence should always allow a person to interact and function as a human being, but for Dolores," or so I reasoned, "the investigation demanded that she submit and respond as a flaccid guinea pig. She might just as well have been a programmed robot."

Not many people would have subjected themselves to the ordeal as did Dolores. Without a single complaint she handed over her life lock, stock, and barrel to me and Dr. Stevenson. And for what? For the sake of science we imposed upon her, using her as a bit of submissive protoplasm that was expected to lay inert and utter a few words in a strange and alien tongue which were then scrutinized and analyzed for hidden meanings and veiled nuances. Worse yet, others, ignorant of the facts, questioned her sanity and muddied her name with slanderous slurs and vicious epithets. And, yes, blast it! though she was the one person I knew to be as honest as the day is long, even I questioned and requestioned her, hinting that possibly she hadn't told the whole truth. And now this: a crazy afternoon in which it seemed she was being told, "To hell with you and your friends! Don't you realize that science insists you be no more than an inchoate blastula to be excised for the glory of others?"

But that wasn't true, not really. Maybe Dr. Stevenson was totally scientific, but he was not unconscionable! Had I paused to think clearly, I would have realized that he assumed Dolores and I were familiar with the rules of scientific procedure; when stunned by the presence of our guests, he simply arrived at the conclusion that we deliberately flouted those rules. But we hadn't. In truth, we had invited our friends in ignorance.

As I continued to look in compassion at my weeping wife quivering on the bed, I wondered whether I had the right to request that she submit to another regression. Really, I wondered, was there any reason, any purpose in subjecting her to further ordeals that day? Had there, in fact, been any meaning to all the other days when she submitted to our probing and prying for a glimmer of light and understanding of the strange phenomena that had come into our lives unasked and unwanted? Was the investigation really worth all the endless days and nights of soul-searching questions?

Silently Punky entered the room. "Daddy," she said, interrupting my thoughts as though reading them from an invisible scroll, "I know you and Momma are hurt, but don't give up now, please!" Then, taking my hands in hers and emphasizing her concern with her big brown eyes, she pleaded, "You've gone too far to quit. Please, Daddy, just one more time!"

Just one more time! Was it worth it?

I began to bend. "Maybe."

"You won't regret it, Daddy."

"Maybe not," I muttered, beginning to realize just how much it meant to her and the other children. Surely, regardless of hurt pride and frustration, Dolores and I owed it not only to Dr. Stevenson and to the world, but to them as well. For them it was imperative that nothing stop us, lest they spend the rest of their lives wondering what might have been, never knowing the truth about the strange phenomenon that had touched their lives as much as it had ours.

Going to the bed and sitting beside the prostrate Dolores, I ventured cautiously, "Hon, can you . . . will you go on . . . just this one more time?"

Wearily she sat up, looking as though the will to live had vanished in tears. "I can't." She sighed listlessly. "It all seems so senseless. She buried her head in tissues. "Oh, the shame . . . the humiliation!"

"The shame and the humiliation!" I exclaimed. "Oh, no! You've done nothing to be ashamed of!"

"It's no use," she wept on my shouder, "I just can't go out there and go through that again. I just can't! I feel like a microbe under a microscope . . ."

"Aaaawww, c'mon now." I tried laughingly to tease her out of the doldrums. "Surely you're not telling me that a mere microbe flirted with me, loved me, and gave us all those lovely children who call me Dad!"

"Now you cut that out!" She drew back sniffling, half smiling despite reddened eyes. "That's the way I feel right now."

"Well, maybe so, but look, hon," I entreated, "lie down and rest; relax. Let me put you to sleep, and you'll soon feel better."

"It's no use," she demured. "It won't work this time. I'm so ashamed and embarrassed."

"Ashamed and embarrassed! Of what?" I demanded. "Hang it, girl, I'm telling you for the last time that you've nothing to be ashamed of! Now, lie down and let me put you to sleep," I demanded, gently pushing her back on the bed. "Then, if you still feel the same after I awaken you, I'll personally tell Dr. Stevenson we quit! That it's all over!"

"Oh, I do need help." She sighed. "I'm so tired . . . just washed out, but . . ." she murmured, and began to go limp as I stroked her hair, "we mustn't disappoint Dr. Stevenson. He's been good to us, and surely he simply misunderstood our intentions."

"Just sleep, Momma," Punky encouraged. "Just relax! Forget Dr. Stevenson; forget everything that happened this afternoon, and Daddy will help you. Just rest, sleep! But please, don't give up. You've gone through too much to quit now."

"Yes, rest . . . sleep," Dolores repeated wearily.

Even as she talked and I touched her on the forehead with three fingers, I thanked God when she relaxed and her eyelids fluttered to a close.

Thank God?

"But why?" one little old lady asked me one day. "Why do you waste so much time thanking someone you've never seen? Don't you feel silly thanking someone whom you've never even met?"

"Whooooaaaa, dear lady," I cautioned, "just you hold on for a minute! You're talking about something you know nothing about. To have seen God in the flesh—no, I haven't; but to have met Him in Christ Jesus and to have seen Him—yea, I've seen Him in the glory of a light brighter than the noonday sun. But more important, dear friend, there was a day when I saw His crowning glory as He came to Dolores in the wee hours of the morning to comfort her when she was but a little girl of eighteen lying on a tear-drenched pillow, pleading in the agony of a mother's lament, 'I want my baby! O Father God, I want my baby! Please, Father, give me my baby.'

"You see, my friend, our first son had been born that

morning, the healthy, robust flesh of our flesh, the blood of our blood! And we heard him cry, wailing as all new-born babies do, 'Hey, world, listen! Look at me. I'm here! I'm alive! I've made it, and—' Then silence, the deathly silence that mutes the world when an angel of death descends to claim its helpless victim.

"Never will I forget, nor will time ever silence the tortured screams of my Dolores wailing, 'I want my baby! Why can't I have my baby? . . . My baby . . . my baby,' until the heartrending petitions were forced into silence by the injection of a sleep-inducing drug.

"You see, dear lady, as Dolores and I were told several years later by a nurse who was in attendance at the birth of our son, 'The doctor accidentally dropped the baby, breaking its neck, killing it!' But that night in the hospital, that night as I sat on the edge of her bed and hurt for her more than life itself, she turned to me while reaching out to take my hand in hers and said, 'It's all right, honey. See, He's come!'

" 'He's come! Who's come? Where?'

" 'There.' She smiled as the light of heaven shone brightly in her face. 'There, can't you see Him . . . there . . . at the foot of the bed.'

" 'See who?' I pressed, scanning the room and seeing no one. Then—but, oh, it's so unbelievable—when I turned to look at my wife again, I tell you the truth: Chills so gripped me that the hairs on my arms stood on end as I saw her eyes turn into two pools of blood. 'He lives!' she voiced with angelic delicacy. 'And He told me, it's all right, child. You shall have a son and daughters to love and to cherish.'

"Even now I still see those eyes, not merely bloodshot, but red, red all over—a deep, dark blood-red like nothing I had ever seen before. And no! my imagination had not run wild, nor had I hallucinated. What had happened I don't know. Still, although I was not really a Christian at the time, I often think of the stigmata: the wounds my Christ bore for me on the Cross. So maybe, just maybe, when Dolores saw Him, Jesus the Christ, standing at the foot of her bed, He used the symbol of His shed blood in her eyes as a sign to me that God in Christ was truly alive and present in the world.

"But no matter, it was in that moment of the long ago that I began seriously to change in my thinking toward submitting to the insistent urge that I commit my life to my Lord and His service."

As Dolores lay asleep on the bed, I thanked God for having given me a talent that could be used for good in hundreds of ways, but though I count all the ways, none was more important right then than that I had the ability to quickly induce a few moments of restful sleep, a sleep so restful she would otherwise have required several hours in bed.

"I'm all right now," Dolores said when I awoke her ten minutes later. "You go out there and apologize to everyone while I freshen up a bit. But first"—she stopped me at the door—"I want you to know that this will be the last time I submit to regression. I simply cannot go through anything like this again."

When I returned to the living room Carl had left, thinking that because he was a reporter he was the one not wanted by Dr. Stevenson. Dr. Stevenson and Dr. Rohl had returned to the living room with the explanation that since they had traveled so far just to get here, they decided that it might be best to continue with the regression even though the situation was less than perfect. Certainly it was not scientific, since persons not involved in the investigation were present.

When Dolores returned to the living room, trying bravely to maintain poise and be her congenial self, there were a few moments of taut uneasiness, but after we all looked at her and smiled a nervous apology, she took her place on the couch and I began the induction process. Soon everyone was so engrossed in the procedure that all else was quickly forgotten.

Charles, Dee, and Dr. Rohl were so enthralled that their eyes seemed riveted on the sleeping Dolores, and when Gretchen uttered her first words, all but Dr. Stevenson and I gasped in amazement at the strange, alien voice emanating from Dolores's lips.

"Gretchen," I began, "you know that I cannot speak nor understand your language, that I do not know what you are saying. But I have some friends here, Dr. Stevenson and Dr. Rohl; they can speak your language and would like to talk to you."

"Ich komme wieder [I come again]," Gretchen greeted us.

Stevenson: "Sprechen Sie lauter, Gretchen. Wie geht es Ihnen heute? [Speak up, Gretchen. How are you today?]"

Gretchen: "Ist gefährlich! [Is dangerous!]"

Stevenson: "Gefährlich? Warum? Was ist gefährlich? [Dangerous? Why? What is dangerous?]"

Gretchen: "Sie hören! [They hear!]"

Stevenson: "Gretchen, wiederholen Sie bitte. [Gretchen, please say that again.]"

Gretchen: "Der Bundesrat, Sie hören, Sie zuhören! [The National Council, they hear, they listen!]"

Stevenson: "Und was wird der Bundesrat tun? [And what will the National Council do?]"

Gretchen shook her head fearfully. "Sache . . . sehr schlecht! [Things . . . very bad!]"

Normally Gretchen spoke slowly and softly, and it was often necessary for me to interrupt and encourage her to speak louder. Too, we were never certain at what age she would emerge, so I asked, "Gretchen, how old are you?" And she replied in the girlish voice of a teenager, "Vierzehn. [Fourteen.]"

Stevenson: "Vierzehn, ja. Und wo wohnen Sie jetzt? [Fourteen, yes. And where are you living now?]"

Gretchen: "In Eberswalde."

Dr. Rohl now entered the conversation: "Gretchen, wo ist Eberswalde? [Gretchen, where is Eberswalde?]"

Gretchen: "Deutschland. [Germany.]"

After a few perfunctory questions, Dr. Rohl inquired about the National Council and asked, "Und wo ist der Bundesrat? In welchem Land ist der Bundesrat? [Where is the National Council? In what area is the National Council?]"

Gretchen replied fearfully, "Überall! Sie hören zu! [Everywhere! They listen!]"

Rohl: "Das ist gefährlich? [That is dangerous?]"

Gretchen: "Ja. Sehr beschwerlich. [Yes. Very troublesome.]"

Dr. Rohl was obviously a bit nervous and hesitant,

telegraphing the fact that he had never before questioned anyone in hypnosis. His inexperience showed up especially when he let the conversation drift to irrelevant material, things important in their own right, but which we already knew, such as "What games do you play?" and "With whom do you play?"

My hopes that he would elicit more important material were high simply because Gretchen emerged that day at age fourteen (she usually came through at nine), but when I heard him and Gretchen talking about Mrs. Schilder, and the names of Karl, Karin, Kurt, and Erich coming from Dolores's lips, my hopes sank. "Surely," I thought, "Dr. Stevenson will not let them retrace the same old ground again." But Dr. Stevenson did not intervene, and I began to think Dr. Rohl and Gretchen were doing exactly as I suspected, a fact I later learned to be true when I received the transcript of that session. In truth, I did not have to wait for the transcript, because even Gretchen became so bored and restless as he asked, "What is your father's name?" and "What does your father do?" that she began to stir restlessly and wave her hands before slamming irritably, "Schon Ich habe reden alles! Warum die Fragen wieder und wieder? [Already I have told everything! Why all these questions over and over again?]"

A point we can never emphasize too much is that people in regression are supposedly reliving that portion of their life about which they are being questioned, and, like most of us in the waking state, they become upset when plied repeatedly with redundant questions. Since Gretchen was clearly annoyed, I decided to move her ahead in time, hoping she would become more responsive to Dr. Rohl as she matured. I suggested, "Gretchen, move ahead in time. Please go to age sixteen."

"Nein!" she resisted, with even greater irritation. "Ich nicht kann!"

I had heard enough German by that time to learn that "Ich nicht kann" meant "I cannot," so I pursued the question. "Why can't you go to sixteen?"

"Ich nicht kann," she repeated, but with much less conviction and authority.

"Gretchen," I impressed upon her, "we need to know

about your life at age sixteen, so please move forward in time, now!"

Without further argument she relaxed and lay with her palms together at her bosom in an attitude of prayer and said, "Gretchen . . . tot. [Gretchen . . . dead.]"

"Gretchen ist tot!" Dr. Rohl exclaimed. "Wann ist Gretchen tot? Sechzehen Jahre alt? [Gretchen is dead? When did Gretchen die? At sixteen?]"

Grimacing, Gretchen moaned: "Ich bin krank. [I am ill.]"

Rohl: "Krank? Gretchen ist krank? [Ill? Gretchen is ill?]"

Gretchen: "Nein. Tot! [No. Dead!]"

Rohl: "Sie ist tot! Ist Gretchen fünfzehn Jahre alt? [She is dead! Is Gretchen fifteen years old?]"

Now, having heard much German since Gretchen came into our lives, I learned that "tot," "gestorben," and Gretchen's word, "torpen," referred to death. Additionally, I knew that "krank" was ill, and as a consequence of hearing those words bandied about, I know something was radically wrong. But what?

When I urged Gretchen to move to age sixteen, she rebelled ("Ich nicht kann"), and for good reason. It has been my experience that a person who has once been regressed to relive the traumatic moment of death is inclined to resist moving to that fatal moment in future regressions. Gretchen was no exception.

While most regressed people are just like you and me in that we have no idea what tomorrow holds in store for us in this world, regressed persons are different; there is considerable evidence that they may indeed be talking about a prior life actually lived. And if that be true, then it is a fact that the memory of their entire existence from birth to that plane of existence we refer to as "afterlife" is recorded somewhere in their subconscious. Thus, even though a person may not have willingly moved to a time period that the questioner wants to discuss, such as the moment of death, that person may either move spontaneously through the not-altogether-understood actions of hypnosis or may speak from a memory acquired in previous regressions. That is, people may remember reliving their death in a previous regression.

This, I believe, is what happened to Gretchen when she exclaimed, "Gretchen ist tot! [Gretchen is dead.]" Remember that I had asked her to move to age sixteen, near the age of her death, and while she may not have actually moved to that actual moment, she may have remembered that she would be dead at sixteen and expressed this with "Gretchen . . . dead." Or there is the possibility her spirit may have started to move toward that fatal moment but had not had time to complete the move when Dr. Rohl asked in surprise, "Gretchen ist tot?" This would explain why she seemed to be contradicting herself in the preceding conversation.

Obviously Gretchen could not have been, as the conversation indicated, first dead and then ill; an understanding of the actions of a person in hypnosis should clear up any misunderstanding.

Most people in regressions will respond quite readily to suggestion, either moving mentally or letting their spirits move to the designated point in time on request. However, comparing them to you and me, were we to take what we knew to be our last, long walk toward death, most likely we would move rather slowly. This is also true of persons in regression, such as Gretchen, who have previously been moved in time until they relived their death in a supposed prior life: They are most reluctant to be advanced again to that point in time, because they either remember or in some way sense what happens when they reach that moment in time. Thus, when I urged Gretchen to move to age sixteen, she did not want to go to that age, which she knew to be the year of her death. Still, when I insisted that she move ahead in time, she began to comply, absent-mindedly voicing what was in store when she got there.

How does that explain her statement that she was ill after saying she was dead? Well, when she said, "Gretchen . . . tot," Dr. Rohl exclaimed in surprise, "Gretchen is dead!" But Gretchen, moving in spirit slowly to her fatal end, had progressed in time only to the moment when she was attacked (she always described the beating as an illness: headache), and she corrected him, saying, in effect, "No, right now I am ill—I haven't yet gotten to the time of my death." Naturally, not understanding what was happening, Dr. Rohl could only answer in perplexity, "Ill?" But again, because Gretchen continued to progress in time, she soon passed beyond her headache into death and was forced to say, "Nein. Tot! [No. Dead!]"

Along this same line, many people assume that because a regressed person is discussing a supposed prior life, that person should know everything there is to know about the previous life. Indeed, one does, but factually, the questioner should never ask a question about anything in the prior life that is not consistent with the exact period of life being discussed. More explicitly, don't ask me about anything that happened to me at age sixty-five, for I have not yet attained that age. So it is with people in regression: The chronology is most important and should never be mixed up. Just as Gretchen emerged at age fourteen, she normally would not answer questions about events that occurred when she was fifteen or sixteen. To get information about an older age, the subject should be moved to that age by the hypnotist. At times questions are asked of a person concerning a year being relived at that moment and almost always the answer, if there is one, will be distorted or rambling.

When I finally realized what was happening to Dolores, that she was not reliving the time period being discussed, I quickly began the process of moving her back to age fifteen. After allowing her a reasonable time to acclimate, I signaled Dr. Rohl to proceed with his questioning.

"Was macht Gretchen? Ist sie bei Frau Schilder? [What is Gretchen doing? Is she with Mrs. Schilder?]"

"Ja," Gretchen responded, happy to get away from her moment of death. "Frau Schilder kocht. [Yes. Mrs. Schilder cooks.]"

Rohl: "Ist der Vater da? [Is your father there?]"

Gretchen: "Ja. [Yes.]"

Rohl: "Wann wird Gretchen krank? Fünfzehn Jahre? [When does Gretchen become ill? At fifteen?]"

Gretchen: "Ja. [Yes.]"

Let me note that although Gretchen supposedly died at age sixteen, we see here that she "became ill' (was attacked) when she was fifteen, indicating that the fatal moment came shortly after she turned sixteen. This should also help explain why she was so quick to speak of death when asked to move to sixteen.

Rohl: "Was für eine Krankheit? [What kind of illness?]"

Creasing her brows, Gretchen searched for an answer. "Ich weiss nicht. [I don't know.]"

Rohl, trying to be more explicit, asked, "Was ist krank? [What is ill?]," meaning, I presume, "Where do you hurt? Where do you feel sick?"

Gretchen, holding her head, moaned, "Kopfweh! [Headache!]"

For a moment I began to think that Dr. Rohl and Gretchen were going to operate on an even keel, but when he followed his question about her illness with the question "Was sagt der Vater? [What does your father say?]," he confused her, and she mimicked him in disbelief: "Was sagt der Vater? [What does my father say?]" You see, by taking her mentally to the time of her illness, he had moved her chronologically ahead of the time when her father was present with her. Had he asked her to remember what her father had said, she could have done so, but never could she have answered on the spur of the moment a question that was asked in the present tense about something that had happened quite some time before. A person in regression must be given sufficient time to mentally adjust to a time change. This explains why Gretchen seemingly had so much trouble with such an innocuous question about her health—she had not had time to move forward and adjust to the new time span.

Thankfully, Dr. Rohl's next question was one she could answer. He asked, "Wo ist die Mutter? [Where is your mother?]," and she stammered sadly, "Der Mann . . . torpen, mein Mutter. [The man . . . dead, my mother.]" In this instance he was not asking her to explain something that had just been said, but rather to explain from memory something that had happened a long time before. It was as if he said to her, "Remember when your mother left home and tell me where she went."

Seeking a more definitive answer, he then asked, "Der

Mann tötet die Mutter? [The man kills your mother?]"

"Ja," Gretchen replied.

Rohl: "Wann ist die Mutter gestorben? [When did your mother die?]"

Gretchen: "Wann ich bin sehr klein. [When I am very small.]"

But again Dr. Rohl asked her to do the impossible: "Wann stirbt Gretchen? [When does Gretchen die?]"

Obviously she could have answered such a question only after she had been moved forward in time past the moment of her death. Still, possibly because she began moving toward that time, or because she sensed from feedback something of that moment, she cowered into a shell and demurred, "Ich nicht spreche. [I not speak.]"

But Dr. Rohl insisted, "Sie können es sagen. [You can talk about it.]"

"Nein," she argued. "Ich verstehe nicht. [No. I do not understand.]"

Determined to get an answer, Dr. Rohl demanded, "Was passiert, als Gretchen stirbt? [What happens when Gretchen dies?]"

But Gretchen just lay and moaned, refusing to answer.

"Was geschiecht? [What happens?]" he persisted. "Was passiert, als Gretchen stirbt? [What happens when Gretchen dies?]"

"Ah." She moaned and cringed in terror, the feedback memory becoming more real, "Sehr schlecht! [Oh, very terrible!]"

"Was passiert? [What happens?]," he continued to press. "Wie geschieht es? Wie? [How does it occur? How?]"

But Gretchen could only answer, "Ich . . . Ich weiss nicht . . . Ich . . . krank! [I . . . I don't know . . . I . . . ill!]"

Rohl: "Gibt es Soldaten? [Are there soldiers around?]"

Gretchen: "Ja. [Yes.]"

Rohl: "Gefährlich? [Dangerous?]"

Gretchen: "Ja. Manchmal verborgen. [Yes. Sometimes hidden.]"

Rohl: "Wo haben Sie sich verborgen? [Where have they hidden?]"

Gretchen: "In dem Wald. [In the forest.]"

Because Dr. Rohl had let Gretchen spend considerable time on this phase of her life, she was able to speak clearly of what was happening, but when she attempted to tell of going into the forest to her hiding place there was another breakdown in communication, and Dr. Rohl tried to change the subject by saying, "Denke Sie an eine andere Geschichte. [Think about another episode.]"

"Nein," Gretchen rebelled, wanting to tell about the events occurring right at that time. And when Dr. Rohl asked, "Können Sie sich an eine andere Geschichte erinnern? [Can you remember another event?]," Gretchen slumped, shrugged, and threw her hands out in despair, telling Dr. Stevenson and me, "Er nicht versteheht! [He doesn't understand!]"

Flushing with exasperation, Dr. Rohl shouted, "Nicht verstehen? Nicht verstehen! Wir wollen Sie verstehen. Erzählen Sie mehr. [Not understand? Not understand! We want to understand you. Tell us more.]"

He did indeed want to understand, but was unable to because the intricacies of regression were just too much for his newness to the task. Dr. Stevenson subsequently wrote on the transcript, "Dr. Rohl was trying to see inwardly." And while his efforts were extremely commendable, either Dr. Stevenson or I should have taken more time to explain that persons in hypnosis seldom seek an answer introspectively. Rather, they speak the content that flows spontaneously from the subconscious—the only store of information they have, compared to our dual capacity of both conscious and subconscious resources.

Maybe this will explain it better:

Even as I write this book the phone rings. I pause to answer it and converse with a lady who has been coming to me for hypnotherapy. That is a fact—a fact which I relate at this moment because it actually happened. It was an event in time which occurred and is now stored in my memory bank. And, just so, people in regression will tell the questioner of an event that is happening in their lives right at that moment—the event they are reliving! They do not search their heart, soul, and mind for the memory of a scene that has happened. To use a trite expression, "They tell it like it is," even though we receive it as an accounting of something that may have happened a hundred years ago.

Dr. Rohl continued to press: "Erzählen Sie mehr. [Tell us more.]"

Gretchen began, "Ich versuche reden der . . . [I try to speak . . .]"

"Ja," Dr. Rohl encouraged her.

Gretchen: "Ist reiten das Pferd . . . verborgen dem Wald . . . [I ride the horse . . . hidden in the forest . . .]"

Rohl: "Aha, reiten Sie mit dem Pferd? [Oh, so you ride on a horse?]"

"Ja," she replied, in an attempt to lead up to the moment of her death. Apparently she had succumbed to Dr. Rohl's persistence and decided it might be best to tell him about that terrible moment—but then, for reasons I shall never understand, especially after knowing that he had worked terribly hard to get her to that point, he digressed with a series of questions that must have seemed irrelevant to Gretchen, such as: "Wem gehört das Pferd? [Who owns the horse?]" "Wo bleibt das Pferd? [Where does the horse stay?]" "Ist das Pferd auch im Wald? [Is the horse also in the forest?]"

But Gretchen had had enough and stopped him, demanding irritatedly, "Warum die Fragen? [Why all the questions?]"

"Wir wollen es wissen! [We would like to know!]" he began, before stopping to rephrase the question with less irritation: "Erzählen Sie uns, kommen Sie nach Hause, nach Eberswalde? [Tell us, do you come home, back to Eberswalde?]"

Having given up, apparently Gretchen let her spirit move to the afterlife to get away from the cares of this world and our questions.

"Ah," she answered dreamily in the ethereal voice used when she spoke from the afterlife, "Vor langer Zeit. [A long time ago.]"

Dr. Stevenson responded, "An interesting answer," and indeed it was. In fact, when the context of that dramatic statement is weighed with Dr. Rohl's subsequent questions, there can be no doubt that Gretchen had indeed moved into the afterlife. For example, when he asked, "Können Sie sich an die Leute erinnern? [Can you remember the people?]" she replied with complete disinterest, "Nein."

To make certain he understood the full impact of her denial, he then asked, "Können Sie sich an Frau Schilder erinnern? [Can you remember Mrs. Schilder?]"

"Frau Schilder?" she responded, like one searching for a name with a familiar ring.

"Ja, Frau Schilder," he repeated hoping to jog her memory. "Wie sieht Frau Schilder aus? Was für einen Mantel hat Sie? [How does Mrs. Schilder look? What sort of coat does she have?]" But Gretchen just lay with a strained look on her face, not answering; she did not remember Mrs. Schilder because she was not with her in that faraway place.

It is not often that a person in regression, supposedly advanced to the afterlife, will remember persons or events in a prior life. And doesn't this say something good to us? When death comes, were we able to carry with us all the cares, worries, suffering, and torment of this world, even heaven would be hell. Thank God, we don't, and because all that happened in this life is past and forgotten, Gretchen could not recall the specifics of this life.

Apart from Dr. Rohl's inexperience, what other reasons could have brought about the breakdown between him and Gretchen? Well, persons in hypnosis will normally follow only the instructions of the hypnotist unless they have been instructed by the hypnotist to respond to other persons. But sometimes there are exceptions to this rule. If other persons are present during the hypnotic session and make a casual suggestion, even in a whisper, the entranced person may very well follow that suggestion.

Suppose that Charles had whispered to Dee, "I wish Dr. Rohl would hurry up and get Gretchen to a point beyond death so we can see and hear what she would say." I did not hear him say such a thing, but there is the possibility that he could have, and this might explain why Gretchen moved into the afterlife. She might have heard Charles and wanted to please him more than Dr. Rohl. It is common knowledge among hypnotists that a person's hearing may sometimes be increased tremendously in hypnosis, a fact I will elaborate in an actual case history in a subsequent chapter.

There is another explanation: telepathy. And here I must now defend Dr. Stevenson's objection to other persons being present in our home during the investigation. Although Dolores and I were terribly offended and our guests extremely embarrassed, I must emphasize that he was totally correct in insisting that no outsiders be present, a fact we did not fully understand at the time. Although Dr. Rohl did most of the questioning, any one of us in the room could have posed a question telepathically. We could have been concentrating on some aspect of the case, maybe even subconsciously posing a question or answering a question which Dr. Rohl had posed; as in the case of a whisper, it is conceivable that Gretchen could have telepathically received and voiced an answer to our question, or given our answer in lieu of anything Dr. Rohl might have been questioning her about at the time.

Regardless, it now seems obvious that Gretchen did progress far beyond the pace of Dr. Rohl's questions, and since I could not understand the conversation, it might have been better had Dr. Stevenson called upon me to move her back to the forest experience, because the forest experience was clearly the most important period in Gretchen's life. We needed to know what actually happened there, as indicated by Dolores's retrocognitive vision and her rapid bypassing of that period of time when Dr. Rohl questioned her.

Dr. Stevenson was familiar with Dolores's vision, and he certainly recognized its importance, because he had previously informed me that while her vision was not unique, it did tend to lead him to the further belief that retrocognitive visions may be a concomitant part of a bona fide remembrance of a prior life. Other people with whom he has worked have had a similar experience. Moreover, the importance of Gretchen's forest experience was emphasized by the fact that it was in the retrocognitive vision that she first told of being put to death in the forest.

In retrospect I had first thought of Dolores's vision as merely a dream, but remember that I had hypnotized her the day following her dream and she had relived in minute detail in regression all that she experienced in the dream so I could only conclude that it was a retrocognitive vision of a life lived in the long-ago. There were just too many similarities for it to have been the wild imaginings of a sleeping mind. Gretchen had emphasized the forest as the place of her death, so it was imperative that Dr. Rohl or someone else make every effort to let her relive the forest experience in the hopes of acquiring new information.

Returning to Dr. Rohl and Gretchen, she seldom volunteered information, but now she figuratively threw a bombshell by exclaiming, "Gretchen einkerkern! [Gretchen imprisoned!]"

Caught totally off balance, Dr. Rohl picked up only on the last syllable: "Kerkern?"

"Nein!" Gretchen corrected the learned professor. "Einkerkern!"

Rohl: "Aha, ja. Einkerkern. Ja, ich kenne das Wort. Es heisst—[Oh, yes. Imprisoned. Yes, I know that word. It means—]"

"Sehr schlecht! [Very terrible!]," Gretchen interrupted, moaning.

Obviously, Dr. Rohl was trying to determine whether she knew the importance of what she was saying, so he engaged her in a battle of semantics, trying to make certain whether she was talking about a prison or imprisonment. He asked, "Ist ein Kerker ein Gefängnis?" [Is a Kerker the same as a Gefängnis, a prison?]"

"Ja," Gretchen assured him.

Rohl: "Das heisst, Gretchen ist im Gefängnis. [So you are saying that Gretchen is in prison.]"

Surprisingly, although she had assured Dr. Rohl that she understood the semantic difference between Kerker and Einkerkern (prison or imprisoned), she created chaos by answering "Nein. [No.]"

Taken aback and clearly rattled by her apparent statement of contradiction, Dr. Rohl turned hastily to our guests and exclaimed insistently, "Sie ist im Kerker! Sie ist einkerkert, nicht wahr? Warum ist Sie einkerkert? Warum? [She is in prison! She is imprisoned, isn't she? Why is she imprisoned? Why?]"

"Shhhhhhh," Gretchen whispered while putting a finger to her lips and opening her eyes to hurriedly survey the room, "Sie kommen! Sie horchen! [Shush! They are coming! They are eavesdropping!]" Then, with an urgent note of solicitous fear for Dr. Rohl, she warned, "Du müssen verborgen! [You must hide!]"

Pleadingly Dr. Rohl encouraged her, "Erzählen Sie mehr. [Tell us more.]"

But Gretchen cringed. "Sie kommen hier, Stille. [They are coming here, silence]," she whispered. "Stille, sehr gefährlich! [Silence, very dangerous!]"

Dr. Rohl, attempting to allay her fears, comforted her: "Das ist jetzt vorbei! [That's over now!]"

Oh, if only he had not said that! But he had, and unintentionally he had told her that that period of her existence was over and done with. You see, most persons in hypnosis will respond to the slightest cue, and Gretchen, wanting to get out of a dangerous situation, took him at his word and subconsciously moved forward in time until she began to show signs of tiredness and weakness, mumbling with a sigh, "Gretchen ist müde . . . Kopfweh. [Gretchen is tired . . . headache.]"

Recognizing her condition and thinking that the sound of my voice might comfort her, I intervened. "Relax, Gretchen. Relax! In a moment your head will quit hurting, and as it does, I want you to move ahead in time. I want you to go to the age of sixteen."

"Ahhhhh," Gretchen moaned, "Gretchen ist tot! [Ohhhhh, Gretchen is dead!]"

Sadly Dr. Rohl turned to our guests and lamented, "Sie es tot mit sechzehn. [At sixteen she is dead.]"

But Gretchen was already dead, as indicated by her communications from the afterlife. Now, her mention of prison and her complaint about being tired, plus her statement "Gretchen is dead," surely indicate that somehow her spirit had drifted back into life in this world. In fact, her next words, "Der Soldat! [The soldier!]" add to that assumption, but when Dr. Rohl responded quickly with the questions "Der Soldat hat das gemacht? [The soldier did that?]" and "Ist der Soldat böse? Wie lange? [Is the soldier angry? How long?]," Gretchen sighed. "Nicht lange [Not long]," she said, seemingly in response to something altogether different, a point that was emphasized when the conversation continued.

Rohl: "Stribt Gretchen im Kerker? [Does Gretchen die in prison?]"

"Nein," she answered weakly, stirring from a prone position to an attitude of prayer with hands at her bosom, "Gretchen ist müde. [Gretchen is tired.]"

Remembering that Gretchen was talking about imprisonment, soldiers, and dying, yet saying she did not die in prison, let us consider the possibility that in fact Gretchen was not living again in this life. Possibly she was trying to make us understand that while there was a time when she lived as flesh and blood on this earth and was forced to spend some time as a prisoner in a jail made of stone and wood, she was now saying that she was a prisoner in another life.

Such a premise seems plausible to me even though she did talk of prison, soldiers, and death. While I did say a short while ago that heaven would be hell if we took our memories of this life with us into the world to come, I was referring specifically to heaven. As for hell, that's another story. Anything that can add to torment is hell, and maybe our memories of this life are an ingredient that makes hell even more hellish. This does not mean that Gretchen was in hell—only that she wasn't in heaven, a point I will discuss in a subsequent chapter. And since she wasn't in heaven, at one with God, possibly she spoke from a memory of her prior life. This is indicated by her statement that the soldier wasn't angry long, that his wrath quickly abated once his grisly task was done and she was dead, and if she was dead, obviously she was in the "afterlife."

Concerning Gretchen's statement that she was tired, I believe that all who are in the afterlife and not in heaven will be perpetually tired. One of the most tormenting things about this life is a continual tiredness that comes from worry, boredom, and frustration, and the Scriptures say that "Whatsoever is bound on earth, shall be bound in heaven, and whatsoever is loosed on earth, shall be loosed in heaven" (Matthew 16:19). So if we hold on to the tormenting tiredness here on earth, it will hold on to us in the life to come.

More important, the assumption that Gretchen was a prisoner in that other world is strengthened when we consider Gretchen's appeal to Dolores from her place in the other world behind the huge portal. Always she was pleading for Dolores to "Come." But why? Well, as she said to

170

Dolores one day, "I want peace." And peace could come to her only if she was released from bondage either by living again through Dolores or in some way advancing onward and upward into heaven.

This brings us to the dichotomy of Dolores's lying on a couch in my study and speaking as though she were Gretchen even as she saw Gretchen standing behind a huge portal, indicating that either Dolores is the reincarnation of Gretchen remembering a past life in regression, even having retrocognitive visions of that life, or, Gretchen coming into our lives has indicated very strongly that her soul—any spirit in the afterlife—does continue to live as an intelligent being after death. We are also given very strong proof that a spirit personality from that world can manifest to persons in this life, even speaking to and through them if not actually entering into them and possessing them completely.

Gretchen's manifestation to us also gives new insight to the many Protestants who have long deplored the Roman Catholic belief in purgatory and limbo, choosing to believe that at death our souls go to either heaven or hell. Conversely, there is much food for thought in this for all Catholics who are contemptuous of the Protestant belief that God does not provide a temporary resting place for the soul before the soul is completely made ready for heaven.

Many reasons can be given why everyone should believe in the future existence of the soul, even those who do not now believe in heaven, hell, purgatory, or the survival of the soul. Why anyone doubts the existence of the soul in the afterlife is beyond me, especially since the world has been told of thousands upon thousands of human experiences involving supernatural events of the survival of the soul after death, such as I experienced following the Christmas holidays in 1954.

My family and I had visited my parents in Clarksburg, West Virginia, and on New Year's Day, 1955, we had no sooner started the long trip back to Hinton, Virginia, than I turned to Dolores and said in tears, "I will never see Dad alive again."

After arriving home that afternoon, I was overwhelmed by an inexplicable fear. Thinking I would feel better if I rested, I went to the bedroom and lay down. But even then my fear possessed me, and I asked Dolores to come and sit with me. Several hours later, a few minutes after the hour of midnight, I felt a rush of peace and contentment flood my soul, I turned to Dolores and told her, "It's all right, now. Dad is at rest—he's dead."

A short time later Dolores left the room to look in on Punky, who slept just across the hall. As I lay there in the darkness, a strange light began to glow in the upper left corner of the room. Soon the light changed into something that looked like a large circular convex mirror. In that mirror I saw Dad, smiling and seeming to say, though no words were actually uttered, "I just wanted to let you know that I'm all right, that everything is just fine."

I saw Dad for only a moment or two before the phone rang. It was my sister, Ruth, phoning at approximately 12:30 A.M. to tell me that Dad had died. "Yes, Ruth, I know," I said, adding, "Tell Mom I'll be home tomorrow."

Six years ago my mother died on the Saturday before Thanksgiving. Although Mom was eighty-four years old, she enjoyed good health. Dolores and the children had gone to visit our relatives for the holidays, but because of my health, I did not make the trip. On the Wednesday before Thanksgiving, the day they left, as I returned home from school at Lynchburg, I had the strangest feeling that when I entered the house Dolores would tell me that she had received word that Mom had died. But, no, she was all packed and ready to go, and the children were excitedly happy about the trip, so I said nothing about my feelings.

On the Sunday morning after Thanksgiving I knew that death would come or had come to a member of my family, but I forced myself to excuse the thoughts of death as mere worry over the fact that Dolores and the children would be driving a hundred and sixty miles homeward on a busy holiday Sunday, when death always stalks the highways. I went to the church, and was talking to Mrs. Mary Barton when I suddenly blurted, "Mom is dead!" Then, looking out the window, I saw our car pull into the driveway. Leaving the church immediately, I met Dolores as she walked toward me. I said, "Mom is dead, isn't she?" and Dolores could only nod yes and embrace me. She and my nephew, Jimmy Jay, had driven to Greenbush to break the news as gently as possible, fearing that a phone call might be too much for my weakened heart.

Death, as we conceive it, is a terrible thing when it comes to those we love, but it need not be. Thousands of people have had experiences comparable to mine, and many have been recorded, but thousands more could become a part of the record if only people would overcome the fear of being branded as "kooky."

One of the healthiest attitudes about death and those that live on in the world of our fathers is expressed by Bishop H. Kenneth Goodson, president of the United Methodist Council of Bishops. He wrote in the July 1973 *Virginia Advocate,* "A few days ago I went to the little town of Salisbury, North Carolina, where I was born and went to the town cemetery. I hardly ever go through my home town without stopping to see my two brothers who live there, but I also usually stop at the town cemetery, for there are three people buried in a plot that has my family name on the stone, and I often stop to talk to them. There are not many people who would understand this kind of behavior, but I still enjoy a visit with my parents and believe that God enables us to live in that mysterious realm of the universe that is out beyond the far cliffs where only free spirits like Jonathan Livingston Seagull are permitted to fly. One of those graves belongs to my brother, Dan, who died when I was a wee little thing, and I have no remembrance of him at all. The second is the grave of my mother. There was a personal matter I wanted to talk to her about, and I did. She approved of my conversation with her."

While it may be true, as Bishop Goodson says, that "not many people . . . would understand this kind of behavior," I beg to believe differently. Wherever I have gone and met people, whether in church, lectures, seminars, or in casual conversations, it soon became apparent that most people, though usually silent on the subject, wholeheartedly believe there is a life after death, a life which permits us to have communication with all who have gone on before. More important, I know that survival of the soul is real, simply because I have talked with personalities in the afterlife without making a trip to the cemetery. Mom, Dad, and countless thousands of free souls did not wait to be lowered into the darkness of a casket, nor did they linger in the moldering clay of the grave, before coming to me and others for the sole purpose of giving us their personal assurance that life does not end with the failure of the flesh.

CHAPTER XI

Our Ancestors Speak

After Dr. Stevenson had conferred with colleagues in West Germany and learned that the only known Eberswalde in Germany was in East Germany, he made a two-day stopover in West Germany on his way to India, hoping to determine if a Gretchen Gottlieb ever lived in that city. As a result of that effort he stated in his "Preliminary Report of a New Case of Xenoglossy" in the *Journal of the American Society for Psychical Research*, Volume 70, January 1976, that "It has not been possible to trace any person whose life corresponds to Gretchen's statements." He then added, "Some of her statements are incompatible with known facts. For example, a real Gretchen could not have been the daughter of the mayor of Eberswalde because Eberswalde has never had a mayor by that name."

While his conclusions may very well coincide with the known facts about Eberswalde in East Germany, and although Dr. Stevenson deems it an absolute imperative to investigate every possible lead, even a casual study of the tapes and transcripts by a casual observer would show that Gretchen tried desperately to direct our attention to a locale with which she was familiar but which was approximately three hundred miles southwest of that city. While the modern city of Eberswalde with a population of some thirty-five thousand people is the only known Eberswalde in Germany today, most native-born Germans with whom I have discussed the case have said that many years ago there were many small towns with that name. So, to say that a "real Gretchen Gottlieb could not have been the daughter of a mayor of Eberswalde because there was no mayor of that city by that name" is to conclude that such may be the case only if one is content to consider that one city in East Germany. Even Dr. Stevenson concedes there may be other places named Eberswalde that could have been incorporated into other cities or towns.

Why look southward? Well, when Dr. Stevenson first entered the case, in 1971, he proceeded immediately to the heart of this problem by asking Gretchen while Dolores was in regression, "Wo wohnen Sie? [Where do you live?]," and Gretchen answered, "In Eberswalde. [I live in Eberswalde.]"

Stevenson: "In Eberswalde. Ja, und ist das in der Nähe von einer anderen Stadt? [In Eberswalde. Yes, and is that near some other city?]"

Gretchen: "Ja, Darmstadt."

Please note that Darmstadt is some three hundred miles southwest of the modern city of Eberswalde in East Germany. On a tape which I sent to Dr. Stevenson in the fall of 1971, Gretchen was asked if she knew of any other cities nearby, and she clearly stated "Wiesbaden" and "Worms," cities within a few miles of Darmstadt. Also, when she mentioned Darmstadt, Wiesbaden, and Worms, she claimed to be nine years old, so wouldn't it seem logical that a girl of that age would most likely make reference to towns and cities near her own home town, which she called a "Kleinstadt [small city or town]"? Moreover, she always described Eberswalde as having only a bakery, butcher shop, church, and school. She described the terrain as mountainous, with a forest and a small stream nearby. So even the topography disputes the possibility that Gretchen may have lived in northern Germany, which is generally level with plains sloping out into the low-lying coastal flats along the northern shores, while the area around Darmstadt, Wiesbaden, and Worms is uneven, with high, flat plains edged by rolling hills and scattered mountain ranges.

Possibly Dr. Stevenson was influenced by the fact that he was unable to detect an accent which would indicate the region where Gretchen lived, but Jurgen Horsch of the German Wire Service and other native Germans were quick to note that Gretchen spoke with an accent suggestive of a particular region near Darmstadt and Wiesbaden, even though they did not know she had mentioned those cities in her regressions.

It must also be remembered that early in my encounter with Gretchen we had considerable difficulty in communicating because I could not speak German. I always asked questions in English, and she would always answer in German. Although I had difficulty understanding her, she could understand me, and often used different words in an effort to make me understand what she was trying to say. Two words she used in those days were "Eberstadt" and "Eberback." Being ignorant of the German language and German history, I had no idea that she was referring to names of towns or cities. After a while, though, I assumed that those two words did refer to specific places. I suggested to Dr. Stevenson early in the investigation that he consider "Eberstadt" and "Eberback," but I remember thinking after making the suggestion that he must have thought I was giving him superfluous information, because he failed to make a notation of my suggestion.

Because he evinced no interest, I took the tapes to school, where several teachers helped me search German maps for Eberstadt and Eberback, but when no such places could be located, we too concluded that Gretchen must have come from Eberswalde in East Germany.

Further listening to the tapes and a study of the transcripts made me discard that idea. Surely, if Gretchen had lived in that northeastern part of the country she would have given me the name of at least one city in the near vicinity. Once when I asked Gretchen to pinpoint the location of her home relative to Darmstadt, she traced a diagrammatic configuration on a map with her finger which resembled an acute triangle that included the cities of Wiesbaden, Darmstadt, and Worms. In an effort to mark the exact spot, she indicated that her home would be west of Wiesbaden and south of Darmstadt.

What makes Eberstadt and Eberback so important? Well, many native Germans have suggested that many, many years ago Eberstadt or Eberback may have been called Eberswalde. Many have said that Gretchen may not have actually meant that she lived in a town named Eberswalde, but rather, since the Eberswalde is a union

177

of two words, "Eber," meaning wild boar, and "walde," meaning woods or forest, maybe she meant to convey the information that she lived near the woods of the wild boars, or the place of wild boars in the woods. This reasoning seems especially plausible and consistent with Gretchen's simple, rural mentality. She may have reasoned that we would understand that she meant Eberstadt instead of Eberswalde, which we would then be forced to translate the "the city of the wild boars," or to assume that she meant Eberback, which would be described as "the place of the wild boar across the creek."

Another conflict is found in the apparent overlapping of the life spans of Loreen Tuttle and Gretchen. Loreen said she was born on January 3, 1851, and died in June 1874. Although Gretchen has never given dates for either birth or death, we assumed for various unproved reasons that she lived between the years 1870 and 1890. But even then we knew that if those dates proved correct, there was a strong possibility that reincarnation would have to be ruled out as a possible explanation of the Gretchen case. However, most parapsychologists insist that dates given in regression are seldom accurate, meaning that we should not put too much credence in Loreen's dates for birth and death. Even if she were correct, nothing in the known facts says for certain that Loreen did not live and die as stated, or that Gretchen did not reincarnate in Dolores after Loreen's death.

How did we establish the dates for Gretchen's sojourn in this life? Gretchen referred to the Bundesrat and religious strife more often than any other subject. Since we thought the Bundesrat did not come into existence until 1867, when it was formulated to designate the Upper House in the council of states which became the North German confederation, it is doubtful Gretchen lived before that date. More important, Gretchen said that Pope Leo was head of the Roman Catholic Church, and indeed he did lead it from 1878 to 1903, giving possible cause for believing she did live for at least a while after 1878.

Bismarck, the empire's Chancellor (Prime Minister), and head of the Bundesrat, ruled until 1890, which narrows the possibility of Gretchen's earthly existence to the years 1867–90.

During Bismarck's reign, he believed two obstacles prevented him from instituting and implementing a nationalistic policy to bring greater unity to the federation of twenty-five states constituting the Empire: the Roman Catholic Church and Socialism. As a consequence, he attacked the Roman Catholic Church, expelled the Jesuits from Germany, and provided for government control of education and the appointments of priests. The Church fought back, and a severe struggle known as the Kulturkampf ensued between the Church and secular authorities, not ending completely until after Pope Leo XIII adopted a more conciliatory tone toward the German government. So, although Loreen may have lived and died, and if reincarnation is still an issue, there is no reason to believe that she could not have reincarnated as Gretchen soon thereafter and lived as Gretchen until 1890, since Bismarck ruled as Chancellor until that date. Many parapsychologists have cited several cases where they believed a person reincarnated very shortly after death. In such cases there would be no overlapping of lives.

But wait: While we based our assumptions on the fact that Gretchen did live after 1867 because the Bundesrat did not come into being until that date, a close reading of the transcripts reveals that when Gretchen once referred to the Bundesrat, she did so very hesitantly, pronouncing the last syllable very softly, as if in doubt about its correct usage. And this makes me wonder whether she planned to say Bundesrat or Bundestag, a term that had come into use earlier. If this is true, we can assume that Gretchen was referring to an earlier period.

Also, Gretchen mentioned Pope Leo as being head of the Church, but it seems strange to me that she could not give the name of the local priest. More important, she often spoke of Martin Luther as though he were alive at the time, which was totally untrue. It soon became evident that she knew little or nothing about the local church, especially the name of the local priest, forcing me to conclude that all her information about Martin Luther and Pope Leo came from instruction given her by her father. Gretchen seemed to have a very limited knowledge about the Church as a whole; everything she said

179

about Martin Luther and Pope Leo seems to be hearsay or partially learned knowledge.

As a consequence, although all the interrogators constantly brought up the names of Martin Luther and Pope Leo, everything said by Gretchen about them should be disregarded, if for no other reason than it was I who introduced their names into the regressions. Too, when it is noted that all the other interrogators continually bombarded her with questions about them, we must conclude that she was almost forced into saying something, be it right or wrong. During my days as a schoolteacher, it was not unusual for a very poor student, one we would call not too bright, to try to give an answer to almost any question asked, even without any idea of what the class was talking about. So I believe it was with Gretchen.

Therefore, assuming she may not have known the difference between Bundesrat and Bundestag, the possibility should at least be considered that she may have lived earlier. This thought is reinforced when we realize that she spoke of living in another regression as Loreen Tuttle at a time which almost forces us to juggle facts and figures just to prove that Gretchen did live during the Revolution of 1874. If Dolores lived as Gretchen, logic demands that she also lived as Loreen, since she gave a verbal account of both lives. To deny the existence of one life necessitates that we deny the other. Conversely, if we accept Gretchen because Dolores spoke German in regression, we must also accept Loreen even though she did not speak German.

In other words, if Gretchen actually reemerged from a former life and relived through Dolores, we must accept that Loreen also lived, that her life is of equal importance, even though her case is a little less dramatic simply because she did not speak German. Supposing evidence should be discovered proving that Loreen did actually live more than a hundred years ago, then what? Such proof may very well exist, according to information I now have, but since it adds nothing to the proof that Gretchen lived, we will explore that evidence at a later date.

More important, Dr. Stevenson says that he is still trying to determine whether other towns named Eberswalde which merged with larger communities formerly existed in Germany. But for the present, or until such information has been uncovered, his main concern in the Gretchen case involves a study of xenoglossy. He wrote in the *Journal of the American Society for Psychical Research* that "the failure to trace a person corresponding to Gretchen's account of herself means that the chief interest of the case lies in the evidence for responsive xenoglossy."

There are two types of xenoglossy: recitative and responsive. Recitative xenoglossy refers to a person's being able to repeat, without necessarily understanding, fragments of a strange language, such as the young man who spoke Oscan; or persons who learned a foreign language as children and then forgot they learned it. It is the ability to speak a known language, but one which the speaker does not remember having learned. Responsive xenoglossy refers to persons who can converse intelligently in a foreign language not previously learned.

Dr. Stevenson says that "from my own knowledge of German I am certain that Gretchen could speak the language responsively, that is, that she could give sensible answers in German to questions put to her in that language . . . that the Gretchen personality could speak German intelligently seems to me established beyond all doubt . . ." The question, then, he adds, "is whether D.J. [Dolores Jay] learned German normally. She denies that she did so and I am convinced that she and her husband have told the truth when they say they had no effective knowledge of German prior to the development of this case. . . . All my efforts, which I think not inconsiderable, to learn of any opportunity D.J. might have had for learning German when she was a young child turned up nothing whatever to support this conjecture. After some years of doubt, I now have no hesitation in saying that I am quite convinced that D.J. did not learn German normally."

If she did not learn the language normally, obviously something paranormal or supernatural caused her to speak the language. But what?

Could genetic memory have played a part? That's possible but highly improbable even though Dolores had great-great-grandparents who immigrated to the United States from Germany. They died several years before

Dolores was born, so there was no possibility that she might have learned the language from them.

Could they have passed the memory of the language down to Dolores? Well, in this rapidly expanding age of science anything seems possible, and we could tentatively say yes, but in accordance with known data, is the concept of genetic memory based on fact?

Apparently it is. Brain investigators have attempted in recent years to define biological bases of memory through intensive research in chemical bases of memory and electrophysiological bases of memory. Psychologist James V. McConnell, at the University of Michigan, used planarians (common flatworms) found in creeks and ponds to determine memory transfer. McConnell flashed a light on the worms and then gave them an electric shock, which caused them to contract. After repetition of the process, the worms soon learned to contract when the light was flashed.

McConnell went a step further. He gathered the worms trained to respond to light, ground them into a purée, and fed the purée to untrained worms The results: The untrained cannibals responded twice as often to the light flashes although they had never been shocked.

Dr. George Unger, a pharmacologist at Baylor College of Medicine, trained animals to perform various tasks; he then extracted chemicals from their brains, and after purifying and isolating the chemical material he injected it into the brains of untrained animals; the untrained animals then acted like trained animals. For example, Unger extracted scotophobin, a protein from memory molecules, from more than four thousand rats which had been trained to fear the dark. When the scotophobin was injected into untrained rats, they also feared the dark. The same processs was used with more than six thousand rats which had been trained to ignore the sound of a bell; when the substance was injected into the untrained rats, they too ignored the bell.

Some will argue that Unger's molecules have nothing to do with memory, and insist that the molecules merely stimulate nerve cells in the brain, as do pep pills, hormones, and other ehemicals. Such refutation of Unger's experiments in no way explains why injected rats follow exactly the same patterns of fear exhibited by the rats from which the molecules were extracted.

In another research project, Ronald Hoffman, a biophysicist at the University of Houston, reports that after teaching goldfish to swim through a triangle to get food, he injected their brains into other fish. All swam through the triangle without prompting. Rodney Bryant of the University of Tennessee reported that he injected synthetic rat scotophobin into the brains of hundreds of goldfish; the goldfish exhibited fear of the dark and resisted learning to swim in the dark.

Thirty-two laboratories in the United States are working in this field. In many instances (especially in goldfish) the instilled learning usually lasts for only six to ten days. Still, the passing of memory from one animal to another is clearly present, indicating the possibility that a parent can pass along the memory trait to an offspring via biological inheritance. Since the addition of memory molecules by injection from donors to rats, earthworms, and fish will make them ape the actions of their donors, does it not suggest that the memory trait is already present in all animals, including humans, but that it is simply not strong enough in most cases to initiate recall on its own?

Now suppose that such persons as Dolores and others who recall alleged prior lives in regression may have inherited a double portion of memory molecules; can it then be said that genetic memory is strongly indicated as a biological fact? More important, when you remember that in the preceding examples the memory trait was present, but only transferable by injection or assimilation, can it be said that because our knowledge of genes (hereditary traits) is by no means complete, it is entirely possible that we are biologically endowed with memory traits through inherited genes, but that as of this date most such genes have not yet become dominant and lie dormant until activated by some special circumstances or activity such as dreams, visions, or hypnosis?

Suppose we go a step further and assume that we do inherit memories genetically; can we say such an assumption proves a valid argument in the Dolores/Gretchen or the Dolores/Loreen case? Well, in the Dolores/Gretchen case the answer could be yes, but in the Dolores/Loreen case, no! Since Dolores does have a German ancestry, biological inheritance is possible; thus, Gretchen being German, the answer has to be a plausible yes. But, since we have not yet traced any German heritage to the Tuttles of Indiana, the answer seems to be no. The only relatives Dolores and I have in Indiana are on my father's side of the family, which would have no bearing on her ability to remember a past life in Indiana. So the genetic-memory theory seems highly implausible as an explanation of her memory recall in regression.

A few years ago it would have been a big help to have had a pat answer to Gretchen's origin. But we didn't. Because Dr. Stevenson had his own timetable for the investigation, and a commitment to his other investigations, we found it hard to continue bucking the pressure coming at us from all sides to prove that Gretchen was more than a witchcraft entity or a hallucination dredge up by Dolores in an occult ritual. So great was the strain on us that I gave serious thought to releasing the Gretchen story to the newspapers when Donnel Nunes of the *Washington Post* called for an interview.

The pressure from some people in the church was hardest to take. For instance, one time I went to Mount Holly church for a Sunday-morning worship service and saw a religious tract on the pulpit Bible when I stood up to preach. I had seen a similar tract before, a ridiculous article written by someone who knew nothing about hypnosis, and even less about Christianity. The tract had been purchased in bulk by our enemies who fought so hard to drive us out of town. They had thought that by reading the ludicrous missive, others would also learn to hate us, eventually helping them to rid Elkton of our evil presence.

The tracts were insignificant, and I could have ignored them had not someone scribbled on them gutter filth such as "You lousy S.O.B. [they spelled it out], you're nothing but a —— —— pimp, and your wife's a stinking whore!!"

"Oh, God!" I prayed as my soul grieved to know that somewhere in that congregation was one or more persons with such a warped, perverted soul. For a few seconds I held tightly to the pulpit as a dizzy, swimming blackness assailed me. I wanted to run, to get far, far away from the filthy, degenerate scribbler, but I couldn't move. I wanted to cry, but no—they would have laughed aloud at my weakness. I wanted to speak, but no words came. And then I got angry. Angry because I had preached to those people with heart, mind, and soul for a salary that hardly paid my gasoline expenses. Worse yet, there were people there in the Lord's house that day whom I helped when their children got in trouble with the law, others who gladly took our money when they were hungry. I did not expect a reward or a pat on the back, but neither did I expect a knife in the back. Even those who benefited from hypnotherapy in my study sat like bumps on a log, knowing what had been done and caring less about what others did to me.

One woman I especially remember. She was the one whom I thought I could depend on through thick and thin. But, no, as all the others did, she too sat looking at the floor, out the window, or up to the ceiling. How different when she, Donna Mills, lay in the hospital in Charlottesville, and sent word that she wanted to see me. For twenty years she had been a diabetic, and at least once a year during all that time she had been forced to the hospital for a stay of not less than twenty-one days because of her condition. When I walked into her room that day, she smiled and said, "Preacher, I want you to help me . . . hypnotize me. I've heard that you have helped others in my condition."

When I asked if she had consulted her physician and gotten his permission, she said no, she didn't want him to know anything about it. "You see," she explained, "he and my father are very close friends, but my father is a religious nut and he thinks that hypnosis is of the Devil, and if he ever found out that I even thought of calling you in, well . . ."

Although Donna had often visited in our home, I apologized and explained that it was not possible for me to hypnotize her there in the hospital without authorization, but she persisted. "Just show me how it's done!" she pleaded. "Please, Reverend Jay, you are my last hope!"

For the only time in my life, I let friendship sway me

into violating my rule of ethics against hypnotizing any-one without a doctor's authorization. I did not really in-tend to hypnotize her. I thought that if I showed her the procedure, she would be satisfied. She was, because she was a somnambulist. She went into a trance easier than anyone I had ever met—within two minutes she was in a very deep trance. Quickly I told her, "Your blood-sugar count will become normal; you will become calm, quite, serene and in a few moments when I awaken you, you will feel rested, relaxed, and refreshed. You will then get up, go to the mirror, and brush your hair. While you are brushing your hair, I will leave, and when you have finished with your hair, you will awaken and know that you have been made completely well."

When I returned to the hospital to see Donna the next day, she had been released and sent home. As I walked down Main Street in Harrisonburg that afternoon, and saw her husband, George, a local banker, he chortled happily, "Preacher, I've never seen anything like it! When the doctor examined Donna yesterday afternoon, he sent her home—her blood sugar was normal."

Donna later told me, "In the past twenty years I have been in the hospital twenty times for my diabetes and they always kept me three weeks. This time, when you came to see me, I'd only been in there six days. And you know what?" she said with a twinkle in her eyes. "I've not been back to the hospital since." Then she added, "Preacher, I don't care what anyone says about hypnotism —if ever there is anything I can ever do for you, I'll do it even if it kills me!"

Sad to say, in church that day when I needed help, just an encouraging word, she cowered and refused even to look toward me. The only help I ever got in that church was from the Lord, and for that I am grateful. In fact, had not the Lord been with me when I visited that church two weeks later, I might not be here today to tell the story.

I had promised the Lord that I would serve Him to the end, that "I'll go where you want me to go, be what you want me to be, and do what you want me to do." No matter what was said to me or my family, no matter what was done—draining my gas tank, putting sand in the gas tank, slashing my tires, or cutting the water hose —I continued to pray that God would give me the grace to forgive my persecutors and I'd return there on my next preaching assignment.

Maybe that was a mistake. When I entered that church on my next preaching assignment, I noticed that one family who attended regularly was absent. I assumed that since they had been unable to drive me out of the church, they had decided to quit coming so long as I was pastor. But just before going to the pulpit I glanced out a window which had been opened two or three inches and I saw a car similar to that family's car parked next to mine. Naturally I rejoiced and assumed they were merely late. I was mistaken—they never did come to the service, and when I left the church that day the car was gone. I felt terrible. It always hurt me to think that I might be the cause of anyone not attending church. Still, there was nothing to do but get in my car and start home, a ride of about five miles along an old country road.

I had not gone far when I heard a strange noise under the front seat. At first I thought the children had left an empty pop can under the seat and it was rubbing against the springs. Though I do have something of a hearing problem, the noise bothered me so much that I pulled to the side of the road, intending to clean out whatever trash had accumulated under the seat.

As I stood outside the open door and leaned over to look under the seat, something like a bolt of lightning struck straight at my face, and I recoiled so fast that I slipped and fell on the gravel. Quickly picking myself up and thinking "rattler," I looked for a long, long stick. After finding one, I cautiously approached the car and gingerly opened all four doors before beginning to probe under the car seat from a safe distance; and sure enough, soon a rattler at least four feet long, looking more like ten yards, slithered out the other side of the car to vanish into the brush. Even now I break out in a cold sweat remembering that day and some of those people, since I am certain that someone's only reason for parking their car alongside mine that day was to bring me what they evilly thought was a fitting gift.

That was not our only encounter with snakes. A few

weeks later Mary Jo had gone to the bathroom to shower. In a few minutes she bolted from the room half dressed, screaming in mortal fear. Rushing to her aid from the study, I heard her babble hysterically, "There's a snake in there! There's a snake in there!" Quickly I closed the bathroom door and went downstairs to my workbench and got a hammer. Slowly, cautiously, and fearfully, I opened the door and slipped into the room, closing the door behind me. At first I didn't see anything, but as I searched with trepidation, I saw the hideous thing coiled between the commode and the far wall. Slowly I approached it, hammer poised to swing. Then, luckily, as it struck out at me I swung and hit it on the head, stunning it. Quickly I pounced on it and beat it to a pulp.

When it was all over, Dolores and I stood by shakily and wondered what to do with it. Finally we decided to wrap it in newspaper and put it in the garbage can, after instructing Mary Jo never to mention the events of that afternoon to Vonda or Jesse. It took Mary Jo, Dolores, and me several weeks before we quit looking in every nook upon entering a room, and for a long, long time I always threw back the covers on the bed before crawling in, fearful that someone had planted another cold, wriggly snake in our bed.

We could never figure out how that snake got into the bathroom, because the whole house was covered with storm windows and screens, but later I examined the screen in the bathroom very carefully and found a small slit at the side of the screen. Without saying anything, I went to the hardware store and bought a new screen.

A couple of days later a friend remarked, "I see you and Mark York have kissed and made up." When I laughingly asked why he thought so, he said, "Well, a couple of days ago I saw his Vega parked below your house. I just assumed he'd come to visit you." (He assumed it was Mark's Vega because pink Vegas are not too common.)

In truth, Mark had not visited in our home for quite some time. He seemed to abhor the very ground on which I walked, and had made every effort possible to run us out of town, even though I had gone out of my way to be friendly with the man. In a way I felt sorry for him, pitied him, because he was somewhat of a loner who had few friends besides his wife, and I'm not certain she liked him too well. Most of his spare time was spent listening to the more radical radio preachers, who really mixed him up with their many strange doctrines. Actually, he had become so confused that he had developed a messianic complex, even grown a beard "so I can look more like Jesus," he said.

Lamentably, his professed holiness was often punctured by temper tantrums and uncontrolled hatred for anyone who disagreed with his fragmented conceptions of true Christianity. Worse, he felt so all-wise and holy that on more than one occasion he attempted to belittle me to my children, hoping to convince them that he was "their one true friend," concerned only with saving them from a Satanic father. Vonda once said of his efforts, "Daddy, Mark talks like he is sick upstairs." Sick or not, I could not help wondering, since his car was parked just below our house the day the snake was turned loose in our bathroom: Could he have slit the screen and slipped the snake in? Of course, I'll never know for sure. I do know that I had been previously warned that he would "get" me, one way or another.

I had never thought of Mark as being capable of doing such a thing, yet he had destroyed a beautiful friendship between Dolores and me and a beautiful young couple, the parents of a couple of toddlers whom we loved dearly. Herb was a strapping six foot two mass of muscle. Marie was a diminutive black-eyed beauty of Mexican descent. When I first met Herb and Marie, they knew very little about the Christian religion. Our heart went out to them, and we spent months and months of enjoyable time counseling them. Both, especially Marie, had problems too numerous to mention, and progress in getting them to accept Christ as their Savior was slow.

Marie underwent hypnotherapy three times weekly for several months to overcome a melancholic personality induced by constant memories of premarital promiscuity. Her husband had forgiven her, God had forgiven her, but she could not forgive herself. She had begun to make excellent progress after finally accepting that while she was not a saint (nor is any of us), she could be and was a good wife and mother and could function reasonably well as a homemaker, by God's grace.

However, after attaining a measure of peace with herself, her friendship with Dolores and me cooled considerably after she became friends with Mark. After a visit with us, Mark would go to her home and belittle our labor of love and friendship, insisting that I was merely using her, that "there was no way she could be cured and find forgiveness outside the saving grace of Christ." Well, while I believe wholeheartedly in the saving grace of Christ, I also believe in the efficacy of psychotherapy, psychological counseling, and hypnotherapy, especially when incorporated with good religious practices.

Regrettably, our friendship with Herb and Marie ended one day after Marie visited us just to engage in chitchat, then went home and deliberately misrepresented to Herb everything Dolores and I had said. Naturally Herb was upset, and he came in a rampage to the parsonage to tell me off, ending his tirade with the threat "It's all right, Preacher. Someday Mark's going to tear you apart; he'll teach you a lesson you'll never forget!" On that score he was correct, and I learned once again that often it is those whom you love the most, those to whom you give yourself unreservedly, who turn on you with a viciousness more reprehensible than that of the snake that was deliberately loosed in our bathroom.

There are some things so personal that Dolores and I would prefer to keep them secret. Many we have already revealed, because an autobiography necessitates confession. Because that is the nature of this book, I must tell you about an event that ranks as one of the most horrifying of my life.

Some frends who lived in a retreat between Elkton and Harrisonburg had attended a few of our services after the wife had spent several months in hypnotherapy. One day I noticed a coldness in their attitude that puzzled and worried me. As time progressed, that coldness developed into a devastating barrier.

After much worry and prayer about the matter, I decided that maybe if I visited in their home we could sit down as responsible adults and discuss the problem, whatever it was, that was destroying our friendship. So I phoned Art, telling him I would like to come over for a visit.

"Sure, Preacher," he responded, seemingly congenial and enthusiastic, "c'mon! Glad to have you any time."

When I pulled into the lane leading to their home, I was disturbed to see several cars parked under the trees to the right of the house. After I got out of the car, an uneasiness made me pause momentarily to reflect. Maybe going there wasn't such a good idea after all.

But soon I reasoned, "Art is as anxious as I to clear the air and patch things up."

Unable to completely shake the aggravating uneasiness, I forced myself to mount the steps and use the wooden mallet on the horseshoe hung on the door as a knocker.

"Hiya, man!" A young lad of fifteen or sixteen greeted me as a long-lost friend, though I had never laid eyes on him before. "Art and Nadine're tied up, dressing," he explained. "But hey, man! Don't just stand there. C'mon in!" he insisted, grabbing my arm and dragging me across the threshold. "You're among friends!"

Was I, really? Doubts quickly assailed me as I stood inside the door, smelling a cheap, sickly-sweet incense that sent a lazy spiral of smoke upward from a mantelpiece that adorned an open fireplace.

The house had formerly been a hunter's lodge made of rough-cut timber and stone, but it had been neglected, it was in bad repair and sparsely furnished. The inside had never known paint, and the wind often gushed through cracks in the unvarnished wooden-plank floor.

In a corner to my left, lolling against the wall from his nest in a beanbag chair, sat Joe, a tall, gangling boy of fifteen whom I knew to be a frequent visitor in their home. In front of the fireplace a frizzy, buxom peroxide blond lay flat on her stomach in an abbreviated halter and skin-tight short shorts, reading a paperback.

"Whoops," a middle-aged man laughed after opening the front door and hitting me in the back with it, almost knocking me over. I didn't know the man, but I was to learn that he was from Luray, the county seat of Page County, where I had taught school and coached in the early sixties.

"You don't know me, Preacher," he said with a grin

akin to a leer, "but I've seen you around, and I know you like a book."

"Hey, Pops," Joe slurred, "peel your coat and sit."

"Yeah," the older man said, grabbing my coat from behind and stripping it from me. "Park your honkers and rest your weary bones."

"You better do it, preacher man," a young woman named Peggy chimed in, with what she surely thought was a seductive smile, "you'll need all the rest you can get."

"Oh, Lord," I wondered as I looked for a place to sit before settling for the only place available, the floor, "what in the world's going on here, anyway?"

After I had made myself as comfortable as possible, a door at the far end of the room to the right of the fireplace slowly opened, revealing a bedroom, and everyone quickly stood as if on signal as the wheezy strains of a fanfare issued from what sounded like a kazoo.

"All hail the glorious, the mighty Blairs," those in the living room chorused while raising their arms to the ceiling and bowing in what I assumed was mock adoration. "Peace be unto you, O divine shallocks of this sacred abode. With joyful heart we submit to your eternal reign."

Had it not been for the pervasive air of insidious tension haunting me, I would have laughed aloud, especially when Art and Nadine strolled regally from their bedroom as king and queen, he in a gaudy bathrobe and sneakers, she in a cheap chenille robe laid back on the shoulders and open down the front to a tie at the waist. With false eyelashes, too much eye shadow, rouged cheeks, and an overabundance of cherry-red lipstick cheapening her creamy blondness, Nadine made a vain effort to saunter bewitchingly on Art's arm to the smoldering fireplace.

Together they bowed, curtsied, and bowed again, after which Art intoned in mock reverence, "O fire that burneth, but doth not consume;/O light that flickers, but cannot illume,/Speak to me of thy mighty power/In thunderous words, this very hour." With that, he tossed a handful of white powder into the fire, causing it to explode and burn with a blue intensity. Then, turning to face us, they slowly sank to sit rigidly, Buddha-style, bare legs crossed, hands on knees.

"Sit!" Art commanded.

"Aye, holy potentates," the motley group responded. "Allikaaa, Allikaaa, Allikaaa!"

When all had returned to their places, lolling, lounging, sprawling, and lying on the floor, Art looked at me and ordered me to scoot on the floor until I sat directly in front of him and Nadine.

"Well, pucky pronouncer from the pulpit, what brings you to our holy sanctum?"

Everyone snickered. Even Nadine let a faint smile curl the corner of her mouth before diverting her eyes from mine—in embarrassment I presumed, over her tawdry appearance.

"I had hoped that . . . uh, well, I thought that . . . uh . . . we could . . . uh . . ."

"C'mon, man!" the young boy ordered. "Speak up! Answer the man!"

Again I tried to explain my purpose in coming, after a quick glance at the boy, wondering who he was and what the whole charade was about.

"I just thought that you and I might—"

"You just thought," Art interrupted, scowling, "that you could come here tonight and flimflam me like you did Nadine"—he paused to lay a hand on her bare thigh—"when you put her to sleep and tried to make out with her. Ain't that right, buddy?"

"Oh, come, Art!" I half smiled, thinking he was putting me on. "A joke's a joke, but look"—I glanced around at the shabby scene—"aren't you carrying things a bit far?"

"This ain't no joke, mister!" he grated, eyes glaring, burning in hatred. "I know how you tried to lay my wife!"

"Now, Art, that's ridiculous. You know very well I never dreamed of touching your wife!" I rebutted with holy contempt. "How can you even think that I would ever consider such a contemptible thing?"

"You calling him a liar?" the man from Luray challenged, grabbing my arm. "Why, I ought to—"

"Hold it, Fats!" Art stopped him. "You'll get your turn at him. But now, Preacher," he spat out, "you'll answer to me."

Joe, Peggy, and the buxom blond all grinned gleefully as Fats leaned back and pouted. The boy urged, as though to a mad dog, "Get him, Artie! C'mon man! Lay it on him!"

"Look, folks," I said reasonably, starting to get up, thinking to leave.

"You stay put, dog meat!" Fats yelled, laying heavy hands on me and slamming me to the floor like a slab of bacon. "Don't you dare move again unless you're told to!"

"The trial's over, folks. Is he guilty?" Art called.

"Yeah!" they chorused.

"O.K., so that's it!" he said, looking from one to another. "What's his punishment?"

"Beat him!" cried one. "Whip him!" screamed another. "Stick him in the gut, man!" the boy drooled hopefully as he flipped a switchblade and rammed it hard against my belt.

"Back off, boy!" Fats ordered. "We powwow first."

All gathered around Art and Nadine to debate the punishment in hushed whispers. Finally the circle broke, and the frizzy blond stood draped over Fats. Together they stood looking at me till the blond looked up and whispered in Fats's ear.

"Hey, Artie." He turned with an evil glint in his eye. "Blondie's got a better idea, and man, is it good. Whoooeee." He bellowed and guffawed. "She says she knows how to fix him so's he can't ever lay with another woman."

"Whatta you mean?" the boy protested. "You done said I could carve and salt and pepper him!"

"Yeah, I know, boy," Art agreed, "but let's hear what Fats has got to say."

"Well," Fats simpered, relishing the idea as his own, "he's a preacher man, and—well, we's all Christian, so let's do it religious like."

"Yeah," Blondie added, looking at me like a hungry cannibal, "then we can make a mark of the cross and sprinkle the altar with the blood—his blood!" She laughed fiendishly.

"What you talking about, man?" the boy queried jealously. "I was gonna give you blood, lots of it!"

"But we's Bible people," Fats argued, "and we got to do it the Bible way."

"I don't understand," Art said, like a little boy listening to his parents debate which toy to give him.

"We're gonna make him a eunuch!" Blondie explained.

"A what?" Joe asked.

Peggy spoke, still wearing that same silly smile. "It means they're gonna cut his—"

"We's gonna castrate him!" Fats interrupted, wanting to be the first to tell Art.

"Oh—but . . ." Art seemed to be weighing whether that idea was better than the first.

"Don't you see," Fats explained, "this is best. He's a preacher, we's Christian, and the Bible says that in the old days that there were eunuchs who worked around the king's palace, and to protect the queen from those bastards, they dehorned them—"

"They what?" the boy asked, confused by all the talk.

"Like I said," Peggy explained, "they cut of his privates—see?"

"Yeah," Fats added. "And best of all, there ain't nothing wrong in doing it, 'cause the Lord wanted it done—it's in the Bible."

"But who's gonna do it, Fats?" Joe asked, a bit scared by the idea.

"Me and Peg!" Blondie shrilled, thrilled in anticipation.

"That's right," Fats agreed. "So, Joe, you get that arm and I'll get this 'un till he's flat on his back. And, boy, you—Dammit, Preacher!" He hit me in the mouth. "You quit your fightin'—there ain't no way you're gonna get out of this, so you just behave!"

"Whatta you want me to do, Fats?" the boy asked, crawling around on his knees, hunting something to do.

"You take that there leg—that's it—and you hold it tight. And, Peggy, you and Blondie take turns holdin' the other—Dammit, Preacher!" He rammed a knee into my side. "I done told you once, and I ain't gonna tell you no more! You behave yourself or I'm gonna stomp your guts out!"

Winded and choking with pain, I could only pray that somehow God would send a miracle. Only a miracle could stay the hands of that savage mob.

"O.K., baby doll"—Fats looked at Blondie—"he's yours. Strip him and have your fun."

Realizing that my only hope was in diversion, I called to Nadine, who sat as if in a happy stupor as Blondie began unfastening my belt. "Nadine, please, remember the times when you were coming apart at the seams, when your whole world was going to pot, how good you felt after looking at the circle of perfection?"

I had touched my forefinger with the thumb of my right hand, forming what I called "the symbol of perfection," and I urged her to look at it.

"Thank you, Lord!" I breathed a sigh of hope as I saw her eyes on my hand, the glint of excitement beginning to fade and the lids to droop and blink.

"Remember, Nadine," I said encouragingly, with renewed hope as her Buddha stance began to wilt and her shoulders slumped. "Thank you, Lord," I breathed, with even greater hope as her face muscles went slack, her eyes flickered shut, and her head sagged to droop on her chest.

"Nadine!" Art screamed, grabbing her. "Nadine, speak to me!"

"Everything's all right, Nadine," I assured her. "Relax, that's it. Let yourself go."

"Stop it, Preacher!" Fats raged, grabbing me by the neck. "Stop it or I'll choke the hell out of you!"

"No you won't, Fats," I bluffed, "not if you ever want to see Nadine awake again."

"Whatta you mean?" Art said, fear beginning to consume him.

I dared to lie in desperation. "I mean I'll fix her so she'll never awaken if you don't let me go right now!"

Now frantic with fear, Art screamed, "Let him go!"

"But, Artie," Peggy said reproachfully, "you promised!"

"Yeah!" Blondie whined. "You said we could cut him."

"Let him go, I tell you!" His fear was turning to feverish anger.

Slowly the hands loosened, and I sat up, shaking myself to straighten my clothes. "Now, Art, you do exactly as I say and everything will be just fine."

"What do you want me to do?" he asked in childish helplessness.

Standing up and fastening my belt after zipping the fly, I told him, "I'm going to leave—"

"No! You can't!" someone screamed, and others shouted equally strong negatives.

"Shut up and listen!" I ordered with new-found bravado. "Now, Art, after I leave, lay Nadine on the floor. Then . . ." I waited for the full force of my orders to sink in. "All of you—and I do mean all of you—get down on your knees and pray."

"But you got to help Nadine first!" Art objected.

"I am helping her, and you will be helping her by praying. Prayer is what she needs right now—prayer, that's the only thing that will awaken her." I looked around, making sure they understood. "Now you do as I say," I demanded as I edged to the door.

"Will she really wake up?" Blondie asked, a mixture of disbelief and wonder in her voice.

"Yes," I assured her, "but only if you pray for thirty minutes, and by prayer I mean for you to ask God to help her and to forgive you."

Cautiously I opened the door and slipped out backward, keeping my eyes on them as they stared at me with a mixture of disappointment and trembling fear.

"Lord," I prayed as I backed the car out of the driveway and headed down the long lane to the highway, "forgive me for lying. And thank you, Lord. Thank you for keeping me cool to think clearly."

What had I really done? Basically, Nadine was a somnambulist, and all during her therapy sessions I had used the forming of a circle with my thumb and forefinger as a posthypnotic suggestion. In lieu of using normal hypnotic procedures, a posthypnotic symbol such as my use of three fingers on the forehead, a word, the forming of a circle with thumb and forefinger—anything suggested by the hypnotist—will serve as a cue for the subject to enter a trance.

My fear that Nadine might not respond to the suggestion lay in the fact that she was highly excited, normally not the best condition for hypnosis. Yet posthypnotic suggestion had been sufficient to put Dolores into a trance after her chest was crushed in an automobile accident. Besides, in a pinch any weapon will do. In this instance, I had no choice but to use a posthypnotic suggestion as a tool—a weapon to save my skin.

As for prayer and the statement she would awaken in thirty minutes, I had hoped that Nadine heard me talking to them, and that she accepted that conversation as a posthypnotic suggestion to awaken. But whether she took the suggestion was immaterial, really. Certainly prayer might do them all some good. As for Nadine's awakening, when a person in hypnosis is no longer attended by the hypnotist, the subject will either awaken immediately or slip into a natural sleep, awaking when the nap is completed. But, please, to the inexperienced, this does not suggest you try it, or that you enter into hypnosis because there is no danger to the subject because while the person will awaken, it may be with posthypnotic traumas.

How, then, had I lied? Only by bluffing that she would never awaken.

CHAPTER XII

Gretchen Goes Worldwide

When *Washington Post* news correspondent Donnel Nunes phoned long distance seeking an interview with Dolores and me on a cold, wintry day in December, I thought for a moment his call was the answer to a prayer. Dolores wasn't so sure, and after a short discussion with her, I asked him to call back in a few days.

When the children came home from school that evening we gathered in the living room to discuss whether we should let another story of our involvement with Gretchen be published. The children voted yea, but Dolores and I were reluctant to go ahead right at that time; the memory of the bitterness spawned by our story in the Harrisonburg *Daily News-Record* made us a bit shy of any more publicity. After a bit more discussion, it was decided that each of us would seek a divine answer in prayer.

For the next several days the children spent a great deal of their time in their rooms, Dolores in our bedroom, and I in the study, in prayer. For my part, I felt a closeness to God in those prayer sessions more real than I had experienced in quite some time, but wanted more assurance as to what I should do; like the ancient Israelite judge Gideon, I sought a sign from the Lord and waited patiently for Him to speak.

The trials of parents often rub off on their children, sometimes causing family rifts and great personal anguish. So it happened to us, but to a great extent we consider ourselves fortunate. Ours have been good children, never having caused us a moment's worry through disobedience or bad behavior. But a few people in the community would have had it otherwise as they sought to bring trouble into our home through the divide-and-conquer method.

(Even at this writing this is still going on among some people in that area. Although we moved from Elkton years ago, the vicious rumor was started that our son, Jesse, had been arrested and sent to a boys' home for the incorrigible. Friends from that area, on hearing the news, called to ask us if the story was true. When I assured them, "No! He's never even received a ticket for speeding," they said, "Well, you know how it is around here—they've got to be crucifying someone."

At the time the rumor was in full force, Jesse was reaping rewards as an honor student and outstanding athlete. He was elected an officer in the Gretna High School SCA, and was awarded a plaque by the Woodmen of the World for Outstanding Proficiency in American History. He was awarded trophies for excellent play in football and baseball, is president of our church's Youth Fellowship, and was our "guest" preacher on Youth Sunday. This year (1977), although school has not yet started, he will be one of the tri-captains of the Gretna Hawks football team.

When we moved from Elkton, we had thought that the old adage, "Out of sight, out of mind," might hold true for those people, but apparently something has been bred into them that gives them pleasure only when they can make someone else unhappy.)

The last place we expected trouble was from the people we thought really believed themselves to be ultrareligious. Sadly, we soon learned that an unusual religious movement was in full force in Elkton, and while I have the greatest respect and admiration for the truly devout, including those who call themselves charismatic, honesty demands that we report that many of the supercharismatics involved in that movement zeroed in on the youth of the community, causing much heartache.

At first glance their purpose seemed especially good and I supported them wholeheartedly. For example, a young couple new to Elkton, Robert and Ava Hollen, began having the youth of the community meet in their home one night each week for prayer and Bible study, and it seemed wonderful to me that people like Bob and

Ava would gladly give of their time and efforts to the youth. Soon, though, I was forced to question their motives.

All three of our children attended the first few meetings, but Vonda, a high school senior and very mature for her age, stopped attending the services after the third meeting. When I inquired, "Why?" she refused to comment, saying only, "The meetings were not to my liking." Not long after that I went to Mary Jo's room for a reason that now escapes me, and saw a spiral notebook lying open on her bed, the same notebook I had seen her take with her the night before to the youth services at the Hollens'; on that notebook, lying back side up, the following words were written in longhand: "Why won't my father tell me the truth about the Bible?"

That cut like a knife. For the longest time I could only stand and stare at that bold handwriting which flashed at me like a bubbling neon sign. Always I had tried to be honest with my children, faithfully tried to teach them God's Word as it was written as well as by example. Never had I forced them to swallow my conceptions of truth by cramming religion into them. Believe me, it was a long, long day before Mary Jo came home from school. Maybe that was good. While anxiously waiting for her, I searched heart, mind and soul for a hint of where I had failed to teach her Biblical truth. In the end I could only pray and wait until I could sit down with her and hear what she had to say.

No sooner had she come home than I went to her and in the privacy of her bedroom inquired, "Just what truths in the Bible have I withheld from you?" Surprised, she looked at me wide-eyed and said, "None that I know of, Daddy. Why?" Pointing to the notebook lying on her bed, I asked, "Can you explain what you mean by that?" Quickly she grabbed the notebook and stared in disbelief at the writing before turning to me with teary eyes. "Daddy, I never wrote that! I've never even thought such a thing!"

Brushing the tears from her eyes, she opened the notebook and exclaimed, "That isn't my writing. Look!" she cried, comparing her notes with that written on the back. "See, I couldn't have written that!" It was true. The writing was completely different. When I asked if she had any idea who could have written such a thing, she thought for a moment and said, "No." However, on second thought she said that she always took that notebook with her to all youth meetings and Bible-study classes. "Oh," she exclaimed in a flash of memory, "last night I let Ava look at it—but no." She paused thoughtfully. "I didn't see her write anything on it."

"Maybe Ava didn't write it," I said, "but someone did, so can you give me just one good reason why anyone would do such a thing?"

"Well," she confessed reluctantly, "most of the kids in that group are interested in speaking in tongues, but because I knew you didn't approve of such things, I didn't say anything about it to you."

Later I confronted Jesse about the youth group and the tongues movement. "Yes," he admitted, "they believe in speaking in tongues, but no one forces you to."

Whether the tongues movement was forced on the children is immaterial: Their power of suggestion that came from these meetings had the force of a sledgehammer, and it was not long before many of the youth began exhibiting bizarre behavior for this day and age. Many carried their Bibles wherever they went, even to school and to ball games. One lad about Jesse's age walked into the gym one night during a high-school basketball game, sat down, and proceeded to begin reading the Bible, or at least pretend to do so. Not once did he look up at the action on the floor. Even during the halftime festivities he kept his eyes glued to the book, making a somewhat blushing effort to ignore the taunting gibes hurled his way by giggling teenagers who thought he was overdoing the religious bit.

Other students became so zealous in their missionary efforts that they accosted teachers in the school hallway, demanding that they confess whether they had been "baptized by the Spirit," which the young people declared would give the teachers the ability to speak in tongues, the "only visible sign of salvation." Teachers who said no, and every teacher did, were ridiculed and told "You're lost and going to hell! Repent! Repent and be baptized right now!" Naturally, most teachers were appalled. To my knowledge, only one teacher invited the missionaries to visit him in his room after school to discuss his need of salvation and the ability to speak in tongues.

One lad, about fourteen, and his sister, a year or two older, who had been caught up in the movement though they never attended church and would not darken a church door after their "baptism by the Spirit," because "there ain't no church worth attending." But that's beside the point. To my amusement, they often put on a good show. One day as I took my daily walk I was startled to see the girl, Lolly, run screaming from the house as though chased by marauding banshees. "O God, I'm lost!" she wailed, in wide-eyed panic. "The Devil's got me and I'm going to hell! Help me, Teejay!" She pleaded with her brother at the top of her voice while slipping to her knees, writhing in torment. "Call Amos, Teejay. Call Amos to come cast the demons out!" Amos, another young boy, supposedly had powers to exorcise demons.

"What for?" Teejay asked, only mildly concerned. "What are they doing to you?"

"They took me over," she gasped, "and, dammit, they made me forget! See! They made me do it again."

"Forget what? Do what?"

"Oh, Teejay," she wailed, "they made me forget my baptism, and I let the word 'damn' slip off my tongue. I can't keep from saying 'damn,' dammit!"

I kept on walking, not wanting to embarrass them, but on another occasion I was walking down the street and was mildly amused to see Teejay being exorcised by Amos. It was comical. Teejay was lying on his side, propped on an elbow, one leg bent back under him. He was reaching out with the other arm as though trying to ward off a host of demons struggling to possess him. Standing astride him was Amos, tears streaming down his face as he held Teejay's head in one hand, raising the other toward heaven, beseeching in a high, shrilly pitched voice, "Jesus! Jesus! Jesus! In your name I command you to cast out these demons from Teejay!" Then, laying both hands on Teejay's head, he ordered with the authority of a pompous prelate, "Hear me, thou evil one! Depart from this child of God!" Then, like a pleading, frustrated schoolgirl, he shouted, "I command you in the name of Jesus: Go! Git! Scat!"

Slowly Teejay began to relax, pleading voicelessly with Amos, pulling his pants leg and pointing to his open, gaping mouth while gurgling a gosh-awful "Aaaaagggggghh-hhh . . . uuuuuuggggghhhh."

"O Jesus, dear Jesus," Amos begged in tender compassion as he looked down to Teejay. "Heal him, Lord! You've taken the demons from him, now heal him. Give him his voice!"

"Aaaawwwhhhoooooeeeee!" Teejay shrilled, jumping to his feet and embracing Amos. "He did it! Praise the Lord, He gave me my voice. Hallelujah!"

"Glory to God!" Amos chimed as he laughed and cried and danced a jig with Teejay. "Hallelujah! Whooooeee! Hallelujah! Praise His holy name!"

Another young person who had joined the movement came to the parsonage one day and said, "Reverend Jay, if you really want to know the Lord and the true joy of salvation, you've got to be baptized by the Spirit and begin speaking in tongues. Believe me, without the baptism of the Spirit, all your learning and years of service in the church can only lead to complete and utter destruction."

"You don't mean," I queried increduously, "that all my years of trying to live the good life, all my prayers, my reading the Bible and trying to practice what I preach, will go for nought?"

"That's right! Without the baptism of the Spirit you are lost!"

Well, well, well! Maybe she was right, but if my family and I had had to contend only with fanaticism, life would have been all roses and cheesecake. As for all our trials, a change was coming, that I knew! But I still think Elkton is a good town and that its reputation is not deserved by its many good people.

My family and I had continued in prayer, seeking God's guidance. One day, a week before Christmas, as I drove into Harrisonburg, a blinding light filled the car and I heard music, celestially beautiful—not the canned Christmas carols that emanated from every store and street corner, but rather an angelic chorus present with me in the car, serenading the presence of God! He was alive and I knew it, but never more so than in that moment when His presence was so clearly revealed to me!

Quickly I pulled to the side of the road and wept in praise of His goodness, His love and mercy. In that one moment I knew that our prayers had been answered, that the story must be told. Hurriedly I turned around and headed home to await the phone call that I somehow knew would—and did—come from Donnel Nunes that day, even though he had not specified a certain time or date when he would call back.

A few days later Mr. Nunes and a photographer came to our home, and we told him the story of Gretchen. On January 20, 1975, the *Washington Post* published the story, sending our name and Gretchen's story to the ends of the earth.

I had just started to read the story at 7:00 A.M. when Mrs. Fannie Oliveto of Kensington, Maryland, called at 7:05 A.M. A flood of calls ensued that did not abate until two weeks later. At 9 A.M. we got Vonda and Mary Jo out of school to answer the telephone; at noon we called Punky to come from Hagerstown, Maryland; and after school Jesse was kept busy directing traffic around our home.

It was unbelievable! We had thought the *Washington Post* would run a story that would appeal only to the people of our immediate area, hoping that once local residents knew the true story, all those on a witch hunt would desist. But, my, oh my! How wrong, how naïve we were!

By 9:30 a New York radio station was on the phone. NBC, ABC, and CBS quickly followed. Jerry Smith of the Associated Press phoned at 10 A.M; then Dina Modinet of NBC News made arrangements for Douglas Kiker and his TV crew to come to Elkton. Immediately following came calls from Amanda Patton of Mutual News Service; Jurgen Horsch of German Wire Service; Tom Ferraro, United Press International; Eric Engberg, Westinghouse; Jeffry Blythe, British Broadcasting Corporation; radio station CKWX, Vancouver, British Columbia; WWL, New Orleans; WSB, Atlanta; David Hawkins, CBC, Canada; Tim Jernigan, WRR, Dallas; Mike Whorf, WJR, Detroit;

WJR, Union City, New Jersey; and Jim Alton of WKAT, Miami. There were hundreds of calls from smaller stations all over the United States and networks in Canada, England, Italy, France, and Australia.

That was only the beginning. On the third day after the story broke, Carl Schumacher sat in our living room listening to a group of reporters fire questions at us. He then joined Punky in the study to time the phone calls. They were coming in at the rate of one every three minutes; as soon as Punky hung up, the phone rang again.

Not all callers were reporters. Hundreds of people wanted to be hypnotized. Some wanted us for lectures. Publishers were looking for a book. Many agents insisted they would make us rich. "You don't need to know a thing about writing," they said, "we have plenty of people who will gladly do the book in your name." What a revolting thought that was!

Many people tried to exploit us by promising great riches, but we refused all offers. Outside of appearing on the TV program *To Tell the Truth* and a few talk shows, such as *The Tomorrow Show* and *Lou Gordon's Show* in Detroit, we decided to let the story die down until we could tell the entire story fully in this book.

It was more than a year since Dolores had been regressed when Douglas Kiker came to our home for an all-day taping session, and when he asked Dolores to let me hypnotize her, she refused. "I don't ever want to be regressed again," she said. The trauma of too many suggestions was just too much.

Since the story had gone worldwide, I felt that people might consider the whole thing a hoax if they did not see a demonstration of her in regression as Gretchen. But Dolores was adamant in her refusal until after Kiker and his crew had gone downtown for dinner. "All right," she finally agreed, "you may put me to sleep and try to contact Gretchen, but don't be surprised if she has already found peace and refuses to emerge."

But such was not the case. By the time Kiker and his crew returned, Dolores was in a deep trance on the couch in the living room, and when Kiker stepped through the door and saw her stretched out on the couch, he almost fainted. "Oh my God!" he gasped. "She—she's—is she dead?" he stammered, white as a sheet.

I laughed. "No, she's merely in a trance. Now," I instructed everyone, "if each of you will take your place, I will try to bring Gretchen through." Soon Gretchen was talking to us, but, as usual whenever Dolores has not undergone regression for a long time, she spoke very softly and sluggishly. She did that evening, too, when a German reporter who came with Kiker and his crew tried to converse with her.

That was a strange day and a strange session, one seemingly fraught with supernatural interference, a fact we did not fully appreciate until after the TV crew had returned to Washington and previewed the tape. When Gretchen was emerging in the session at our home, Kiker and his crew had sensed an unseen presence in the room and had heard an unearthly, ethereal moaning. (Of course, Dolores was in a trance and my hearing problem prevents me from hearing subtle sounds.)

The next day Kiker called me and asked if he and his crew could come back on Friday for another taping session. "It seems," he said, "a stray hair had attached itself to the camera lens, slightly marring the picture. And," he added in awe, "that spooky sound which almost curled my hair when Gretchen was talking can be heard on the tape." So on Friday, in addition to the more than eight hours of taping on Wednesday, another three hours of taping were necessary.

I did not hypnotize or regress Dolores on Friday, yet the same hairlike image showed up on the Friday tape, even after the cameraman had taken every precaution against hair, dust, and anything else that could attach itself to the lens. What caused the hairlike image? Your guess is as good as mine.

The strange noise, I like to think, can be traced to our dog, Candy, a French poodle who would never stay in the room when I regressed Dolores. But that day, according to Kiker and members of his crew, when I began talking to Gretchen, Candy slipped into the room, her tail between her legs, and lay under the coffee table, apparently wanting to be as close to Dolores as possible. During the taping session, not one person thought the weird moaning came from Candy; only afterward, when we sought a rational explanation, did we assume that she could have been the cause. Plausible answers can always be found; whether they are valid answers or not is another story.

The town's reaction to the horde of reporters, photographers, and TV crews was one of amazement. Never before had Elkton been exposed to such a phenomenon. Gossip flew like wildfire, and the radicals became even more radical. Thank God, ninety-five percent of the local residents were on our side, and because of their goodness, love, and concern they let us know in one way or another that they were supporting us in their prayers.

There were a few, though, whom we had considered our friends, who rode the fence or turned tail and ran when they saw us on the street. Harold Chaplin is a good example. Probably more than anyone else from that area, Harold came often to my study to sit and talk. We considered him a tried and true friend, even though he sometimes became angry and pouted if we teased him about his beloved Washington Redskins. Not the brightest person in the world, yet consumed with an insatiable curiosity, Harold asked thousands of questions about hypnosis and regression, often insisting that someday he would like for me to "put him under." He encouraged me to continue with my regressions and investigations, saying that "If I were in your shoes, I would do exactly as I pleased. And if the people didn't like it, they could go to and stay put!"

But Harold was a kinky kind of wishy-washy. When we went with the NBC crew to the town shopping center for filming, Kiker asked me to get some local person to stand with us. Fortunately for us, or so we thought, Harold happened to pass by right at that moment. When I reached out the right hand of fellowship, as I always do, and asked, "Harold, would you like to be on national TV with us?" he continued walking, grunting, "Nope, I've been on TV before, and I don't like it one bit."

The truth was Harold was merely a fair-weather friend, as others in the community were to tell us later. Later Harold came to us and excused himself by saying that some of his relatives from up in the mountains had let him know that if he feared for his skin he would be better off "not to have anything more to do with that heathen preacher!" Knowing Harold's relatives, I can't really blame him. But Dolores was hurt, terribly so, and with tears brimming she asked, "If we can't depend on Harold, who in the world can we trust?"

"I don't know, hon," I replied cheerfully, suppressing the sickness in the pit of my stomach. "Just trust in the Lord, and—"

"Hey! You snobs," Raymond Mobray yelled as he came running from the Elkton Cleaners, where he worked. "Won't you even stop and shake hands with us common folk anymore?"

I laughed with a joy that knew no bounds at finding just one friend who was not afraid to be seen on the street with us. "Raymond, do you know that right at this moment you are being filmed by a TV crew from NBC?"

"Oh Lordy, no!" He wheeled and looked for the cameraman, still holding on to my hand.

"What's the matter?" I inquired, afraid that he too would turn and run. "Don't you want to be seen on the street with us either?"

"Hell no!" he thundered angrily. "You're my friend, and I don't give two toots in a mud pile what anyone thinks. I'm your friend—you can count on that, buddy!"

And he was a friend, through thick and thin. As we stood there in the bright sunlight, the townspeople gathered in the doorways and windows of the shops and stores to stare, and eventually Dolores and I went home happy, happy because we learned in that moment that if you have but one friend who will stand with you in a time of trial, that friend and the Lord can help you overcome a thousand enemies. Never again were we afraid to walk the streets of Elkton and hold our heads high. Really we had no reason to be afraid or ashamed, because it's a fact: Elkton is a good town, and Dolores and I soon learned that there were very few in town so flip-floppy as those that came from the outside, like Harold.

CHAPTER XIII

Our Life an Open Book

All told, reaction to the national exposure of the Gretchen story was a mixture of good and bad, acceptance and rejection, and although it would be foolish to attribute all the blame for troubles to one person, it is a well-known fact that our problems in the community were multiplied when Manley Milton, a layman who became pastor of a local nondenominational church, added his support to the radical religious element which had spent the previous two years tormenting us.

Dolores and I had thought Manley was our friend, especially after he came to me and said, "Carroll, while I don't know anything about hypnotism, I know you, and I believe you to be a good, God-fearing man." He added, "Because I live strictly by the word of God and His word tells me to judge no man, I will never judge nor criticize you and Dolores."

Grateful for his seemingly sincere assurances of fidelity to us and the work we were doing, I thanked God for Manley, valuing him as a friend in a time of need.

Sadly, we soon learned that what Manley said to us in private and what he said in public did not quite match. When Donnel Nunes of the *Washington Post* inquired of all Elkton ministers concerning their personal feelings about my activities in hypnosis, only Manley exercised the privilege of speaking out in enmity. "I think it's the work of the Devil!" he proclaimed. To explain his animosity, he added, "In the book of Deuteronomy God forbids the children of Isreal to consult with familiar spirits, and I think Carroll is dealing with familiar spirits."

Obviously Dolores and I were shocked and hurt by his accusations in the *Post,* but even then we determined in Christian love to not bear him ill will, preferring to be charitable in our thinking. Manley spurned our love and friendship, even though he telephoned me to deny ever making such a statement to Mr. Nunes. However, before that conversation ended, Manley seemed compelled by some strange compulsion to set himself up as a divine judge and said, "Carroll, even though I did not say such a thing to that reporter, I must say that until you have been baptized by the Spirit, I cannot know salvation as given by Christ."

But theologically, for the Christian, and I am a Christian, salvation comes only through God's love in the saving grace of Christ, and the Spirit is represented in the Scriptures as the active Person of the Godhead who establishes a new nature in sinful, unregenerate man, a nature which is a creation of God and which is activated by a new will, receptive to the grace of God given through faith in our Lord Jesus Christ; and every person saved by grace comes under the hand of God and is baptized by the Holy Spirit. As an indwelling Spirit, He carries out His work of sanctification in the life of that person. But Manley was not interested in theological concepts of salvation. Rather, because I did not speak in tongues, he insisted without equivocation that I was merely going through the motions of pretending to be a Christian. And for that I am sorry. Sorry that he is so naïve theologically, and sorry that he concluded I was unsaved just because I conducted my ministry as did Jesus. That is, I preach, pray, and minister without babbling in tongues.

Most regrettably, only moments before Manley phoned me to deny his statement to the press, his son, Manley, Jr., went to a local authority on the press and the law and asked, "If a person makes a statement to a news reporter, can that reporter print what you say?"

The man queried, "Why do you ask?"

"Well," Manley, Jr., said, "when that reporter from the *Washington Post* came to see my father, Dad accepted him as a friend, never dreaming he would print everything that was said."

"And did your dad say those things about Reverend Jay?"

"Well, yes"—he paused, blushing—"but he never expected them to be printed in the paper."

As a matter of fact, Manley did try to get Donnel Nunes to make a retraction, but was told that the statements had been made and the paper stood behind what was written! As the local authority said, "If you don't want something printed, don't tell it to a reporter."

Still, Dolores and I wanted to be Manley's friend, and still do, and I tried to explain to him that we were merely conducting a scientific experiment, that we never once dreamed of contacting familiar spirits, nor did we for a moment doubt God's love in granting us salvation.

"Carroll," Manley argued, "how can you say you are not consulting with familiar spirits when you admit that you may be talking with the dead?"

"Look, Manley," I tried to reason, "how many times have you stood in a funeral home and heard someone weepingly speak to a loved one lying in a casket?"

"Oh, lots of times!" he replied.

"And would you say that they were consulting with familiar spirits just because they spoke to the dead?"

"Oh, my Lord, no!" he exclaimed, aghast.

"Then pray tell me, Manley, since my wife is merely in a hypnotic regression—a form of sleep—how can you possibly accuse me of consulting with familiar spirits?"

"But that's not the same!" he responded.

"Technically you're right, Manley. But listen for just a moment. You took a verse of Scripture from the Old Testament and used it to accuse me of being evil. In fact, you said, 'There shall not be found among you a consulter of familiar spirits.' A perfect example of what you are trying to accuse me of can be found in Samuel 28 in the story of the Witch of Endor. Remember that Samuel, King Saul's mentor, was dead, and King Saul was about to lose his throne to David. In an effort to get help, Saul went to the Witch of Endor, who was said to have a familiar spirit because she could raise up the dead. In fact, at King Saul's request, she did call forth Samuel from the dead, and Samuel rebuked her for 'disquieting me'—disturbing his rest in the afterlife. But remember this too, Manley: King Saul wanted to talk to Samuel because the Philistines were about to defeat him in war and Saul wanted advice from Samuel as to what to do."

"That's right," Manley agreed.

"Well, at least we agree on one thing. But tell me, have you or anyone else ever seen me regress Dolores and then ask Gretchen to advise us on anything? In other words, I have never tried to call anyone from the dead, and neither has Dolores. You cannot even call Dolores a medium; she has never attempted to contact the dead. Specifically, Manley, a consulter of familiar spirits is one who tries to rise up the dead or to talk with the dead either privately or in a séance."

"Yeah, I know," he said. "But when you talk with Gretchen you've got to admit that possibly a dead girl is speaking through your wife."

"That may be true, Manley. It may very well be that Gretchen is a spirit, but all we have ever done is to ask her questions about her prior life here on earth, if indeed she did live at one time as a physical being on this earth. But hear me clearly: If it should be that we eventually do learn that she did live and die and now speaks to us through Dolores, we will have done nothing more than prove what the Church has been trying to prove for two thousand years. That is, we will then have provided fairly good proof that the soul does continue to live on after death."

"Yes," he agreed, "but when you talk to Gretchen, you are acting as a consulter of spirits!"

"Are you saying," I inquired seriously, "that anyone who talks with the dead is a consulter of the spirits?"

"Yes, sir! I do!" he exclaimed, in a tone indicating absolute knowledge.

"Then tell me, Manley, when you speak from the pulpit about Jesus calling forth Lazarus from the dead, do you refer to Jesus as an evil consulter of the spirits? Or when you describe that glorious moment on the Mount of Transfiguration when Jesus spoke with Moses and Elijah, do you refer to him as that evil man who consulted with familiar spirits?"

"Of course not!" He began to hedge. "But that's different!"

"Is it, really?" I debated. "If merely talking with the

213

dead or to the dead is evil or makes you a consulter of spirits, then obviously Jesus Christ would be, as you define the term, a consulter with familiar spirits."

Maybe I should have quit at that point, but I thought that if I injected a little humor into the conversation he would laugh it off and forget the whole thing, so I said, "Manley, if you had used the past tense in reference to Dolores and familiar spirits, I would have agreed with you wholeheartedly. You see, for the past thirty-five years I have consulted with a familiar spirit—my wife—and if that be evil, so be it."

"Oh, Lord! Carroll!" he responded, aghast. "It's sacrilegious to joke like that."

"Why, Manley?" I asked, amused at his inability to engage in lighthearted banter and his lack of understanding that we are nothing more than spirit (soul) clothed in a body of flesh. In an effort to reason with him and to help him overcome his tendency to become indignant over things not really that important, I said, "'Manley, while it's true there are times when I probe my wife's subconscious when she is in a trance, technically there is little difference between that and when I seek to learn her deepest, most intimate thoughts when she is awake."

And that is true in every area of life. Consider the psychiatrist who probes the thoughts and memories of the patient lying on the couch in his office, seeking root causes of the patient's problems through verbal catharsis. Or consider the wife of a successful businessman who walks through a department store picking up several unneeded articles which she puts in her purse. When her husband becomes enraged or worried half out of his mind after learning of her sticky-fingered habit and demands of her, "Good gracious, woman! Whatever possessed you to do such a thing?" is he not seeking for her deep-seated motivation, searching for her subconscious cause for kleptomania? In most instances, the enraged or heartbroken husband will not settle for superficial answers. Rather, in the discussion or argument that follows, he may beg, browbeat, and cry in an effort to uncover her deep-seated motivation.

The same is true of marriage partners who seek the advice of marriage counselors, who listen to both sides before determining the underlying cause for a couple's incompatibility. And what about the parents whose children get into trouble despite all the loving upbringing and parental care? Do not they often inquire of the errant child, "What in the world made you do such a thing?"

What about the wife, Jean, who turns a quickly perked ear to the sleeping husband who mutters amorously, "Mary . . . please, Mary . . . just one more time!" Does she not rise up and lean over him, demanding with bated breath, "Mary? Mary who?" Is she not hoping to get an answer about a name that slipped from her husband's subconscious, an answer she probably could not get from him in his waking, conscious moments?

But Manley wanted neither jokes nor explanations, so he came up with a rationalization: "If you are not consulting with familiar spirits," he charged, "you are at least working against God by being a charmer."

"Oh, c'mon, Manley, you've got to be kidding!"

"No sireee!" he bellowed. "Deuteronomy 18:10–12 plainly says, 'There shall not be found among you any one that maketh his son or his daughter to pass through the fire, or that useth divination, or an observer of the times, or an enchanter, or a witch, or a charmer, or a consulter with familiar spirits, or a wizard, or a necromancer. For all who do those things are an abomination unto the Lord . . .' "

I laughed at his efforts to find a Scriptural basis for indicting me. "Manley, if I were a charmer, believe me, the very first thing I would do would be to cast a spell upon you and all those who oppose me, making you and them my strongest supporters."

That only made him more angry, and he vowed in a screaming crescendo, "I'm going to get you, fellow!" And he almost did. From that day forward he denounced me at every opportunity: from the pulpit, on the radio, on the street, and to people who had been our friends for a quarter of a century.

Still, Dolores and I prayed for Manley and his followers, especially since we thought their usage of the Old Testament passage of Scripture absurd. While we fervently believe in life after death, and we do take Jesus' Word literally ("Since I live, you shall live also"), we have never engaged in spiritualism's practice of conjuring up the dead (consulting familiar spirits), nor have we ever attended or conducted a séance. Never in my discussions with Gretchen have I ever asked her about the welfare of anyone abiding in the afterlife.

As for being a sorcerer or a charmer who conjures up magical spells, the charge is even more ridiculous—although I must confess there have been times when I wished I could work a few magic tricks to make life a little easier, as has everyone else, including Manley.

Manley didn't stand alone in his denunciation of us. The Reverend David C. Lowenstall, a United Methodist minister, an ardent and active teacher in the "speaking in tongues" movement, sidled up to me during a meeting and said, "Carroll, I know you are under a lot of pressure, that you are getting a lot of guff from a bunch of nincompoops, but I want you to know that I have instructed the people of my church that they are not to judge or condemn you or Dolores. I explained to them," he added, "that the Lord works in strange and mysterious ways, and possibly this may be the Lord's way of using you to help build His kingdom."

For those kind words of assurance I was most grateful. Shortly thereafter, however, David wrote in a "Letter to the Editor" of a Virginia newspaper: "Rev. Jay contends he does not believe his wife to be evil or that he believes in reincarnation, and I admit that he has the right to believe this or any other theory."

To say the least, my family and I were shocked to know that a fellow minister of our denomination would say such a thing in print. But, even more to the point, I was puzzled. Even now I wonder what he really meant by that statement. Was he telling the world that I merely wanted people to be deluded into thinking that I did not believe in the theory of reincarnation? Or, horror of horrors, was he saying that I was merely spouting a theory when I contended that I did not believe my wife to be evil? Believe me, David, if my wife were evil, the many members of my church would have known that fact long ago, and all my contending would not have changed things one whit.

That was only the beginning. He then stated, "The one area in which I have not heard any comment is the area of demon possession." In this he was saying that at the time he wrote the letter, he had not yet heard anyone accuse either Dolores or me on the radio of being demon-possessed; neither had he read such an indictment in the paper, a situation he determined to change by insinuating in his letter to the editor that if our names were substituted for the name of the man in Luke 8:26– 36, we would surely be seen to be demon-possessed. Not content to insinuate that we were unbelievers because we had been blinded by the cunning subtlety of demons that made us carry on Satan's work with great skill, he added the following bit of amazing information: "The possession of extraordinary knowledge always characterizes the demon as he speaks through the body of his victim."

Well, now! Imagine that! He not only implied we were possessors of extraordinary knowledge, he said that "the possession of extraordinary knowledge always [!] characterizes the demon as he speaks through the body of the victim."

Now, do you understand what that means? Did you know what you were writing, David? Oh, say it ain't so, please! For if your assertion is true, I have no choice but to believe that Pasteur, Einstein, Schweitzer, and, yes, even my Lord and my Savior Jesus Christ, possessed extraordinary knowledge only because demons spoke through them.

David didn't stop with that ludicrous statement. He said, "Perhaps the most striking characteristic is the demon's ability to speak languages unknown to the subject." Oh no, David! Not again? As a minister in the church, surely you believe in the Day of Pentecost. If you don't, you contradict everything the Church has ever believed about its birthday. Worse, you are an avowed leader in the "speaking in tongues" movement, so how could you even conceive of such a foolish thing and still claim that when you babble in tongues the Holy Spirit is speaking through you?

For those not familiar with the Day of Pentecost, permit me to note that in Acts 2:1-8 it reads, "When the day of Pentecost was fully come, they were all in one place and all were filled with the Holy Ghost, and began to speak with other tongues, as the Spirit gave them utterance . . . Now when this was noised abroad, the multitude came together, and were confounded, because . . . every man heard them speak in their own language, and all were amazed, saying one to another, behold, are not all these Galileans, and how hear we every man in our own tongue" (the language of Parthian, Medes, Mesopotamia, Libya, Cyrene, Asia, Pontus, Cappadocia.)

Specifically, St. Luke, the author of the Book of Acts, is saying that those gathered together in an upper room in Jerusalem, after they had received the Holy Spirit, were miraculously endowed with the power (ability) to speak foreign languages. If David's assertion is correct, the Holy Spirit had nothing to do with it. Rather, they were all filled with demons who spoke through the body of their victims. If that be true of all those on the Day of Pentecost, what must we believe about David and all others who babble in tongues today?

David also demonstrated his lack of knowledge about hypnosis. He said, "I cannot agree to hypnosis insomuch as one has to submit his will to another."

I regret that I must once again be repetitious and emphasize that there must be good rapport between hypnotist and subject, but this in no way implies that a person must submit their will to the hypnotist. To the contrary, as I stated previously, people in hypnosis will never do anything in violation of their own moral character.

Again: Hypnotism is a form of sleep—the word "hypnosis" itself is derived from the Greek word for sleep. Yet we know that scientifically it is more, much more that mere sleep. The proof is that many wonderful things can be done for a person in hypnosis that cannot be done in normal sleep. For example, many persons have undergone major surgery without pain under hypnosis, something that cannot be done in ordinary sleep.

Incidentally, does the Bible anywhere indicate that possibly hypnosis can be used as a valuable tool in surgery? I think it does. Genesis 2:21 says, "And God caused a deep sleep to fall upon Adam, and he slept; and he took one of his ribs, and closed up the flesh."

Knowing that the first step in hypnosis is a trance state comparable to sleep, it would appear that God, regardless of the method used to induce sleep, did indeed use a form of hypnosis to remove the rib. Such an assumption is enhanced by the fact that analgesia, another wonderful characteristic of hypnosis, had to be induced to prevent Adam from awakening due to the intense pain that always accompanies the separation of flesh, whether by incision, tearing, or other methods. Certainly it is highly unlikely that anyone could enter into a normal sleep deep enough to inhibit nerve cells from transmitting the presence of pain to the brain and back to the point of trauma.

As for reference to the "tongues movement," a brief explanation between tongues and xenoglossy is in order. Speaking in tongues (glossolalia) is usually a religious experience in which a person speaks in a strange language, or uses speech with unrecognizable sounds without meaning, usually uttered in a state of ecstasy. Linguists claim that "tongues" do not have the ingredients of language.

Dr. John P. Kildahl, a psychiatrist and minister, in research initiated by the American Lutheran Church states: "research indicates that the gift of speaking in tongues is taught rather than caught, and it cannot be understood." To emphasize this point, in his research a tape recorder was used on several groups of people speaking in tongues; when the tapes were later played for persons claiming to have the "gift of interpretation," not one of the interpreters could give an interpretation of what was said that bore any similarity to any other interpretation. Dr. Kildahl even reported the case of a man who was raised in Africa by missionary parents who had attended a tongues-speaking meeting. He was a stranger to the group, but during the meeting he stood up and spoke the Lord's Prayer in the African dialect he had learned in his youth. When he sat down, an interpreter of tongues offered the meaning of what he had said: a message concerning the Second Coming of Christ.

Many involved in the "tongues" movement say that the revelation of the meaning of the message is in the ear of the listener rather than the speaker, that the message will be revealed to the listener by the Holy spirit.

Xenoglossy, on the other hand, deals only with known languages; as I have already explained, it can be either recitative or responsive.

Let me now interpolate that possibly I should never have mentioned the Gretchen story to anyone. Certainly we would have avoided much antagonism and persecution. Possibly we should have used pseudonyms instead of our real names, but we honestly felt we were engaged in a scientific-religious investigation, certainly nothing to be ashamed of. Despite all the heartache and misery we have endured, we still feel that this was the Lord's will for us, even to the decision to let the story be published in the *Washington Post*.

Dr. Stevenson had strongly opposed our desire to release the story; even more important to us, he was also very reluctant to proceed with the case at a more rapid pace. He had spent twelve years on the Jenson case, and he explained to us that he did not like to be rushed, that he wanted time to think and contemplate and make decisions without haste. But Dolores and I could not wait twelve years. In the Jenson case the husband was also the hypnotist, but unfortunately he did not live to see the results of the case published, and because I had been so near death on several occasions, the possibility that I might not live long enough to see the investigation to its ultimate conclusion made us anxious to proceed with all reasonable haste.

True, I had survived eight heart attacks and surgery and our future looked brighter than it had in years, but besides our optimism for a long life, we had no assurance that the operation would guarantee a long life. Saphenous-vein bypass operations were relatively new at that time, and not enough people had undergone the operation to afford medical science an opportunity to study postoperative results and longevity of patients. It was believed that if I lived two years beyond the date of surgery and transplants, I could expect to live a fairly normal life. But again, there were no guarantees.

In addition to suffering the strain of ostracism and persecution by religious radicals, the many long years of illnesses and hospitalizations, combined with the tremendous expenses incurred in the investigation of our work in hypnosis, we were forced into debt, to the extent of several thousands of dollars. We had hoped that, if the good Lord so willed, we might recoup and get back on an even keel financially through writing and lecturing. But even that hope led to further criticism and frustration. We were accused of being mercenary. Some even said Gretchen was a hoax to make money.

All my life I had read about people who had worked hard, lived through unusual experiences, and then told about those experiences in books, lectures, and seminars, and I am fairly certain that all were compensated for their time and effort. But when Dolores and I attempted to tell our story, we were accused of trying to capitalize on our strange but wonderful experience. Especially those in the field of medicine intimated that I should cease practicing hypnosis and lecturing on the subject. To a great extent I agreed with them, especially after meeting some of the unlearned and unqualified persons practicing hypnosis. For many years, in all my lectures and seminars I proclaimed from the depth of my heart that no one without a solid educational background in psychology should ever attempt to practice hypnosis, or be hypnotized unless the hypnotist had such a background.

I began the study and practice of hypnosis in 1954, four years before the American Medical Association acknowledged hypnosis as a legitimate tool. Once I started with hypnosis, I studied everything available on the subject, even working on a master's degree in guidance and counseling at Shippensburg College and a Ph.D. in counseling and psychology at the University of Alabama. Unfortunately, because of my weakened heart I could not withstand the rigors of advanced graduate study, and in the final year of my doctoral studies my health deteriorated so rapidly that I was ordered by my doctors to drop out of school before dropping dead in class.

No person ever lived who admires the men and women in the medical profession more than I, nor will I ever launch a tirade against them as a whole, but the facts do demand that I report that the American Medical Association has been terribly shortsighted in not giving hypnosis a higher priority, especially since they claimed it as their own baby years after some of us had practiced it as an art and a science. While it is true that a few of their members do practice hypnosis, the number is exceedingly small in proportion to the number of members in the AMA. Worse yet, even to this day there is no true medical residency in hypnosis anywhere in the United States, a deplorable indictment of a profession which sits in judgment on anyone outside their own organization who has made a diligent study of the science solely for the purpose of helping others live a more healthy, happy life. If nothing else, the AMA should at least make use of serious practitioners as medical aides (paramedics) or interns under their supervision.

To defend my use of hypnosis: Hundreds of people have benefited from my ministry, and not one has ever lodged a complaint as a result of treatment received. I do not mean that everyone who came to me was helped. Such a claim would be absurd, since not everyone can be readily hypnotized. Even more important, despite the cry of those who labeled us as mercenary, not once did I ever charge anyone for services rendered, nor did I ever refuse to help anyone who had a legitimate need (excepting, of course, those with physical problems requiring medical attention rather than hypnotherapy.)

While I would not for one moment detract from Dr. Stevenson's greatness as a scientist and an investigator of the paranormal, I must confess that ever since Dr. Stevenson's visit to our home with Dr. Rohl, Dolores and I had lost much of our desire to continue with the investigation. He had not meant to offend us—we had simply caught him off guard by foolishly inviting outsiders to be present. As he later explained, "If my colleagues were to learn that others were present during the regression, it would surely prejudice their opinion of the case." Dr. Stevenson also felt I should cease lecturing, especially if I was to continue speaking about the Gretchen case.

At the time I thought his objections were voiced because he was a psychiatrist and a member of the medical profession. I now know that such was not the case. I did cease lecturing, because it would have been pointless for me to lecture on hypnosis and not mention the one thing everyone wanted to hear about: the Gretchen case.

Dolores and I now realize that Dr. Stevenson was totally correct in asking us to limit our public discussion of the Gretchen case; we also know that much of our hurt and frustration came about because we were not cut out to be used as scientific guinea pigs. For five years Dolores submitted without complaint to the many tests, regressions, and interrogations. Even now I cannot understand how she put up with as much as she did. For example, when Dr. Stevenson and I would discuss the Gretchen case, we usually did so when she was not present; or if she was present in the room, we often asked her to leave, which she did without ever once rebelling.

Why would we not discuss the case in her presence? Because the less she knew about the case, the less she knew about what she said in previous regressions as Gretchen, the less chance there was that she might be influenced to add to or take away from the Gretchen story in subsequent regressions. You see, although Dolores could never remember what she said or did as Gretchen, there is always the possibility that a person in regression might add to (or alter) information given in a previous regression as a result of information acquired in the conscious state.

Being the subject of an investigation is a terrible ordeal. To begin with, a person's life becomes an open book. Everything one has ever said or done is open to scrutiny. Our lives were microscopically examined; Dr. Stevenson investigated Dolores's past back to the moment of her birth. A portion of his official report of his investigations says, "In Clarksburg, West Virginia where both the Jays grew up, I interviewed nineteen relatives and neighbors of Dolores Jay. The principal informants concerning her childhood were her parents and a younger sister. They all affirmed that they had no German-speaking persons in their family or among their acquaintances in Eastview, the suburb of Clarksburg where they lived. They also denied having any German books in the house when Dolores was a child. They were equally certain she could not have gone off from home by herself, perhaps visiting some German-speaking residents of the area, without their knowing of such wanderings." (Actually, there are no German-speaking residents in the immediate area).

Two persons among the nineteen friends and relatives questioned were Mrs. Daisy Nolan and Mrs. Verna Blackshire, who were Dolores's closest friends from infancy through high school. They were certain that Dolores never learned the language as a child, and they stated that because they knew Dolores to be a totally honest person, "If she said she never learned the language, then she didn't!"

Dr. Stevenson also learned that German was not taught in any Harrison County schools during the time Dolores and I attended them.

Even worse than the indignities of the investigation, Dolores was forced to suffer tremendous vexation in church. One beautiful spring Sunday she accompanied me to the morning worship service at Mount Nebo, a small chapel on the side of the Blue Ridge Mountains. We had partaken of the Lord's Supper in a service of Holy Communion that morning, and the worshippers had knelt at the communion rail with Dolores and partaken of the elements after I had issued the invitation: "All ye that do truly and earnestly repent of your sins, and are in love and fellowship with your neighbors . . . walking from henceforth in His holy ways, draw near with faith and take this sacrament to your comfort."

It was a beautiful service. Everyone seemed filled with the love of God, and I was certain that as Christ looked down from the right-hand throne of the Father that morning upon that congregation of pious Christians, He rejoiced in the knowledge that His sacrificial death upon Calvary's cross was not in vain. "Yea, Lord," I thought, with joy bells ringing in my soul, "these people would crawl on bended knee to the ends of the earth if need be to prove that they were born anew in God's own image." They seemed to be such good, decent, kind, humble, loving, and forgiving people that I loved them with all my heart and soul. But when the service ended and Dolores joined me in the vestibule to extend the right hand of fellowship to each parishioner leaving the Lord's house, only two of the nearly forty persons present that day would shake hands with Dolores; the others looked straight ahead, stone-faced, saying nothing or muttering through gritted teeth, "Witch!"

Probably the hardest pill to swallow was the attitude of Raden Moore. Raden had given us a hard time, but the night before he had come to the parsonage and said, "God told me in answer to prayer that you and Dolores are on His side. And, Preacher," he added, in seemingly sincere humility, "from now on you can count on me. I will defend you and your family to the death if need be." However, on that Lord's day he walked from the church with his face mirroring a glowering hatred, after which he and a few others went through the whole of the community with a petition which they intended to present to my Superintendent, Eugene Woolridge, thinking he would kick us out of the church immediately. To their chagrin, they succeeded in getting only sixteen signatures from among almost four hundred members of the charge.

As Dolores and I drove down the valley from Mount Nebo that day, her heart strings snapped and she wept as though her soul was in torment. Oh, God, I hurt for her —it wasn't fair! Just that morning before the service started I had said once again that if anyone had anything against us, "Speak up and we will leave immediately and resign from the charge without protest." But no! They had come to church, sung with holy fervor, and knelt humbly beside Dolores at the altar as being at one with her and the Lord, and then—it was unbelievable—in the name of all that is holy, the cruel, inhuman shamelessness of glaring and hissing directed at her after that service bespoke a sickness of soul unworthy of the most blatant sinner.

In the almost forty years I have known Dolores, not once have I heard her speak ill of anyone; not once has she ever said a cross word to any member of our churches or our neighbors; never would she offend anyone intentionally. To be cut to the core by the rancid bitterness of so-called Christians was the most terrible thing that could have happened to her. Worse yet, when she later learned that many members of that church literally rejoiced in exultation upon learning that their heathenish actions had caused her to suffer the torments of hell, she became ill —ill because she spent all her time praying and fasting for that church, certain in her heart that the Lord would in some way intervene and save those people from themselves and their own destruction.

For days the children and I watched over her and prayed. Then one night, shortly after I had gone to bed, Dolores sat up and reached out, seemingly embracing someone at the side of the bed, murmuring softly in angelic love, "O Jesus, my Jesus! You've come . . . you've come! I knew you would. Thank you, Jesus. Thank you," she exulted as tears trickled her cheeks.

"Yes, my Lord," she continued after a moment's pause, listening to what seemed to be words of assurance. "Yes, I remember." She smiled as the full moon glistened on her tear-streaked face, reflecting a radiant joy reserved for angels. "Thank you, Jesus," she said before turning to me. "Ked, honey," she said, in a melody reminiscent of Mary in the Magnificat, "my soul doth magnify the Lord, and my spirit rejoiceth in God my Savior for the Lord has heard and answered my prayers. And He comforted me!" She shouted in ecstasy. "Oh, He comforted me with His words of assurance, 'Weep no more my child. As it is recorded in my Word, "Well done, thou good and faithful servant: thou hast been faithful over a few things, I will make thee ruler over many: enter thou into the joy of the Lord" ' " (Matthew 25:21).

Then, lying back against the headboard, she looked at me in radiant joy. "Remember how we used to gather around the piano with Ruth and Ira [Whitmore] and Norman and Betty [Howdyshell] and sing? Remember," she said, and began to sing in melodious reverence:

> If when you give the best of your service,
> Telling the world that the Savior is come;
> Be not dismayed when men don't believe you,
> He'll understand and say, well done!

So great was our grief for the trouble in the church that I went the next day to Raden's home, to the young man who had turned in one night from "dying" for us to driving us out of town with a petition. He would not come to the door. I wrote a note and left it lying on the kitchen table, since the back door was open and the screen unlocked. In the note I pleaded, "Raden, if I or any member of my family has wronged you in any way, just say the word and I will apologize. If you want, I will even stand in the presence of the congregation and apologize."

Sadly, Raden did not want an apology, even one that was not owed him. He had made up his mind to run us out of town at any cost and would let nothing stop him.

Sick at heart, I went home, praying with every step. Thank God, there is indeed a silver lining to every cloud. Sitting in our living room was Carl Schumacher. Seeing me downcast, he said encouragingly, "Perk up, boy! Things are never as bad as they seem." Just looking at Carl, I knew that to be true. At that time Carl was deaf, yet he heard every word I said.

Some months before, Carl had come to me and handed me a note written by his doctor: "Carl, you are deaf and there is nothing more that can be done for you. Go to a psychiatrist and learn to live with it."

He was too much of an optimist to accept such a prognosis, so he said to me: "Carroll, I want you to hypnotize me and make me hear again."

Despite my admiration for Carl, I was certain he was reaching for the moon. He had lost not only his hearing, but his sense of smell, taste, and touch several months previously in an accident that required extensive hospitalization. Although most of his senses had been reactivated, I knew that if he had suffered nerve damage to the auditory nerve the possibility of his ever hearing again was practically nil, whether he submitted to hypnosis, hocus-pocus, or sophisticated surgery. But he needed help, and even though his doctor had told him that there was nothing more they could do, I agreed to try to do what I could for him. So I asked him to come back later that evening, giving me a chance to pray and think about what I ought to do.

I then devised an aid to determine whether he could hear by improvising a makeshift test. I recorded Vonda playing a musical scale on the piano, the scale ranging from high C, four octaves above middle C, to the lowest A, the fourth A below middle C. When Carl returned that evening and lay on the couch, I hypnotized him, a feat some people would have believed impossible. Then, turning on the tape recorder, I played the scales full blast after plugging his right ear and putting an earphone in his left ear. On a note pad I wrote, "Carl, can you hear anything?"

"Yes," he said, "a very faint sound." Then, with the left ear plugged and the earphone in his right ear, he heard absolutely nothing. Turning off the recorder, I prayed for Carl, as I always prayed for everyone whom I hypnotized, before reading him the following statement:

"Your subconscious mind will keep all noises generated inside your head [a constant roaring and ringing common to many people with hearing problems] from reaching your subconscious. The sounds will gradually diminish as your subconscious mind brings them under control. In a few minutes the sounds will be completely gone; they will never be any louder than they are right now, but even if they should return even that much, you will be able to reinforce this suggestion by rubbing your left ear lobe with your finger. This will always work.

"Your subconscious mind will be particularly sensitive to the sounds between middle G and C two octaves above it. Your subconscious mind will reinforce these particular frequencies so that your hearing in your right ear will appear to be essentially flat between fifty and two thousand cycles. Your subconscious mind will in the same way make the sounds of the letters S, C, V, and Z easily distinguishable, and all consonants will be easily heard and distinguished. These suggestions will be automatically reinforced every time you hear Joyce's voice [his wife], and her words will be easy for you to understand."

Although it would be impossible to explain how Carl and I expected the psychodynamics of hypnosis to facilitate his hearing, I fervently hoped that God's dynamics, sought in prayer, would accomplish the task if all else failed.

Since Carl was deaf to the extent that he could hear sounds in his left ear only if they were extremely loud, how could he possibly hear my prayer and instruction? Well, as for the prayer, Carl did not need to hear it, since it was offered to God and only He needed to hear; as for the statement, Carl read it before being hypnotized, and certain tactile signals were arranged and discussed before we began the hypnotizing. My hopes were based on the known fact that some people in hypnosis have increased sensitivity to the external stimuli of smelling, tasting, touching, seeing, and hearing.

In any event, a few moments after I read the statement to Carl while he was in a trance, I retested him with the recorder blasting away at full pitch. He screamed, "Turn it down!" Quickly obeying, I reduced the volume until he could hear it in the normal conversational range.

After giving Carl posthypnotic instructions and bringing him out of the trance, I walked with him out into the cool moonlit night. After a few minutes of conversation in normal voice under conditions making it impossible for him to read my lips, he interrupted me: "What's that strange noise?"

I had heard nothing, but Carl was scanning the sky and said, "I hear an airplane." So he did. A plane was flying through the night sky far, far to the east of us, but I could not hear it.

A week or so later, Carl returned to the same university hearing clinic that had told him he was deaf. When all tests were completed, his doctor said, "Carl, I'm sorry. You are deaf. Again I suggest that you go to a psychiatrist and learn to live with it."

"But, Doctor," Carl replied, "if I am deaf, how come I hear every word you say?"

"You can't possibly hear me!" he exclaimed.

"Oh, but I can! In fact, I don't need a psychiatrist; I've found the help I need."

With eyebrows raised in skepticism, his doctor asked, "What kind of help?"

"Hypnosis! I went to a hypnotist, and now I can hear everything you say."

"Impossible!" scoffed the doctor. "You only imagine you can hear."

Carl laughed. "Maybe so, but as long as my imagination gives me the ability to hear you, the telephone, and my wife's endearing words, life will be a great joy."

Please, this does not mean Carl was healed. He wasn't! But this much is certain: He regularly follows my posthypnotic instructions and uses autohypnosis, and his hearing problems have been reduced to a minimum, permitting him to function normally as he conducts his business as owner and editor of the *Valley Banner*.

Carl is only one of hundreds I was privileged to help through the use of hynosis. Dolores and I felt comforted by remembering them when the full force of hatred issued from those around Elkton who opposed our use of hypnosis in bringing health, happiness, and a surcease of pain to people who sought our help.

It had been quite some time since Gretchen had manifested to Dolores in spirit form, and we had begun to believe that we would never again see or hear from her unless I regressed her. But one day after I returned home from a trip, Dolores seemed pensive, even melancholic. When I inquired why she seemed so low in spirit, she informed me that Gretchen had visited her that day.

"I was standing at the kitchen sink, washing the dishes," she explained, "and I felt a presence in the room, and when I looked around, Gretchen was standing at the snack bar."

"What did she want? Did she say anything?"

"No, she didn't say anything, but she waved to me as if bidding me, 'Come go with me.'"

"Come? Go? Go where?"

"I don't know," she answered sadly. "I only know that Gretchen wants peace. I think that's all she ever wanted!"

Dolores had often voiced the opinion that Gretchen had spoken through her in an effort to get help, "to get out of that void—that lonely, lonely place of nowhere."

"If she wants peace," I asked, "why did she come to us? How can we help her?"

"I don't know, unless . . ." She paused thoughtfully. "Isn't it possible she is in purgatory, that her spirit had wandered all these years in the land of nowhere, waiting for someone to hear her story, someone to pray for her and help her?"

"If that be true," I responded, "why didn't she come through to a Catholic priest? Why through you and me, a Protestant minister and his wife?"

"Oh, Ked, don't be silly," she admonished, half seriously. "Maybe there are no Catholic priests who are hypnotists, and I doubt very much that many of them have ever been regressed."

I had to agree that possibly she was right. Maybe Gretchen did need help in her search for peace; and it was true that I knew of no Catholic priests who had hypnotized and regressed anyone. "So what do we do, Dolores. Do we . . . ?"

"We pray. It makes no difference whether we believe in the concept of purgatory; the fact remains that Gretchen is real, so terribly real, and she needs our help!"

Thus, we prayed. We prayed for Gretchen, and for God to give us understanding, patience, and love. Especially we prayed for all who did not understand our motives. And yes, we even prayed for the woman who called us at all hours of the day and night to babble drunkenly, "Could youse hypatize me, an . . . an brings me backs as . . . as da Queen of Sha . . . Shebsha?"

CHAPTER XIV

How Do the Dead Communicate?

When Dr. Stevenson phoned in March 1974 to request that Dolores and I come to his office for a regression and word-association test to be administered by Dr. Hilda Huntz, Professor of German at a large midwestern university, we were most reluctant to go. The stress of the investigation was having such a deleterious effect on Dolores's health that I was reluctant to ask her to submit to even one more session. (This seems to contradict my assertion that hypnosis per se has no adverse effects on anyone when applied by a competent therapist, but serious regressions do cause wear and tear on the emotions, since the subject does relive the role of the life being revealed through the subconscious. Quite naturally, if there has been tragedy in that life, the effect on the nervous system is bound to be cumulative.)

Even though Dolores never remembered what she said or did in regression, the strain on her was reflected in a fatigued appearance. In some strange way the constant fear and flight to avoid death and the trauma of the severe beating that preceded Gretchen's death somehow seeped through, as if by osmosis, to the surface of Dolores's conscious mind, plaguing her with vague apprehensions. Still, Dolores was always a strong defender of Dr. Stevenson, and often referred to him as "a good man, a man of the highest ideals." So we agreed to make one more trip if he would agree that it would be the last time he would request she submit to regression, which he did readily.

Basically the session was to be devoted to a word-association test, administered by Dr. Huntz, but due to the nature of the test it would be necessary to ask Dolores questions while she was in regression so as to establish good rapport between the hypnotized subject

232

and the interrogator. That is easier said than done. Some subjects just do not respond well to an interrogator no matter how congenial, or how well-laid the plans.

So it was with Gretchen and Dr. Huntz. Obviously the tests were excellently prepared, but Dr. Huntz had never before worked with anyone in regression. And although Dolores really liked and respected Dr. Huntz, when Dolores became Gretchen it was a different story. It now seems prudent to believe that because of Gretchen's fear of the Bundesrat and her mistrust of all strangers, it would have been wiser and infinitely more beneficial if she had been given more time to get to know them before they interrogated her as Gretchen.

I also think that because Dolores and I misinterpreted something Dr. Stevenson said to us, a serious misunderstanding developed, causing Dolores to be extremely apprehensive even before the regression started. He had said that many people would like to conclude that telepathy was the complete answer to the whole Gretchen case. In itself this was a perfectly innocent statement, but shortly after we entered his office that day he suggested that after I hypnotized and regressed Dolores I should leave the room. Naturally we thought he was hinting there might be collusion (if not telepathy) involved, but Dolores and I were completely innocent of any hoax and secretly resented what we thought was an insinuation that telepathy was involved, which we considered an absurdity.

As the moment for the test grew near, Dolores became extremely nervous and asked that I not leave the room. "There's no need for you to go; and I do not want to be left alone with them." I assured her, "Relax, hon, everything will be perfectly all right," even though I myself was a bit apprehensive. But I shouldn't have been. As Dr. Stevenson later explained, he and Dr. Huntz didn't want me present because they were afraid I might interrupt and interfere with the investigation.

No matter. I did as he requested and retired to an outer room, where I sat apprehensively twiddling my thumbs. As I said earlier, Dolores and I have a unique relationship, a telepathic communication that seemingly informs one or the other that all is not well. So it was that day. Psychic vibrations told me that all was not going well in that room where she lay alone in regression with Dr. Huntz and Dr. Stevenson.

Possibly I was letting my emotions run amok. But, no, fate, for lack of a better word, seemed to conspire against Dr. Huntz and Dr. Stevenson. Remember that I said personalities in regression do not always emerge at the same age in regression, and that Gretchen normally came through at age nine. Well, that day she did something she had never done before: She emerged as an entity abiding in that realm of existence between life and death at age sixteen, the age she departed this world. Naturally, that created serious problems; the transcripts reveal that Dr. Stevenson had considerable trouble engaging Gretchen in meaningful conversation.

Gretchen's first lucid statement was "Ich bin schlecht [I am bad]"—a real shocker. Never before had Gretchen even intimated that she had been anything but a sweet, decent young girl, and possibly our surprise was occasioned by the knowledge that moral indiscretions committed by a subject in a prior life are not often kept from the hypnotist. I was certain that had Gretchen been a "bad" girl she would have revealed her moral indiscretions in earlier regressions.

But wait! Let us reason for a moment. Since we know that Gretchen emerged that day at age sixteen, possibly later in the year when she died, meaning that she spoke to us from the afterlife, it seems reasonable that she was not saying she had been bad in her earthly life; rather, because she obviously had been confined to a place which we here refer to as purgatory, it seems logical that she was saying in essence "I must have been a bad girl or I would not have been confined to this place of no escape for more than a hundred years."

But let us not permit our minds to descend into the gutter. You see, in the Roman Catholic Church it is a tenet that the lack of baptism is sufficient cause for confinement in purgatory. In other words, her sin may have been the failure to consecrate herself with the sacrament of baptism and she did not find rejection in heaven because of moral indiscretions.

Other evidence abounds that all did not go well that

day in the regression. Most obvious is the fact that Dr. Stevenson was forced repeatedly to insist "Sprechen Sie lauter, bitte [Please speak louder]," "Wiederholen Sie [Say it again]," and "Das ich nicht gehört. Können Sie es wieder lauter sprechen? [I couldn't hear that. Can you say it again?]"

Gretchen tried desperately to make them understand that it was impossible for her to speak as one of them because "Ich bin schläft [I am sleeping.]" But anyone who has been involved in any kind of investigation soon learns that the full import of statements made by persons at any given time are not always fully understood immediately, and I am certain neither Dr. Huntz nor Dr. Stevenson immediately grasped the meaning of Gretchen's statement when she said, "Ich bin schläft!" I am of the opinion that if they had stopped to contemplate momentarily, they would have realized that she was using the word as it is often applied in funeral eulogies, meaning "I am in the eternal sleep of death." Even Dr. Stevenson's next question indicates that he did not stop to think of it in that way, especially when he said, "Schläft? So, könnten Sie nun wieder aufwachen?" [Sleep? Well, could you wake up now?]"

"Nein," Gretchen replied mournfully, remembering her last days on earth, "nicht wollen zurück. [No, not wanted back.]"

Clearly Gretchen was saying that she was not then asleep in Eberswalde, nor did she believe in her own mind that the authorities wanted her back, else they would not have killed her. But apparently Dr. Stevenson had not yet realized that her soft ethereal voice indicated that she was one speaking from the other world, and he urged her, "Gretchen, sprechen Sie ein wenig lauter. [Gretchen, speak a little louder.]"

As usual, unless Gretchen was extremely tired or confused, she tried to comply, and she said hopefully, "Ich versuche. [I'll try.]"

Finally satisfied that he was making progress, he said, "Ja, versuche. [Yes, try.]" Then he added, "Nun gehen wir nach ihrem Hause, ja? So. [Now let's go to your house, all right?]"

But Gretchen suddenly realized that Dr. Stevenson

did not understand after all, and said, "Vor länger Zeit [A long time ago]," stunning Dr. Stevenson into replying, "Vor länger Zeit? [A long time ago?]"

"Ja," Gretchen concurred, hoping he would understand. And apparently Dr. Stevenson did begin to suspect that she could not return to her earthly home, and he asked, "Wo ist Hause? [Where is house?]," meaning, I presume, "Is your home in the afterlife or on earth?"

"Vor länger Zeit [A long time ago]," she lamented, "Ich bin schlecht [I am bad]," indicating that she is now confined to that place in the afterlife and cannot go back to her home on earth. Then, almost as an afterthought, as if in curiosity, she asked, "Warum zurückkommen? [Why I come back? or, translating Gretchen's simple vernacular, Why do you want me to come back?]"

Although others may disagree, I see no possible reason for entertaining any cause for believing that Gretchen was indicating that she was merely in a natural sleep such as we mortals enjoy in this world, but rather she seemed to make it abundantly clear that her "schläft [sleep]" is the sleep of death in the afterlife. She emphasized this very thought when she refused to repeat her last statement for Dr. Stevenson, saying, "Nein! Sie verstehen nicht. [No! You do not understand.]"

My experience with hundreds of people in regression makes me believe that Gretchen tried to tell Dr. Stevenson, "I am what you would call dead." I reason thus because I have heard many persons in regression exclaim at the moment of their death, "Oh, I died!" I often heard them describe the moment of death, but never have I heard anyone in regression make the statement "I am dead." Really, there is no reason why anyone should proclaim to be dead, because every personality in the afterlife is alive, far more alive, I believe, than are any of us in this world.

Although the Bible speaks of those who cease to exist in this world as dead, and although we use the word "death" to refer to those who have preceded us into the afterlife, there is no such thing as death except for those in hell, who can never know the true joy of living. Thus, we say that the word "death" to those in the afterlife has no meaning; it is nonexistent. True, I have heard a person passing from this life to the next exclaim at the moment of death, "I have died!" but after having said that, the death experience is quickly forgotton, and apparently such persons have no memory of the event, nor will they speak of it again unless moved back chronologically to that time in regression.

It has also been my experience that those in the afterlife who have not yet reached perfection—become one with God—often speak of their present existence as sleep, an existence conceived of as thought, an interlude that precedes advancement to Myer's seventh stage, known as Timelessness, or the state referred to by the reincarnationists as nirvana.

Constant experience in working with people in regressions is a prerequisite for understanding the fine nuances inherent in regressed subjects' expressions, and if you prefer to call it ego instead of experience, I honestly feel I would have known intuitively what Gretchen was trying to say, I would have made inquiries that may have led to more fruitful experiences had I been present in the room with Dr. Huntz and Dr. Stevenson that day. For example, on one occasion Dr. Stevenson said to Gretchen, "Erzählen Sie uns eine Geschichte. [Tell us a story.]" Had I been there and known what he said, I would have been forced to interject, "That is a no-no!" I would have done so because experience has taught me that he had asked her to do something she would never do.

You see, subjects in hypnosis almost always respond to the literal meaning of a word, phrase, or question, and since Gretchen was not accustomed to telling stories, she would not begin doing so at that time. Persons in hypnosis tell it like it is. That is, they reveal only the events they are experiencing right at that time, a fact Dr. Stevenson knew well but momentarily forgot. This, then, is merely to say that two experienced heads are better than one, that my presence in the room might have saved Gretchen the needless conflict of trying to solve an unsolvable problem.

One other situation needs to be discussed. At one point Dolores started to open her eyes, and Dr. Stevenson quickly instructed, "Nein, machen ihre Augen zu. [No, close your eyes.]" Now, normally Dolores lay fairly passively with eyes closed as if in sleep, but some of the most rewarding information given to us by Gretchen came when she opened her eyes, got up, and walked around, giving animated action and response to things she was seeing or doing at that time. Dr. Stevenson may have thought she was coming out of the trance, and he did the sensible thing under the circumstances, but since I had worked so closely with her, I could quickly have discerned whether she was in fact awakening or merely looking around in a trance, in which case I could have said "Gretchen, tell us what you see." It would have been most interesting to see what she would have said.

As for Dr. Huntz, she is a wonderful person and an expert linguist, but I felt she was so anxious to help and so absorbed in the drama that she mistakenly thought she could regress Gretchen to her childhood by saying "Gretchen, ich möchte mit dir spielen. [Gretchen, I'd like to play with you.]" But since Gretchen, right at that time, did not know Dr. Huntz, she had absolutely no interest in playing.

"Spielen? [Play?]," she asked in disbelief. "Nein!" she rebelled, shaking her head adamantly.

To one living in the afterlife, play is an absurdity. As I will elaborate later, those poor souls in the afterlife are concerned only with escaping an eternity of unhappy boredom and frustration. Besides, Gretchen had lived and died more than a hundred years ago, and one thing was certain: Hilda Huntz was not one of her playmates. So in a sense it was incongruous for her, living in this day and age, to think she could suddenly go back more than a hundred years and automatically become Gretchen's playmate.

Thankfully, Dr. Stevenson intervened immediately, realizing that if anything worthwhile was to be accomplished, Gretchen would have to be moved chronologically back in time until she became a resident of Eberswalde at a younger age. But Gretchen resisted his efforts, possibly because he tried to employ a method with which she was unfamiliar. On two other occasions in other regressions he had attempted to move Gretchen from one age to another and failed, but it must be remembered that Gretchen was usually fearful of the Bundesrat, especially so when strangers were present.

Gretchen always thought of me as her friend. Even though Dolores was my wife and Gretchen spoke through Dolores, Gretchen never once thought of me as any more than a friend. Gretchen did not know Dolores, and when asked if she had ever heard of Dolores Jay, she always answered, "Nein," a logical answer since no Dolores Jay lived in Eberswalde when Gretchen lived in that town as a young girl. No matter how many times Dolores's name was mentioned, Gretchen would not admit to knowing her, which was only natural because Dolores had not been a part of her natural, physical existence on earth.

Neither did Gretchen know me, Dr. Stevenson, Dr. Klaus, Dr. Rohl, or Dr. Huntz. Always she referred to me as "Mein Freund. [My friend.]" Since first emerging through Dolores, Gretchen had been dreadfully fearful of the Bundesrat and would talk to no one for fear of being betrayed, fearful she would be reported to the Bundesrat. More important, in regressions she would not talk to anyone unless I first introduced the person to her as "My friend, someone you can trust." And that was not an easy task. Not until after her third or fourth emergence did she finally accept me as her friend, someone she knew she could trust, who would not betray her to the Bundesrat. Possibly that, more than anything else, made her quickly reject Dr. Huntz's offer to be a friend, someone with whom she could play. That trust and rapport had not really been developed.

Such an explanation does not tell the whole story. As a child Gretchen lived in the small town or place called Eberswalde, and her friends were limited to her neighbor's children: Karl, Kurt, Karin, and Erich Schilder. So while it was commendable for Dr. Huntz to say "Gretchen, I want to be your friend and play with you," this could only have made Gretchen suspicious, since she knew no Hilda Huntz during her childhood days on this earth. As I redundantly insist, Gretchen could discuss only the things, people, and events that were an actual part of her earthly existence. Had she done otherwise, facts would demand that we conclude that Gretchen was fabricating figments of Dolores's imagination, an imagination which would incorporate any suggestions put forth by her questioners.

Here lies an interesting fact. When Dr. Stevenson attempted to move Gretchen back to a younger age, he asked, "Wie alt sind sie? [How old are you?]," and she replied, "Ich bin sechzehn. [I am sixteen.]" That was a strange answer, strange in the sense that while many of our modern theologians insist that death is the end of physical life, the dissolution of the body, many will sometimes insist most adamantly that even in death one will grow and mature into full manhood or womanhood. If that be true, why did Gretchen say she was only sixteen when we knew she had been dead for more than a hundred years?

I once heard a minister assert most dogmatically at an infant's funeral, "Dearly beloved, rejoice in the knowledge that when you meet your beloved child in heaven, she will be a most beautiful young woman." I thought, "Now that's a nice comforting thought." Then I continued to reflect: "I do believe that life continues after death, but while we do continue to grow in knowledge and learn about things eternal, there is absolutely no reason to live in the false hope that we will mature physically as we do in this life."

If we did, consider what it would mean. If, as the pastor said, "Your child shall grow into a beautiful young woman," what then can we say about us older people who are already ugly and wrinkled? Do we grow uglier and wrinklier? What about Moses, Elijah, and David? Are they now nothing but ancient, unrecognizable relics?

Of course not. I'm being facetious. Besides, the Bible tells us we shall be given a new body, "fashioned after His own likeness." More important, as the Apostle Paul says, "For now we see through a glass darkly; but then face to face: Now I know in part; but then shall I know even as also I am known" (I Corinthians 13:12). Please note, this does not say anything about growing older—it merely says we shall know . . . even as we are known.

Returning to the regression with Dr. Huntz, Dr. Stevenson, and Gretchen, the fact that Dr. Huntz was a novice was also a blessing, because she injected new thoughts normally by-passed by those of us who worked so long and hard at the task. For example, she asked a question that would never have occurred to me: "Gretchen, hast du schon etwas von Wiedergeburt gehört? [Gretchen, have you ever heard of reincarnation?]"

"Ja," she replied matter-of-factly, "Ist Geburt von mein Mutter. [Yes, it is the birth of my mother.]"

That was a most interesting question and an even more astounding reply. But Dr. Huntz's inexperience prevented her from pursuing the response to its ultimate conclusion, and we are left to wonder: Do all or even a majority of personalities in the afterlife conceptualize reincarnation as birth, or do they associate reincarnation with birth?

Certainly many reincarnationists insist they do the latter. Centuries of religious and philosophic tradition suggest that human existence is a series of rebirths. Our prehistoric ancestors believed not only in the survival of human personality after death, but in the return of the soul in another body into this life. The Yorubas of Nigeria believe that dead children who were mistreated by their parents are reborn over and over again within the same families.

The ancient Greek writer Herodotus tells us that the Egyptians were the first to teach that the human soul is immortal, and at the death of the body the soul enters once more into a human body at birth. Gretchen, although she associated reincarnation with the birth of her mother, never referred to her own birth as reincarnation. Opinions on this subject may suffer great difference, but I would suggest each should be left to form an opinion.

In his book *Is Death the End?* Dr. John H. Holmes, a New York divine, says, "Nobody can study the evidence given in this particular field without noticing the triviality, almost inanity, of the communications received [from psychic communicators]. Here we come," he adds with faint praise for the communicators, "for evidence of future life and for information as to what it means to die and pass into the great beyond. And what do we get? First of all there are frantic efforts on the part of alleged spirits to prove their identity by the citation of intricate and unimportant details of where they were and what they did at different times when they were among men on earth, and again and again there is a descent to obscurity and feeble chattering."

On the other hand, in the communications of Patience Worth, a discarnate personality who began speaking through a St. Louis housewife in 1913, there were no efforts on her part to prove her identity, and only rarely did she speak about herself and the past. "About me," she says, "yesterday is dead." The same is true of Gretchen. She claimed to have been no person of great importance, nor did she boast of doing anything great. More important, she spoke only of the things which occurred at the moment to which she was regressed.

It was neither birth, reincarnation, or world-shattering events that Gretchen wanted to talk about that day, but death! Yes, death and life in the great beyond were the things occupying her mind. She was so preoccupied with the subject that she finally volunteered, "Ich . . . ich mit meine Mutter. [I . . . I am with my mother.]"

"Ihre Mutter? [Your mother?]," Dr. Stevenson asked in surprise. "Wo ist Ihre Mutter [Where is your mother?]"

Happily Gretchen said, "Im Himmel. [In heaven.]"

"Wo? [Where?]," Dr. Stevenson asked incredulously. Gretchen: "Ist . . . ist tot. Vor langer Zeit. [Is . . . is dead. A long time ago.]"

Stevenson: "Was ist ihre passiert? [What happened to her?]"

Gretchen ignored his question and said, "Jetzt Gretchen mit ihr. [Now Gretchen with her.]"

Stevenson: "Und wo ist Ihre Mutter? [And where is your mother?]"

This time Gretchen smiled. "Im Himmel. [In heaven.]"

Intrigued, Dr. Stevenson asked, "Und kommt Sie wieder zurück? [Will she be coming back?]"

Gretchen refused to say yes or no. She replied, "Ich gehe mit ihr. [I go with her.]"

Huntz: "Ja, du gehst zu ihr. In den Himmel. Wann kommst du in den Himmel zu ihr? [Yes, you go to her. In heaven. When do you go to heaven with her?]"

"Vor länger Zeit [A long time ago]," Gretchen repeated, for the fourth time.

Dr. Huntz then asked, "Und warum kommst du in den Himmel? [Why do you go to heaven]."

Thinking as a minister and meaning no disrespect for Dr. Huntz, had I been Gretchen I would have been tempted to answer, "Because it's a lot better than going to hell." But Dr. Huntz's question cannot be read in the cold light of print, because she obviously meant "What caused your death?"

But Gretchen quickly forgot the traumatic specifics of death and dying and answered rapturously, "Es ist sehr schön! [It is beautiful!]"

Dr. Huntz smiled at the thought and agreed. "Ja, es ist sehr schön. [Yes, it is beautiful.]"

Then, for some unknown reason Gretchen was apparently transported in spirit back to her last moments in the forest, and she wept. "Warum der Mann stechen mir? [Why the man stab me?]"

"Bitte?" Dr. Huntz screamed in shock. "Sag's nochmal! [What? Say that again!]"

Gretchen could only cringe and plead in terror, "Helfen Sie mir!" [Help me!]"

Dr. Huntz assured her sympathetically, "Ja, ich helfe dir. Was soll ich tun, Gretchen? [Yes, I'll help you. What shall I do, Gretchen?]"

Gretchen: "Es ist sehr schrecklich! [It is very terrible!]"

Huntz: "Was ist schrecklich? Sag's mir, damit ich dir helfen kann. [What is terrible? Tell me so that I can help you.]"

Gretchen continued to writhe and moan in pain.

Huntz: "Ich helfe dir, Gretchen. Sag's mir. Was ist schrecklich? [I'll help you, Gretchen. Tell me. What is terrible?]"

Beginning to lose her hold on life and sinking rapidly, Gretchen whispered as if knowing the end was near, "Alles schwarz. [Everything black.]"

Sympathizing as a loving friend, Dr. Huntz asked without thinking, even though she knew Gretchen had been stabbed, "Has du Wuden, Gretchen? [Are you wounded, Gretchen?]"

"Es ist sehr . . . [It is very . . .]"

"Ich sehe [I see]," Dr. Huntz said consolingly. Then,

trying to determine the seriousness of the wound, she asked, "Ist etwas an deiner Hand? Is da Blut? [Is there something on your hand? Is there blood?]"

Continuing to moan, Gretchen whispered, "Mein . . . Kopf! [My . . . head!]"

"Am Kopf? Aber warum, Gretchen? Du bist ein Kind [In the head? But why, Gretchen? You are a child]," Dr. Huntz lamented, almost in tears.

"Nein," Gretchen rebutted, thinking herself a woman, and indeed she was old for her age, the strife making her life a hell on earth.

Suddenly remembering that she was an investigator, that she was not actually present with Gretchen in her final moments, Dr. Huntz assumed a more professional tone and pressed Gretchen for needed information.

HUNTZ: "Was tut die weh, Gretchen? [Who is hurting you, Gretchen?]

GRETCHEN: "Männer, [Men,]" she sighed, resigned to pain and death.

HUNTZ: "Der Mann? [The man?]"

GRETCHEN: "Ja. [Yes.]"

HUNTZ: "Aber warum? Ist der Mann böse! [But why? Is the man angry?]"

GRETCHEN: "Ja. Sehr böse! [Yes. Very angry!]"

HUNTZ: "Aber warum, Gretchen? Du bist lieb. [But why, Gretchen? You are sweet.]" Dr. Huntz spoke with love, again forgetting her role as investigator, touched by Gretchen's winsomeness even in tragedy.

GRETCHEN: "Ich weiss nicht. Ich . . . [I don't know. I . . .]"

HUNTZ: "Du weisst es nicht? Wie sicht der Mann aus? [You don't know why? What does the man look like?]"

GRETCHEN: "Der Mann . . . reiten das Pferd. [The man . . . rides the horse.]"

HUNTZ: "Ist er Soldat? [Is he a soldier?]"

GRETCHEN: "Ja, ja. [Yes, yes.]"

HUNTZ: "Ist der im Wald? Und du bist auch im Wald verborgen? [Is he in the forest? And are you hidden in the forest?]"

GRETCHEN: "Ja. Hinter dem Baum. [Yes. Behind a
   tree.]"
HUNTZ: "Gretchen ist verborgen? [Gretchen is hidden?]"
GRETCHEN: "Verboten. Sprächen mit . . . [Forbidden.
   Talking with . . .]"
HUNTZ: "Mit wem darfst du nicht sprechen, Gretchen?
   [With whom mustn't you speak, Gretchen?]"
   But Gretchen just lay and moaned. She would talk no
more.

Remembering that Gretchen spoke of blackness, it
seems appropriate to inquire what really happens when a
person's subconscious reveals to them a view of life in the
other world.

Most people wonder if there is a set pattern. Do all
experience the same phenomena?

Not really. Some may see a place of bright and glorious
beauty; they may see a bright light, or they may dwell in
a gray fog shaded in black; most important, most are consistent in their insistence that life continues in spirit form.
Many have described in great detail encounters with long-
gone relatives and friends with whom they communicate.

How? If they are spirit and do not possess physical
equipment such as vocal cords, how do they speak?

Dolores always said when passing into that mysterious
realm, "I am not, therefore I do not exist." When I reminded her that she did indeed exist, else she could not
communicate with me and the spirits around her in that
other world, she would say, "We live and move and have
our being through thought."

"Then you do exist and communicate through
thought?"

"Yes," she patiently explained, "we are thought."

Some people might think Dolores was merely dredg-
ing up a concept of life from the reservoir of her subconscious, an idea acquired in past classes in philosophy.
But, no! Her formal education ended at Roosevelt Wil-
son High School a long time ago, and it is certain that
philosophy was not one of the subjects in her business-
administration classes. Too, while Dolores is an inveter-
ate reader, she does not engage much in heavy stuff, and,
obviously, serious reading is an absolute must if one is

to develop a workable theory of philosophical concepts.

Let us consider Dolores's contention that in the after-life she existed as thought. Her statement "I am not, therefore I do not exist" is a comparable antithesis of Descartes' *Cogito, ergo sum* ("I think, therefore I am"). In this search for absolute relatives to his identity, René Descartes began a quest for a certainty of his own existence which became for him the science of reality. That reality came to him only after he proposed to doubt everything, even the product of his own experience, the learning of schools, the traditions of the West, and the special insights of Christianity. Eventually, Descartes was able to verify the truth of his existence to his satisfaction by his new (and what he thought to be infallible) method. He satisfied himself that he proved his thesis of reality by ultimately believing that though he doubted all else, he could always depend upon one indisputable fact, namely: "I think, therefore I am."

Well, then, are we mortals, as Descartes concluded, nothing more than flesh and blood endowed with thought, thought clothed in flesh?

If we accept such a postulate, must we not then totally reject the two weighty premises by which many people have lived and died? That is, can we any longer claim that each of us is a supreme being of God's creation, a creature whom the Almighty endowed with an immortal soul, a soul that returns to its Maker and Creator for reward or judgment when life on earth is done; or can we look at the other side of the coin and believe that we are flesh-and-blood organisms which happened to evolve from the lowly ameba, organisms which eventually die without the hint of a thought that there is any existence whatsoever beyond the grave?

We must go a step further and say that the concepts of heaven, hell, and purgatory, where the soul abides after death, are mere fabrications of our minds if we admit we are mere thought or the apex of Darwinian evolution. If we believe, as most Christians do, then we reject such assumptions and live by the faith that heaven, hell, and pugatory are actual places of existence, the abode of the soul in the life to come.

Many concepts about our final end embrace only a

part of the preceding concept, such as the belief that heaven sans hell is the final resting place of the soul, a product of the assumption that a loving God would never permit anyone to be tormented in hell. Then there is the belief that proclaims "From dust thou art, and unto dust shalt thou return," with neither reward or punishment, nor even a future existence of the soul.

Finally, although I cannot list all the concepts in this work, it seems imperative at least to mention the reincarnationists' premise, which proclaims the existence of the soul, and according to Dr. Stevenson, many even go so far as to express a strong belief in heaven, hell, and purgatory. But basically, reincarnationists believe that ultimately we shall all attain perfection after many trips through many planes of existence in the afterlife, coupled with many incarnations on earth, thus achieving perfection and allows us to attain nirvana, conceived of as becoming at one with God.

For all who cannot believe that anyone will ever reach a state of perfection in this life, or that we do not merely "return unto dust," the question must be asked: What do we do with heaven, hell, and purgatory? What about the ultimate disposition of the soul?

Let us consider the soul first. Is the soul the spirit of us human beings only so long as we live and move and have our being in this life? Or is the soul that part of the human race which lives on eternally as spirit in the world to come? Is it the same as "thought"? If we are mere thought, are thought and spirit one and the same?

Gretchen says that she is thought, that she communicates by thought. Descartes said, "I think, therefore I am." Does this mean that thought is indestructible, that thought lives on even after death of the body? Does thought exist in the afterlife and abide in that world until it, thought, decides to think itself into existence in this world, coming into this world to a new life in a new body? Remember: God thought, and creation was the product of His thought. No, I do not equate Descartes with God—I merely emphasize the ultimate power of Descartes's concept of power.

Carl Jung formulated a theory of personality which may help us to arrive at answers not normally considered by too many people. He saw every individual's personality as the product and container of ancestral history. He believed that you and I have been molded into our present form by the accumulation of traits or thoughts from past generations extending far back into the dim, unknown origins of our race.

Jung conceived of total personality (self or psyche, as he called it) as consisting of separate but interacting systems. The principal ones are ego, the personal unconscious, and its complexes: the collective unconscious and its archetypes—the persona, the anima or animus, and the shadow. The ego is the conscious mind and is made up of conscious perceptions, memories, thoughts, and feelings. It is responsible for one's feeling of identity and continuity.

The personal unconsciousness is a region adjoining the ego and consists of experiences that were once conscious but which have been repressed, suppressed, forgotten, or ignored. The contents of the personal unconsciousness are accessible to the consciousness, and there is a great deal of two-way traffic between the personal unconsciousness and the ego.

The collective unconscious in Jungian psychology seems to be the storehouse of latent memory traces which individuals inherit from their ancestral past. It is the residue of our evolutionary development, a residue that accumulates as a consequence of repeated experiences over many generations. For example, people are predisposed to be afraid of the dark or of snakes because supposedly primitive man encountered many snakes and other dangers in the dark.

More important, the unconscious (subconscious) holds possibilities which are locked away from the conscious mind because it has at its disposal all sublimated contents, all those things which have been forgotten or overlooked, as well as the experience and wisdom of the uncounted centuries. Is it not possible that hypnosis is the key to that vast reservoir of experience and wisdom?

Genetically, it is. When a new life is conceived in the zygote, every trait in the mating parties is passed on to the new creation, and though the parents eventually cease to exist in this life, there is still something of their lives living in their offspring.

Since many of us believe in life after death and evidence abounds that there is a life after death, it surely seems reasonable that there *is* life after death. Yet much doubt has been cast on its reality, because the Church itself has been wishy-washy on the subject. Most churches include life after death as a tenet of faith, but many of our ultramodern ministers deplore the preaching of a gospel that ignores the amount of money received and the efforts expended on a social gospel. Life after death is, for them, the moving of minorities from the ghettos to high-rise apartments or the raising of their salaries to a professional level.

Immortality has been an innate desire of most people in all times, but the Christian Church bases its belief on many of the Scriptural sayings of Jesus, such as "Because I live, you shall live also" (John 14:19) and "I am the resurrection and the life: He that believeth on me, though he were dead, yet shall he live: and whosoever liveth and believeth in me, shall never die" (John 11:25, 26).

I John 8:51 says, "If a man keep my saying, he shall never see death," and I John 3:14 tells us, "We know that we have passed from death into life." Then again, I John 5:11 reveals, "And this is the record, that God hath given us eternal life."

There is considerable debate about what happens immediately after death—do we go directly to heaven or hell? But many shout, "Neither!" insisting there is no immediate reward or punishment since the body must lie in the grave until the Second Coming of Christ at the Rapture, the Parousia, when Christ comes for His Church and the resurrection of the dead occurs.

Atheists do not believe in God, hence no heaven, hell, or resurrection. "Dust thou art, and unto dust shall thou return," they proclaim, even intimating that our only usefulness is to someday become a tater patch or a cornfield.

For the reincarnationist there is neither reward nor punishment. Although some do claim they believe in heaven, hell, and purgatory, for them death is an interlude between lives, with each incarnation supposedly allowing them to pay karmic debts until a succession oi incarnations allows them to become so perfected that they become "at one with God."

Now a few words of explanation are needed. The authority for those who believe we enter either heaven or hell immediately after death comes from two Biblical passages. The first of these is found in St. Luke 23:39-43 and concerns only heaven: "And one of the malefactors which were hanged railed on him, saying, If thou be the Christ, save thyself and us. The other rebuked him, saying, Dost not thou fear God, seeing thou art in the same condemnation? And we indeed justly! For we receive the due reward of our deeds; but this man has done nothing amiss. And he said unto Jesus, Lord, remember me when thou comest into thy kingdom. And Jesus said unto him, Verily I say unto thee, Today shalt thou be with me in paradise." Meaning, of course, that Jesus was saying, "Son, today, soon after you die your soul will be in heaven."

The second, dealing with the possibility of both heaven and hell, is found in St. Luke 16:19-31: "There was a certain rich man which was clothed in purple and fine linen, and fared sumptuously every day: And there was a certain beggar named Lazarus, which was laid at his gate, full of sores, and desiring to be fed with crumbs which fell from the rich man's table . . . And it came to pass that the beggar died and was carried by the angels into Abraham's bosom: the rich man also died, and was buried; and in hell he lifted up his eyes, being in torment, and seeth Abraham afar off, and Lazarus in his bosom. And he cried and said, Father Abraham, have mercy on me and send Lazarus that he may dip the tip of his finger in water and cool my tongue; for I am tormented in this flame."

Clearly we can say that the preceding passages refer to the states that are known as heaven and hell, but for the third group of believers, who insist that we enter neither heaven nor hell immediately after death but lay in our graves until the Second Coming of Christ, we need to look at I Thessalonians 4:13-18: "But I would not have you to be ignorant, brethren, concerning them which are asleep, that ye sorrow not, even as others which have no hope. For if we believe that Jesus died and rose again, even so them also which sleep in Jesus will God bring with him. For this we say unto you by the word of the Lord, that we which are alive and remain unto the coming of the Lord shall not prevent them which are asleep. For the Lord himself shall descend from heaven with a shout with the voice of the archangel, and with the trump of God: and the dead in Christ shall rise first: then we which are alive and remain shall be caught up together with them in the clouds, to meet the Lord in the air: and so shall we ever be with the Lord. Wherefore comfort one another with these words."

I pose a fourth possibility: When we have eliminated those who either go to heaven or hell, become mere dust, or wait patiently in their graves until the Great Judgment Day, is there a fourth group to be considered? In other words, is there life *between* deaths? I think so!

Life after death and life between death are clearly indicated during the three days that Jesus supposedly lay dead in the tomb. I Peter 3:19-20 says, "For Christ also hath once suffered for sins, the just for the unjust, that he might bring us to God, being put to death in the flesh, but quickened by the Spirit: By which also he went and preached unto the spirits in prison; which sometimes were disobedient." The Living Bible says more plainly, "Christ also suffered. He died once for all us guilty sinners, although he himself was innocent of sin at any time. But though his body died, his spirit lived on, and it was in the spirit that he visited the spirits in prison and preached to them . . ." "Prison" here refers to Hades or those in the grave.

If there is not life after death, Jesus would have made that trip into the place of afterlife merely to preach just for the sake of making noise. I don't believe that, nor did those in prison in the afterlife (death) who heard him speak. More important, what did Jesus himself have to say about the matter? St. John 5:25-29 says, "Verily, verily, I say unto you, He that heareth my word, and believeth on him that sent me, hath everlasting life, and shall not come into condemnation; but is passed from death into life . . . I say unto you the hour is coming, and now is, when the dead shall hear the voice of the Son of God: and they that hear shall live . . ."

In St. Luke 4:18 Jesus said, "The Spirit of the Lord is upon me, because he hath anointed me to preach the gospel to the poor; he hath sent me to heal the broken-hearted, to preach deliverance to the captives [in the graves] . . ." And in Ephesians 4:18-10, Paul wrote, "When he ascended upon high, he led captivity captive, and gave gifts to men. (Now he that ascended, what is it but that he also descended first into the lower parts of the earth? He that descended is the same that also ascended up far above the heavens, that he might fill all things)."

How could he fill all things? Romans 10:6-13 says, "But the righteousness which is of faith speaketh on this wise. Say not in thine heart, who shall ascend into heaven [that is, bring Christ down from above]? or, who shall descend into the deep [that is, bring up Christ again from the dead]? But what saith it? The word is nigh thee, even in thy mouth, and in thy heart: that is, the word of faith which we preach; that if thou shalt confess with thy mouth the Lord Jesus Christ, and shalt believe in thine heart that God hath raised him from the dead, thou shalt be saved. For with the heart man believeth unto right-eousness; and with the mouth confession is made unto salvation. For the Scripture saith, whosoever believeth on him shall not be ashamed . . . For whosoever shall call upon the name of the Lord shall be saved."

To me, all this means that our Lord descended between His passion and resurrection to preach to the spirits imprisoned in Hades and offer salvation to sinners who had died without hearing the gospel or getting a chance to repent.

As to "What about life between deaths?", obviously if Christ descended into Hades to preach, He did so because He knew there were souls there that could hear and accept the salvation offered. To argue differently is to say that Christ was a fool to preach to the dead, who could not hear or make a decision.

If then Jesus preached to those who had fallen asleep in times past, cannot we believe that He does so today, especially when we read in Hebrews 13:8 that Jesus Christ "Is the same yesterday, and today and forever"?

In other words, what He did for one, He will do for another; what He did yesterday, He will do today.

Other illustrations of proof of survival, life between deaths, are plentiful, but one more example should suffice at this time. In Matthew 17:1-3 we read, "And after six days Jesus taketh Peter, James and John up into an high mountain apart, and was transfigured before them; and his face did shine as the sun, and his raiment was white as light. And, behold, there appeared unto them Moses and Elijah talking with him."

Since Moses and Elijah appeared and talked, they were alive, proving survival after death and between deaths. But why do we keep talking about "between deaths"? Well, if we believe, as do the reincarnationists, that we all live many lives upon this earth, it naturally follows that we must spend time in another world between deaths. But that is not our only purpose. Even those who do not believe in reincarnation face the possibility of two deaths. John the Revelator tells us in Revelations 20:12-14 that after the Second Coming of Christ, following the Great Resurrection, "I saw the dead, small and great, stand before God; and the books were opened; and another book was opened which is the book of life: and the dead were judged out of those things which were written in the books according to their works. And the sea gave up the dead which were in it; and death and hell delivered up the dead which were in them: and they were judged every man according to their works. And death and hell were cast into the lake of fire. This is the second death." If judgment is final at death and there is no chance to accept salvation offered by Christ in the afterlife, why are there two deaths?

So you see, according to the Bible there are at least two deaths for some people. Of course, we Christians hope to escape that second death because of our faith in Christ. We hope to escape because Romans 10:13 says, "Whosoever shall call upon the name of the Lord shall be saved"—saved because we have believed in Him in our hearts and have confessed Him with our mouths. (True, righteous living must follow confession and acceptance, but for present purposes I merely list the basics.)

What, really, has been the importance of all this

Scripture? Apart from showing that strong reasons exist for believing in survival of the soul, it gives us opportunity to reason that since we in this life are endowed with free will, this free will apparently continues after death, as indicated by the fact that Jesus preached to the spirits in captivity, giving them an opportunity to repent and accept full salvation.

Many theologians insist that Jesus spoke only to those souls who became imprisoned at the time of or before Noah and the Great Flood. If that be true, how can we reconcile the impartiality of God toward those who lived and died between the time of Noah and the coming of Christ into the world? If God did not give the same opportunity for salvation to those who lived and died between Noah and Christ's coming, then we could not possibly say that God was the same yesterday, today, and forever. We must also note that if free will does exist after death, and if reincarnation is indeed fact, it is surely logical that many souls could, through free will, reject God's offer of immediate salvation after death and elect to incarnate for another go-around in this life, which I will discuss more fully in the next chapter.

I have merely raised questions about a person's continued life after death, between deaths, and reincarnation; while I am very much aware that many will reject the premises put forth I feel these thoughts were necessary to bring the questions out in the open for discussion.

Now let us renew our discussion on "thought," since it is a biological fact that at the moment of death the body begins to decay, a fact known even in Biblical days and attested to after Jesus made preparation to raise Lazarus (not the same Lazarus mentioned in the parable of the rich man) and Martha cried, "Lord, by this time he stinketh, for he hath been dead four days" (John 11:39). Still, the Bible asks us to believe that both Lazarus and the saints who arose after the crucifixion of Jesus Christ (Read St. Matthew 27:52, 53) were both mentally and physically complete. This raises the question: Though they had been dead, does not their death indicate that death comes only to the body? That there was something attached to or within those bodies which did not die, which will never die and decay, such as the soul, which continues to abide as spirit, which can conceivably be translated as thought, which has knowledge and consciousness, as indicated in the response of Lazarus to the call of Jesus?

Yes, I think so. More important, according to the Biblical illustrations, they lived twice: once before and once after the death of the physical body. But as for those who believe that the grave is the end, are we to believe that those already dead have not enjoyed existence while abiding between those two states of existence? Would it not seem reasonable that their existence was comparable to that which I enjoyed while doctors worked frantically to restore life to my body when I lay dead in Christ's Hospital in Cincinnati? I, for one, will always believe in the affirmative.

CHAPTER XV

Searching for Gretchen's Roots

As Dolores and I sat in the Parkhaus Hotel in Darmstadt, Germany, an inexplicable atmosphere of optimism made us feel extremely encouraged; maybe we might soon know the origin of Gretchen's life on earth.

Never before had Dolores or I been outside the United States, except for a couple of afternoon drives into Canada, but when the Lufthansa jumbo jet lifted to the heavens from John F. Kennedy International Airport in New York and headed out across the Atlantic toward Frankfurt, Dolores gazed up at me with a childish wistfulness that bespoke a lifelong dream come true. "Honey, down there is the land of my birth, and I love it dearly, but"—she paused with a hesitancy born of deep emotion —"somehow I feel like a person who's been on a long vacation and is finally going home."

Germany had been the subject of many long conversations in our home during the past seven years, but never in all that time had Dolores intimated that that faraway land would ever be anything more than an interesting place to visit. Though we knew Germany to be Gretchen's homeland, never had she evinced any greater interest in going there than had thousands of others who fantasized about touring strange lands.

As the revved-up jet roared its thunderous blast of farewell to America, Dolores again tugged at my arm, as a pensive child might. "Honey, I wonder what it will be like if—well, you know, if we actually find the place where Gretchen lived and died."

The possibility of finding those places was very remote, especially since Gretchen had stated over and over that she was born and reared in Eberswalde, Deutschland, the place we readily found on the map in East Germany.

Since Dr. Stevenson had researched that city and concluded that the possibility of her ever having lived in that city was almost nil, why were we on our way to Germany? Were we so conceited as to think we knew more about parapsychology than Dr. Stevenson?

Hardly! Few people will ever be able to claim that right, least of all me. But as I previously stated, I had what could be called a gut feeling that that northeastern city of Eberswalde was not where Gretchen directed us, possibly because I may have empathized just a little more closely with her than Dr. Stevenson did. After all, she was my baby, born into this age through my wife's subconscious.

Anyone who has read this book knows that Gretchen was not what we would call exceptionally bright mentally, that she sometimes had problems putting into words what she really wanted to say. Maybe, being somewhat like her, I reasoned, she wasn't really designating an actual town or city by that name: maybe she was referring to a small community or a specific locale such as Eberstadt, "a place where pigs or boars are kept," which she called a city or town simply because a few people inhabited the area.

Gretchen always described Eberswalde as a "kleines Dorf [a small village]." Because she had also mentioned an Eberstadt and Eberback, I felt that if we would find those two towns we might hit pay dirt. Although Dr. Stevenson had informed me that a colleague in Mannheim, Dr. Heinrich Wendt, had investigated an Eberstadt that had been incorporated into Darmstadt's boundaries a few years ago and had concluded that it could not have been the Eberstadt to which Gretchen referred, I still thought a personal investigation by Dolores and me might turn up something new, evidence previously overlooked. There were other places called Eberstadt and Eberback in that general area of Germany. These had not yet been investigated. If necessary, we would thoroughly research each town.

No matter; we were there, and found Germany to be a lovely place. Dolores tingled from head to toe at just being there to walk the streets and ride in the country and see all the old houses and castles that somehow made her feel at home again. Sometimes I had to chuckle when Dolores would respond to me with "Ja" or "Nein," or when she caught herself counting her change at the market: "Eins, zwei, drei . . ." She stopped and giggled self-consciously. "What in the world made me do that?"

Other things had an equally profound effect upon her, although there was nothing that could really be called a *déjà vu* experience in the truest sense. The language seemed to her especially romantic, something she could not understand or explain—and no, she could not suddenly speak the language. Also, once, sitting in a restaurant, although Dolores had always been a total abstainer from all alcoholic beverages, she said to me, "A glass of wine is awful tempting right now." And that seemed natural, since don't all Germans have wine or beer with their meals? Then there were times we walked the streets in old, old communities and she found her eyes glued to the intricate design of the woodwork, and touching moments when I saw her run her hands across the stones in old buildings almost caressingly.

Back home in Virginia Dolores had grown extremely weary of the investigation and dreaded the thought of being regressed again. Yet during our first night in Darmstadt she lay on the bed and said, almost longingly, "Maybe you ought to regress me again just to see what would happen."

So I hypnotized and regressed her.

"How old are you, Gretchen?"

"Neun [Nine]," she responded, seemingly more secure and bolder in speech than ever before.

Dolores was not the only one affected. No sooner had Gretchen spoken than I remembered that first regression in 1970, when she said, "Ich lebe Bergenstrasse," and I felt compelled to ask immediately, "Gretchen, when I first spoke to you many years ago, you said you lived in Bergenstrasse. Now tell me, did you move from Bergenstrasse to Eberswalde?"

"Nein." She smiled as if enjoying a secret joke. "Ich lebe Eberswalde in Bergenstrasse."

That didn't make sense. Or did it? Clearly I remembered the day in 1970 when I stood with Dean Fawley in his classroom at Lynchburg-Clay High School, where he taught world history and geography, and I remembered how we had searched his maps of Germany in vain, hoping to locate the town of Bergenstrasse.

"But, Gretchen," I confronted her that evening in 1970 during regression, "there is no city in Germany called Bergenstrasse."

"Nein"—she shook her head—"Verstehen nicht. [No, you do not understand.]"

I didn't, but I pleaded with her, "In some way, Gretchen, explain it to me in a way I'll understand."

"Ich lebe Eberswalde in Bergenstrasse," she had said, waving her arms as though indicating the area around her.

Still not understanding, I said, fishing for an answer, "Are you trying to tell me that you live in the city of Eberswalde in the state of Bergenstrasse?"

"Eberswalde, ja," she replied, thinking I understood; and from that day on she almost always said she lived in Eberswalde.

When Dr. Stevenson entered the investigation, she told him a slightly different story. When he asked, "Where do you live?" she replied, "Eberswalde."

"Ja," he responded, "und also wohnen Sie in einer Strasse? [Yes, and so do you live in a street?]"

"Ich lebe in Bergenstrasse [I live in Castle Street]," she answered.

For confirmation, Dr. Stevenson said imply, "Bergenstrasse?"

"Ja."

Since Dr. Stevenson spoke German, I presumed he had asked the question in such a way that she understood more clearly what he meant, and I accepted Bergenstrasse to be Castle Street instead of the name of the state in which she lived.

That night in Darmstadt I felt that Gretchen was not saying that she lived on a street as you and I think of street, so I asked what seemed like a contradiction: "Do you live in Bergenstrasse on Eberswalde Street?"

"Nein." She frowned. "Ich lebe in Eberswalde auf Bergenstrasse."

While I sat in deep thought trying to figure out just what she meant, Gretchen began to babble, or so it sounded to me. Only one word seemed to stand out: "Heffenhine." Unable to understand what she was saying, I soon ended the regression.

Rising early the next day, Dolores and I spent the day researching the Eberstadt within Darmstadt, where we met the Reverend Wolfgang Weissgerber, who had authored *1000 Jahre Eberstädter Kirchengeschichte*. Father Weissgerber, with his daughter-in-law, Mrs. Rosemarie Weissgerber, quickly convinced us that no Gottlieb had ever been mayor of Eberstadt, and that no Gottliebs had ever lived in the area.

The next day I went to the Darmstadt Archives and was introduced to Hans G. Ruppel, a long-time employee, who provided tremendous assistance for the remainder of our stay in Germany. First, he informed us that there were three other Eberstadts, one in Giessen, one in Büchen, and another in Wiensberg. Too, he gave us the location of several communities called Ebersback.

His greatest help, though, was yet to come. When I told him that Gretchen had told me the night before, as she had in the first few regressions of 1970, that she "lived in Bergenstrasse," he smiled at our ignorance of German geography. "That may very well be true," he said, quickly getting a map and pointing to two words: "Bergstrasse" and "Burgenstrasse."

"But what does it mean?" I queried, since those two words did not seem to be marking any particular city or town.

"The Bergstrasse," he explained, tracing the map with his finger along a highway that lay parallel to the east side of the Autobahn and the west side of the Oldenwald Mountains, "is a road or route that runs from Darmstadt to Heidelberg; and Burgenstrasse"—he paused, making certain I noted the difference—"is merely a word used to denote the route of the castles which line the Oldenwald Mountains and the rivers Rhine and Neckar."

Then and only then did much of what Gretchen had said make sense. It now appeared that she could have been correct in saying that she lived in Bergenstrasse: the road or route of the castles, but not on a street!

"But, Hans," I asked, still somewhat perplexed over her claim to have lived in Eberswalde, "how can we explain Eberswalde, especially since she said on so many occasions that she lived in Eberswalde on Castle Street?"

He mused for a moment. "Well, as you now know, Eber means a place where pigs or hogs are kept, and Wald is woods or forest. So you see"—he again smiled—"she was possibly saying she lived in a place where pigs were kept in the forest of the Oldenwald mountains on the Bergstrasse or Bergenstrasse."

"But where," I wondered, "just where in those mountains could she have lived?" Then I remembered that strange word Gretchen uttered the night before, and I asked, "Hans, does the word 'Heffenhine' mean anything to you?"

"No," he began thoughtfully, "but . . ." He paused reflectively. "Could she have said 'Heppenheim'?"

"Well, yes," I confessed. 'You see, in addition to being unable to speak German, I do have somewhat of a hearing problem."

That night I again regressed Dolores and asked Gretchen, "Did you tell me the last time we talked that you lived in Heppenheim?"

"Nein." She shook her head. "Auf Heppenheim. [By Heppenheim.]"

"Can you tell me anything about Heppenheim?"

"Nein." She shrugged. "Gretchen Dummkopf."

I chuckled. "No, Gretchen, you're not stupid. Now tell me, where is Heppenheim?"

Pointing as if I should be able to see for myself, she said, "Ist dort."

Quickly I opened the medium-size dictionary I had purchased that day, hoping it would help me understand what she was saying.

"Dort . . . dort . . . Ah, I see," after finding the word, " 'over there.' Good! Now, Gretchen, evidently you can see Heppenheim from where you are, so . . . can you tell me anything about Heppenheim?"

"Ein Schloss. [A castle.]"

Again I could not understand, and was forced to ask her several times to repeat her answer. Finally, though, I was almost certain she was trying to say "Schloss auf [or Hof] Heppenheim," and I made a notation to check it out with Hans the next day.

Then, surprisingly, especially since she had seemed so calm, Gretchen became frightened—terrified, to be accurate—and began to cry hysterically, "Helfen Sie, keine mehr . . . Umwälzung!" which Hans was to translate as "Don't help someone more because of revolution!"

I had no idea what she was talking about, so I ended the regression. The next day, poring over my notes, Hans clarified the picture considerably after again getting a map and tracing the Burgenstrasse on the Bergstrasse, stopping at a small town called Heppenheim. "There it is," he said with conviction. "Somewhere in that area is the answer to Gretchen's existence."

"No, Hans," I objected. "Gretchen could not have lived in that area. Father Weissgerber said the Kulturkampf did not extend this far south, and without Gretchen dying in a revolution, her story does not make sense."

"But it does," he corrected me, running to get a history of the Hessen in the Revolutions of 1830–34 and 1848–49. "True, the Revolution of the eighteen seventies did not extend to that area, but there were two revolutions there in 1830 and 1848."

"Even then, Hans," I continued, "Gretchen always spoke of the Bundesrat, but the Bundesrat did not come into being until 1867."

"Yes, nationally there was no Bundesrat till then," he agreed, "but when you know the whole story you will learn that a Bundesrat was formed, and did in fact meet at the Half Moon Hotel in Heppenheim in 1848 to 1849. Look," he said, "suppose that tomorrow afternoon you, I, and Dolores ride down to Heppenheim and I'll show you proof."

Things were beginning to look up again, especially after Hans filled me in on the details as we walked to a bookstore, where I bought two maps showing all the small towns concerned with our investigation. Incidentally, until I took those maps back to the hotel and showed them to Dolores, she had never heard of Heppenheim, the Revolutions of 1830 and 1848, or the Castle of Starkenburg, which Hans said Gretchen was referring to when she said "Schloss auf Heppenheim."

Unable to wait until the next afternoon, Dolores and

I drove to Heppenheim, and when we got out of the car to visit the Rathaus, St. Peters Kirche, and other ancient buildings, Dolores was stunned. As we walked the cobblestone streets and she looked toward the old castle on a nearby mountain, her eyes took on a dreaminess that seemed to carry her back in time. So touched by the scene was she that as I walked to the huge doors of St. Peter's she lagged behind, protesting, "Maybe we shouldn't go in . . . maybe we should get permission first . . . somehow it doesn't seem right."

As I looked at my Dolores, for a moment I thought I saw another little brown-haired, blue-eyed girl in weskit and long dark skirt, her hair braided in a bun, holding back in wide-eyed apprehension, fearfully reluctant to go any farther.

Cathedrals have always been the first thing Dolores wants to see in our travels; she is always anxious to enter and stand in reverent awe, drinking in breathlessly the glorious beauty of stained-glass windows, finely chiseled statues, and ancient altars, which somehow always seemed more holy than their modern-day counterparts. That day in old Heppenheim I had to go back and take her gently by the arm. "C'mon, Dolores, this is just like the hundreds of other churches we have been in before."

"No . . . not really," she protested, even as she relaxed enough for me to lead her through the narthex into the nave, where she stood in silent awe trying to hide the trembling of her hands, holding them at her bosom as though praying, as Gretchen had done so many, many times. For the first time in my memory, she would not go past the pews into the transept for a closer look at the altar. As we exited old St. Peter's, she sighed, seemingly in relief to again be in the warming sun that brought a welcome comfort, stilling her trembling body.

The ride back to Darmstadt was made in comparative silence, each of us occupied by thoughts too deep to mention.

The next day Hans, Dolores, and I returned to Heppenheim, and after a short visit with a couple of local officials to check town records, we proceeded to the lobby of the Half Moon Hotel, where the Bundesrat had met almost a century and a half ago. There we read from a wall plaque that on May 13, 1849, not far from Heppenheim, the Hessians fought a battle against the troops of Baden-Württemberg, leaving three officers and twelve to fifteen men dead. Although no figures were given, the troops from Baden-Württemberg must have lost more. The account did not state that civilians had been killed, but the battle did take place near Erback, and it is conceivable that Gretchen's father and Gretchen herself might have been casualties of either that encounter or one in the earlier years, 1830–34.

Although Heppenheim records clearly reveal that no Gottlieb was ever mayor of that town, there is a strange anomaly: In the revolutions of both 1830–34 and 1848–49, two men who served as mayor of Heppenheim were named Gottfried, a strikingly strange coincidence, or so I thought. Yet I do not believe that Hermann Gottlieb was ever mayor of Heppenheim, simply because Gretchen never said or even hinted that she ever lived within the town of Heppenheim. And never had Dolores said that she received anything from her subconscious that made her really believe she had lived in Heppenheim in a prior life.

Still, I am somehow convinced that Gretchen had been to Heppenheim, or at least close enough to see the town. Her statement "Auf Heppenheim" meant that she had been by or near Heppenheim, and she did say that she saw "Schloss Heppenheim" (Starkenburg Castle), which sits on a mountain at Heppenheim. Too, she said of Heppenheim, "Ist dort [It is over there]," while pointing, indicating that if I looked I could see Heppenheim.

Both Hans and I were inclined to believe that Gretchen had at one time been involved with the area, because of what she had said and because of Dolores's strong affinity for the castle, St. Peter's, and the older part of Heppenheim, so we drove out of Heppenheim to the top of a mountain near Erback where the revolution was fought, and there I hypnotized and regressed Dolores.

I am well aware that such a regression is of no more scientific value than one conducted in my own study in the United States. A person in a trance sees only the events relived by the subconscious. Still, I reasoned that if in the waking state Dolores saw anything in the area that had existed during Gretchen's time, it might very well prompt her subconscious to reveal new and vital information to us. Gretchen did indeed seem to come through more readily in Germany than she ever had in the States.

From our vantage point high on the mountains near Erback, the tower of Heppenheim Castle was clearly visible, but it was a cold, blustery day, and I feared the weather might have some effect on the regression. Apparently not. Gretchen seemed comfortable in that weather—she often spoke of snow in previous regressions. In any event, when the trance was sufficiently deep I led Dolores to the middle of the road and asked, "Gretchen, what do you see?"

"Mein Vaters Haus [my father's house]." She pointed down the road toward the castle.

"What else do you see, Gretchen?"

"Dort ist Kleiner Fluss . . . das Wald. [There is little river . . . the forest.]"

"Tell us more, Gretchen."

"Nein." She cowered. "Gehen weg! [Go away!]," she ordered Hans, fear beginning to show in her eyes.

"Please, Gretchen—"

"Nein." She rebelled, struggling to break loose from Hans and me. "Gehen weg!" she ordered urgently, and began to babble in short, breathless sentences.

It was terribly frightening, listening to her and struggling to hold her and comfort her, as she was obviously gripped with terror. So traumatic had the situation become that her agony was like a red-hot knife in my heart, and I prevailed upon her to forget Gretchen, to let herself again become my wife, merely a visitor in Germany. Soon, thank God, we led Dolores, still in a trance, back to the car, where she collapsed on the back seat. There I began the process of making her forget all that had happened, preparatory to bringing her out of the trance.

As Dolores relaxed more and more, I asked Hans what Gretchen had said when babbling so hysterically.

"Well . . ." He paused, somewhat shaken by the ordeal. "First she urged me to leave because the soldiers were coming. Then she talked as though she had gotten on a horse and rode into the forest to hide, fearing for her life."

"Poor Gretchen," I thought. "Hans doesn't know the whole story. He doesn't know that that would be your last ride, that the soldiers would pursue you and kill you, maybe even bury you, or, worse yet, simply let you lie on the cold, wet ground until covered by the leaves, the twigs, the dew, the frost and snow, until that day more than a hundred years later when your spirit would rise up and speak again as a little girl through Dolores."

When I was certain Dolores was no longer Gretchen and had completely forgotten the events of that afternoon, I awakened her. But to my surprise, after opening her eyes in bewilderment before looking around to get her bearings, she began to sob uncontrollably. Thinking that she had remembered the terrible events that occurred when she relived as Gretchen, I began to comfort her, planning to rehypnotize her and make certain her memory slate was wiped clean. But she quickly stopped me.

"No . . . I . . . don't remember," she managed between sobs. "I . . . I'm only sorry I failed you and Hans! I was so nervous, Gretchen couldn't come through."

But she hadn't failed, and again I emphasize that Gretchen was more real in those frightfully traumatic moments than ever before.

One thing I now know more than anything else: Whether or not Gretchen lived in the Eberswald of the Bergenstrasse near Heppenheim is not important. It is important to know that Gretchen did live as a beautiful young girl in this world at one time. Whether it is reincarnation or spirit possession is inconsequential at this moment, because I am satisfied in my heart and mind that survival of the soul is a reality beyond dispute.

Though we now know Gretchen's story, the search for proof of exact dates and places must go on, because there is no way it can be said that all loose ends have been gathered together and wrapped in a neat little package. For example, Gretchen said in a recent regression that her father had also been a teacher, a fact that I readily accept, because few persons have ever spent their lives solely as the mayor of a small town. More important, we also learned that there was a professor Gottlieb at the University of Mainz in 1773–74. Thus, if we are able to substantiate Gretchen's death as having occurred in 1830–34, that professor could very well have been her father, or at least a very close relative. To have been his daughter, Gretchen would of necessity have to have been a child of his old age—not a probability, but possible.

Many people have argued that Gretchen could not have been a real personality who lived in ninetenth-century Germany because she said she could neither read nor write; especially would this be true if she were a teacher's daughter. But the records indicate that in the early nineteenth century twenty to thirty percent of the people living in the Bergstrasse could neither read nor write. As for Gretchen, I have always maintained that while she was a beautiful young girl, she was also a girl with learning disabilities, a person we would today call a slow learner, or one who was minimally retarded.

Her mental state is not important to this study. It is, however, important to know that her soul, wherever it may be, still lives. And while it may not be true that all of us who sing "I've got a home in gloryland that outshines the sun" will ever really live in that land of unending sunshine, I do believe unreservedly that we will have a home some place in the life to come.

For now, we are obligated to reduce the number of possible answers to Gretchen's emergence through Dolores to the lowest common denominator. If Dolores and I had a choice, we would have preferred to believe that Gretchen was merely a manifestation of linguistic regression. Our life would have been much less complicated had Dr. Stevenson been able to prove conclusively that Dolores had learned the German language early in life, then forgotten it, only to retrieve it from her memory bank in hypnotic regression. But such was not the case—she had not learned the language—so we are forced to search for other causes.

Life would have been even more simplified had we been able to determine without doubt that Gretchen's existence was merely a matter of genetic memory. But as of this day there is little or no proof that memories of past lives are stored in our genes and passed on to our children biologically, despite the fact that some children are prodigies, able to play concerts at age four or five. Apparently such people have somehow been endowed with a combination of control chemicals and genes aligned in perfect patterns during their conception, all of which they inherited from their parents. As yet, even this has not been proven scientifically. As a consequence, re-incarnationists often boast that child prodigies are living proof that reincarnation is indeed fact, insisting that any-one accomplishing great feats early in life must have learned the specialty in a prior life.

Dolores and I also hoped for a while that Jung's col-lective unconscious might offer a satisfactory answer, knowing that ancestral traits, as compared to complete memories of prior lives, can be passed from one genera-tion to another. Sadly, we see no reason for believing that the collective unconscious is anything more than an attractive theory, unsupportable in the Gretchen case.

As for witchcraft, what is there to say except that it is a terrible label to pin on someone in lieu of learned ex-planations? In the old days when ignorance was rampant it might have satisfied some, but today few people will accept fee-fi-fo and Halloween hobgoblins as an explana-tion for religious or scientific phenomena.

Telepathy? A possible but highly improbable explana-tion. To say that Dolores spoke as Gretchen in German because someone managed to transmit the knowledge to her telepathically is to offer an explanation bordering on the absurd. Because there are many people in the world today willing to use even the remotest possibility as an explanation for the Gretchen case, or any case involving the paranormal, Dr. Stevenson took every possible pre-caution to exclude the presence of outsiders during the investigation.

For the many who would offer telepathy as the ex-planation, it must be remembered that Gretchen first spoke through Dolores in our home in Greenbush, and later in Elkton, when no one, not even our children, knew the day or hour we would engage in investigative regressions—meaning that anyone who telepathically prompted Dolores would have had to be attuned to her constantly. Common sense forces us to eliminate telepathy.

What about spirit possession? Is it fact or fiction?

To determine the truth we must first understand the difference between spirit with a small "s" as compared to the capitalized "S" used to denote the Holy Spirit, the third Person of the Godhead: Father, Son, and Holy Spirit.

Spirit with a small "s" may be defined in many ways. Biblically it is used fifty-four times to describe states of being by those possessed with the spirit, such as those with the spirit of wisdom, knowledge, understanding, love, might, jealousy, fear, heaviness, and supplication. Others were described as being filled with the spirit of Elias (Elijah), David, Zerubbabel, Joshua, and Egypt.

Definitively, spirit can be said to be a person's moral, religious, or emotional nature; but spirit may also be the name applied to a supernatural being such as deity, fairy, elf, sprite, ghost, phantom, specter, and apparition, those beings connected with the other world. Although it may surprise all who derogatorily labeled Dolores as spirit-possessed, every human being has at one time or another been possessed by one or more spirits. Without them we would be little more than human robots or limpid zombies.

More to the point, was Dolores, because of her extremely religious nature, so finely attuned to the spirit world that she was able to let Gretchen's spirit replace hers in regression? If this be true, as many will insist, then it must also be true of every other living person, because every person who has submitted to hypnosis and regression under my ministry has told a story comparable to Gretchen's. Somewhere in the subconscious of every living person is a story that will come out under certain conditions and make it appear that that person lived in a prior life, even without being able to speak an unknown language.

Then again, was Gretchen able to manifest simply because her spirit was older and stronger, able to dominate and make Dolores's spirit subservient, enabling it to speak through her?

If Dolores was indeed spirit-possessed, why was Gretchen not able to overwhelm her spirit in the waking state and speak through her?

Why? Because there is no valid reason for believing that Gretchen's spirit could or did dominate and possess her. It must always be remembered that Gretchen had no control over Dolores unless she was in an altered state of consciousness, rendered through hypnosis, or suffered great mental and physical weakness that accrued through long periods of debilitating stress.

Realistically, then, was Dolores any more likely to be spirit-possessed than the rest of us?

I think not! At least, she would not be any more subject to possession than any other person achieving an altered state of consciousness through the ingestion of alcohol, drugs, anesthesia, or those brought on by disease.

Going a step further, can a spirit come from the afterlife, take control of another person, and use that person as possibly Gretchen did Dolores?

Yes, under certain conditions. It must be quickly pointed out that psychology experts will attempt to poohpooh the idea of spirit control and insist on a strictly scientific rationale which says that all apparent lives coming from a person's subconscious are mere products of a person's dissociated personality. On a fundamental level, all of us are more than one person psychologically, if not indeed ipso facto.

We sometimes engage in the tendency to not let our left hand know what our right hand is doing (proclaiming belief in integration while practicing segregation, or love while practicing hatred) without really being conscious that we do not practice what we preach. This is only natural, since every individual is endowed with defense mechanisms designed to keep conflicting attitudes and impulses apart. Going a step further, dissociation allows us to go beyond mere social expedience, in which we adjust our attitudes and behavior to different situations. We often isolate one set of ideas or impulses as a defense mechanism because it would cause us great distress were it brought together with our other thoughts.

This tendency may take unusual or pathological forms. In times of stress, people may not want to face the future, so they escape by assuming a new identity, manifesting a heretofore unseen personality which permits them to act in ways over which they claim no control or responsibility, as is revealed in the somnambulist who walks in his sleep and performs outlandish acts, or in cases where the hand writes without conscious control. In extreme cases there is a complete loss of identity, possibly even the splitting of the personality into two contrasting personalities.

If Dolores can be classified as a victim of dissociation, her condition is not pathological in the truest sense, because her subconscious personality surfaced artificially through hypnosis. Moreover, she never gave the slightest indication of abnormal dissociation prior to entering or following hypnotic regression.

Can anything more be said about these altered states of existence apart from the case histories that link such states of being to the eternal?

Thankfully there is; thankfully, because the basic outline of life after death as I described it in this work was in the publisher's hands when I first read Raymond A. Moody's book *Life After Life*. Now I know that many persons in regression have described in comparable detail the experience of dying without experiencing death per se.

I have acrylic paintings in my study done by artist Rita Jefferson after she requested hypnotherapy and subsequent regression, the latter I think for the sole purpose "seeing what would happen." Something did happen as she felt herself quickly transported through what she described as a trough. "I felt a 'Presence' . . . the bottom of His robe resembling a column from a Greek temple . . . and I saw His arm extended to me, saying, 'Fear not, I will never leave thee nor forsake thee . . . Lo, I am with you always, even unto the end of the world."

When I brought Rita out of the trance, she spoke softly, gently, reverently, tears clouding her eyes. "Oh, it was the most marvelous thing I have ever experienced, Reverend Jay." She looked me straight in the eye. "Believe me, I know now what those people mean when they talk about death and the glorious things that happen after death."

"Rita, do you really think you experienced death?"

"No," she demurred, with the seriousness of a child

271

who had caught a glimpse of heaven, "but when it comes for me, I'll not be afraid, for I now know what it will be like."

Strangely, when Rita handed me her painting of the "Presence," she said, "I couldn't draw His head, so I left Him more like a beautiful column."

"But, Rita," I questioned, "how come I can see the faint outline of His head? Did you paint it, then cover it over?"

"No, I couldn't paint it," she said, straining to see the outline. "I don't see a thing."

"It's there, Rita, believe me."

So it is, as the many who have seen it will testify. I wonder: Did she indeed see Him and did the artist in her make her dwell upon the beauty of His flowing robe, seeing in her artist's eye the stately strength and beauty so often ascribed to Him by men of the cloth over the past two thousand years? I think so!

CHAPTER XVI

To Know Is to Believe

Time after time the good Lord has blessed my family and me with His presence, His love, His goodness and mercy. From among the many precious gifts He has given us, we cherish most highly the one we received when He ordained me to become pastor of the Anderson Memorial United Methodist Church in Gretna, Virginia. Just as "His eye is upon the sparrow" and "He knows our every need," so He surely knew that to live in Gretna would mean joy, peace, and happiness for us.

Gretna is a small town, tiny in comparison to many, but it is not totally unknown. A few years ago one of the television networks focused its cameras on the signs leading into town: WE AIN'T NO BIG THING, BUT WE'RE GROWING. So it is, slowly, surely. For want of a better expression, my family and I are convinced it is the epitome of all towns claiming to be "God's own little acre."

The contrast between the two years of blissful peace we have known here and the blistering hellfire and damnation heaped on us in the preceding three years is too tremendous to describe with mere words. How can anyone put into words a joy that brings a constant melody to your heart? How can one adequately describe what it means to work, worship, and play among people who accept you as one of their own, especially after you have lived for three years in an atmosphere that made you walk with bated breath when going only to the post office? What a joy it is to attend a ball game or a concert without dodging verbal stones and reproaches by wild-eyed radicals. Only the minorities who have now died and gone to heaven after having lived in a segregated community or Jews who escaped from Nazi anti-Semitic hatred can truly experience the joy we now have in walk-

273

ing down the street and not seeing neighbors cross to the other side because they think your shadow might defile their holy robes of righteousness. Aye, it is with humble pride that we now report that it has been our good pleasure to have been invited to join in every community affair in Gretna. I was even elected president of the local Ministerial Association.

Such a thing would have been unthinkable in Elkton. I remember the time when Vonda was to graduate as valedictorian. The ministers in the local Association were selected to speak at graduation ceremonies on a rotation basis, and it was my turn. Yet for some reason the ministers informed school officials that the graduating seniors should select the minister they wanted. Praise God, the seniors selected me and another minister (who did not belong to the Association) as the ones they wanted.

Sometimes I am amazed at the conscienceless perfidy of some people. Though they professed friendship to my face, they denounced me to their friends and deprecated me in their meetings. Some of those same men now pretend not to understand why I resigned from their Association months before we left town.

We should have known Gretna would be different. My former District Superintendent, the Reverend Eugene Woolridge, tried to assure me that Gretna was a wonderful place to live. "You will be accepted in the community without question," he said. Such assurances were not too comforting. We had become so frustrated by ostracism that I could only mumble, "Will we really?" Then, in utter despair, I asked, "Is there actually a place anywhere in this old world where we will be accepted?"

When we first met Susan and Jimmy Hunt, Anderson's lay delegates to the 193rd Annual Conference of the Virginia United Methodist Conference, at Hampton, we approached them with fear and trepidation and inquired hesitantly, "Do you know who we are?"

"Yes." Jimmy smiled, extending the right hand of fellowship.

Still not sure he really knew for certain, I asked, "Do you know that some people consider me a devil's advocate and Dolores a witch?"

"Yes." He laughed aloud, with a warm sincerity that we had forgotten existed. "But where are your horns?" Still laughing, he turned to Dolores. "C'mon, if you can move without your broom, I want you to meet my wife."

For the record, Jimmy—Mr. James L. Hunt, Sr.—is the teacher of our teenagers' church-school class, a man of deep devotion and dedication to the Lord. He is typical of most people in the church and community: never quick to judge another, willing to accept every person at face value.

This does not mean Gretna is made up of pretentious holier-than-thous. They're not, and they would be the first to agree that they are not angels—yet. My high praise of them does not mean that we have not had differences of opinions. Still, I assure you: Never once has anyone questioned our moral or ethical values. We have hypnotized and regressed, counseled, prayed, preached, sung, played, and fasted with them without once ever being made to wonder whether we were acceptable to them and our Lord.

To say that we have not experienced heartache and chagrin in these past two years would be misleading. While we have experienced true joy and peace of mind in the community, a couple of incidents elsewhere disturbed us considerably. On July 28, 1975, four weeks after we moved to Gretna, Warren F. Gorman, M.D., a private practitioner of forensic neuro-psychiatry in Scottsdale, Arizona, pretended omniscience and wrote an article for the *Journal of the American Medical Association* entitled, "Tall Tales and Imaginary Companions," in which he insinuated that Dolores and I were liars who had fabricated the Gretchen story to "accomplish short-term gain." Strangely, he insinuated we were liars because "All of us have a touch of the desire to prevaricate."

Most of us have, I am certain, lied at one time or another, but actually to have a desire to lie? I think not, at least speaking for some of us.

Naturally, my family and I were distressed by the unwarranted insinuations, and my first inclination was to sue the man for making libelous statements in print, but after considering the matter at length Dolores and I decided against such action. We reasoned that if he wanted to confess to the whole world that he had "a touch of the desire to prevaricate," then more power to him.

Dr. Gorman was not the only self-styled judge to imply he knew all the answers without knowing the facts. A Dr. Bruce Danto was quoted in the *Detroit News* concerning the Gretchen story: "I call it a 19-inch fantasy because that's a popular size for TV screens . . . either somebody is lying or she once had some German and this represents a linguistic regression where she remembers what she had forgotten."

These men do not stand alone. The world is full of experts who denounce everyone as a liar, especially if someone makes a report on something that they are not too familiar with.

Dr. Gorman and Dr. Danto did not know anything about Dolores and me and the Gretchen case other than what they had read in the newspapers. Yet Dr. Gorman attempted to psychoanalyze us in absentia.

He said, "if the patients should come to examination, they would be diagnosed as antisocial personalities or psychopathic personalities." Really?

No matter—we didn't go to him or anyone else for examination, not because we were afraid, but because there was no need. And there was no need because we had collaborated with Dr. Stevenson for five years. It may surprise Dr. Gorman to know that, prior to entering the field of parapsychology, Dr. Stevenson was the chairman of the Department of Psychiatry and Neurology at the University of Virginia's School of Medicine, that he is the author of *The Psychiatric Examination* and *The Diagnostic Interview*.

One thing is certain: Had Dolores and I needed psychiatric help, or been dishonest in any way, it is a foregone conclusion that Dr. Stevenson would not have touched the Gretchen case with a ten-foot pole. To the contrary, Dr. Stevenson was very much disturbed and indignant over Dr. Gorman and his article, so much so that he wrote to the editor of the AMA *Journal* and requested that the following rebuttal be printed:

Dr. Warren F. Gorman violated a rule of controversy in scientific matters . . . in that we should always withhold comment about a case or experiment until after a report of it has been published in an appropriate scientific journal or book . . . I have been investigating this case for five years, am now preparing a scientific report about it, and am positive that no other scientist has published, or as of now, intends to publish a report of this case (Dr. Gorman had inaccurately inferred "that competent authorities were unable to verify the case") . . . And in view of Dr. Gorman's wrong impressions and light dismissal of the Gretchen case and the inability of the persons concerned to defend themselves . . . I think it appropriate for me to put into the record . . . that I am convinced that Mrs. Jay did not learn German normally . . . but spoke German exclusively . . .

I conclude that Gretchen could speak German responsively . . . [thus] I see no justification for Dr. Gorman to have disparagingly linked the Gretchen case with antisocial personalities, that is pathological liars and other mentally ill persons. This juxtaposition suggests quite unfairly that the Jays are minimally self deceived and possibly hoaxers. Surely we should expect a higher level of discrimination from a trained psychiatrist.

That is all behind us now—at least until other self-styled omniscients who have never once investigated hypnotic regression start denouncing from superficial wisdom.

Forgetting all that is past, we move into the countdown of our long and hard but marvelous experience. How could Dolores become Gretchen? Or if she did not really become Gretchen, since the transformation occurred only under certain conditions, how can the phenomenon be explained?

First observations seem to indicate reincarnation. Especially does this seem a logical explanation following Dolores's vague *déjà vu* experiences in Germany. But it seems to me that if it were indeed reincarnation Gretchen would not have come to her the day Dolores washed dishes, or the night she was compelled to almost overdose on tranquilizers. If Dolores were Gretchen reincarnated, how could Dolores have seen Gretchen's apparition, her spirit, so to speak?

While in a trance Dolores did say, "I am that girl," and she was able to converse with people in German in such a way that even I had to consider seriously the possibility that she might have been reincarnated. Had I simply closed my mind and said, "No, there's no way I can ever believe such a thing," I would have been saying that I did not want to take a chance on knowing the truth, whatever it might be. I assure one and all that, even now, if I really believed Dolores was the former Gretchen Gottlieb, I would quickly say so. But, and I emphasize this, I see no foundation on which to build such an assumption.

"Ah," you ask, "why did Dolores feel such a close kinship with Germany, particularly the Rathaus, St. Peter's, and all the old buildings?"

Well, for seven long years Gretchen and Germany had been much on her mind, so much so that both Gretchen and Germany had become like old friends. A few times in my life I have heard someone talk so much about another person whom I had never met that when I actually met that person for the first time I felt as though we had been friends a long, long time. So it was and is with Dolores, Gretchen, and Germany.

If not reincarnation, can spirit possession be any more plausible? Can we indeed be possessed, even minimally, by a deceased person's spirit?

The Bible implies we can. It actually gives illustrative examples. Jesus clearly indicated in Matthew 17:10-13 that John the Baptist was Elijah come again. Although many would like to believe that this is an open-and-shut case of reincarnation, St. Luke 1:17 says, "And he [John the Baptist] shall go before him [the Lord] in the spirit and power of Elijah, to turn the hearts of the fathers to the children . . ."

John was not the first to receive Elijah's spirit and powers. II Kings 2:14, 15 reveals that after Elijah had been taken to heaven in a whirlwind, Elisha "took up the mantle of Elijah that fell from him, and smote the waters, and said, where is the Lord God of Elijah? And when he also had smitten the waters, they parted hither and thi-

ther: and Elisha went over [walked on dry ground]."
Please note that it was only after Elisha "took up Elijah's mantle," that is, only after he received Elijah's spirit,
was he able to "part the waters." Note also that Elisha
was able to receive Elijah's spirit only after Elijah had
been taken into heaven, that is, after Elijah had died.
(Death was necessary because, as the Apostle Paul said,
"Flesh and blood cannot enter the kingdom of God" [I
Corinthians 15:50].) This clearly intimates that if the
story on Elijah and Elisha be true (and I believe it is),
all of us may take upon us another's spirit and be led by
that spirit.

Where do those spirits come from? In the last chapter
I discussed briefly life between deaths, the place where
spirits abide. Obviously, not all who have died are in that
place. Revelations 20:4-6 says, "And I saw thrones . . .
and I saw the souls of them that were beheaded for the
witness of Jesus, and for the word of God . . . and they
lived and reigned with Christ . . . Blessed and holy is he
that hath part in the first resurrection: on such the second
death hath no power, but they shall be priests of God
and of Christ . . ."

The preceding refers to those in heaven; verses 12, 13
tell another story: "And I saw the dead, small and great,
stand before God . . . and the sea gave up the dead . . .
and death and hell delivered up the dead . . . and they
were judged every man according to their works." From
these two passages of Scripture, I believe we can infer
three different states of existence prior to the final resurrection. First, those beheaded for the witness are
the saints in heaven; secondly, those referred to as the
dead or death, which are separated in the Scriptures from
those in hell by the conjunction, *and* are those to whom
Christ preached in prison, possibly purgatory, whereas
those in hell are, as it says, "in hell."

Just as there are those in heaven who would not come
back under any circumstances—there is no reason for them
to come back, since they have already received the ultimate reward: perfection, at-oneness with God, which
even the reincarnationists claim as their ultimate goal—
at the other extreme, all those in hell cannot return, although I'm sure they would like to. Of those who cannot

return, we know for certain only about the fallen angels who "lost their first estate" and were "delivered into chains of darkness, to be reserved unto judgment." This, then, leaves that large group in the middle, the "dead to whom Christ preaches." Although it is not apropos to debate the complete issue here, this group may include all who died before the time of Christ, those who lived in remote lands and never heard of Him, and even those who in ignorance rejected His offer of salvation.

Since, as I pointed out in the last chapter, spirits in the "afterlife" are in full possession of their faculties (else they could not hear and make the decision whether to accept or reject salvation offered by Christ), it seems only reasonable to me that some of those spirits were so attached to things on this earth that they cannot or will not let go, that they are in some way able to manifest in spirit form through other people still living in this life.

If this be true, it explains how Gretchen's spirit could speak through Dolores. It even offers an explanation for mischievous poltergeists. This, believe me, is far more important than it seems at first glance. Many Fundamentalist Christians may brand all our efforts in this investigation as evil, even proclaiming that we are possessed by evil spirits, but I believe the Scriptures support my thesis completely.

Hear me clearly: If God has already rewarded the true saints with heaven, then it seems logical to suggest He has already condemned the incorrigibly evil to hell —"and hell delivered up its dead," meaning it has its occupants. But what about those in the middle? Maybe their existence explains why the spirits we call ghosts merely tap on walls, turn out lights, or rattle chains—they are not evil. The evil are in hell, bound "Unto the day of judgment," and cannot come back.

This theory of afterlife which is neither heaven or hell is comparable in some aspects to purgatory, but is of longer duration and not ended by our prayers. It should not cause people to live as they please in this life, hoping for a second chance in the afterlife. Remember, "the things that bind you on earth shall bind you in heaven, and whatsoever thou shalt loose on earth shall be loosed in heaven," indicating that you will be bound pretty much there by the same things that bind you here. Those who hope to live as they please in this life on the assumption thay can or will change in the afterlife are almost bound to be disappointed.

This, then, permits us to assume that possibly the spirits which try to return to this life through another person may do so either because they cannot or will not accept at-oneness with God through Christ, or they do not want to make that choice until after they have completed some unfinished business on earth. Many people have asked, "Why is it that so many of the spirits who supposedly reveal themselves in regression tell of lives that ended with tragic violence?"

Possibly it is just for that reason that they try to return: They simply want to tell their story. Look at it this way: Many times we have all started to say something, only to be rudely cut off, and usually, if what we were about to says was important, we felt frustrated. So must those poor spirits feel, believing that not just their conversation but their whole life had been ended prematurely, impelling them to make some kind of a return to this life.

What does Dr. Stevenson have to say about Gretchen? In the *Journal of the American Society for Psychical Research* he says:

The principal significance of this case . . . derives from the occurrence of a responsive xenoglossy. That the Gretchen personality could speak German intelligibly seems to me established beyond all doubt. The fact that Gretchen's German grammar was defective and that her pronunciation was also poor at times are certainly of interest, but should not detract from the more important fact that Gretchen spoke German and did so most of the time quite intelligibly.

If my statements and those of the native German speakers who helped me are accepted with regard to Gretchen's ability to speak German, then the next question is whether D.J. [Dolores] learned German normally. She denies that she did so and I am convinced that she and her husband have told the truth when they say that they had no effective knowledge of the German language prior to the development of the case. If we set aside fraud as a hypothesis, there remains the possibility that D.J. somehow learned German in her early childhood and afterwards forgot that she had done so, this fact also remaining unknown to her family or having been forgotten by them . . . All my efforts, which I think were not inconsiderable, to learn of any opportunities D.J. might have had for learning German when she was a young child turned up nothing whatever to support this conjecture. After some years of doubt, I now have no hesitation in saying that I am quite convinced that D.J. did not learn German normally.

How then did D.J. acquire the ability to speak German that she showed during the periods of Gretchen's manifestations? In reporting the Jenson case . . . I argued that the ability to speak a foreign language is a skill, that skills cannot be acquired without practice, cannot be transmitted either normally or paranormally, and that if it can be shown that a person has not normally learned a foreign language that he can speak responsively, then we have evidence of the existence and influence on him (or her) of another personality which at some time had learned that language. In short, authentic cases of responsive xenoglossy provide for me important evidence of the survival of human personality after death.

A surviving personality capable of continuing to speak a foreign language and expressing it through an entranced person may do so through processes that we call reincarnation or possession.

With the concept of reincarnation, we can think of a deceased personality which had once learned to speak the language in question as surviving death as an enduring personality which later becomes associated with a new physical body. Under the special circumstances provided by hypnosis, and perhaps at other times, the previous personality could come to the surface—albeit perhaps only partially, but yet with sufficient control to speak its native language.

In considering the hypothesis of possession, we can imagine a deceased personality capable of speaking its native language persisting in a discarnate state until a suitably entranced living person gives it an opportunity to manifest temporarily through that person's body. In the present case this would imply that D.J. became a medium when hypnotized by C.J. [Carroll Jay] and that at such times Gretchen became a communicator capable of controlling D.J. with sufficient power to speak her native language.

If we interpret the case as one of reincarnation, this does not bind us to believing that D.J. is a "one-to-one" reincarnation of a previously living Gretchen. It is conceivable that D.J. lived a previous life in Germany when she could speak German and that the Gretchen personality provided an appropriate dramatic vehicle for the partial expression of memories of that previous life. The Gretchen personality might then resemble an historical novel comprised partly of fact, partly of fiction. Nor does the interpretation of possession oblige us to believe that the manifest personality of Gretchen corresponds exactly, or even closely, with a real person who once lived a terrestrial life and is now discarnate. On this hypothesis also, the phenomenal Gretchen personality could be a mixture blended from parts of D.J.'s own personality and elements of a real discarnate Gretchen lying behind and influencing the manifest communicator . . .

I find myself at this time quite unable to decide firmly between the interpretations of reincarnation and possession . . . I am, however, somewhat inclined to favor that of possession, but with the qualification included in the preceding paragraph. It seems to me enough for the present to conclude that responsive xenoglossy derives from *some* paranormal process. If my assumptions about skills be allowed, then responsive xenoglossy further indicates survival of a human personality after death and its later manifestation in the sessions with xenoglossy.

What does Dolores say?

"I really don't know except that I am me, not Gretchen, not Loreen—just me. I don't know where Gretchen came from, nor do I think I have had a prior life. Truthfully, I have always believed we have just one life to live, and I would not want to say anything that might lead someone to think you can live just any old way in this life and have a chance to repent in the next.

"Gretchen is a part of my life. I did not ask her to come, but she has been wih us so long she now seems like a part of the family.

"There is so much we don't know about life, but if it is true that there is a place called purgatory, and if Gretchen is there, it is my prayer that she has at last found peace. If the telling of her story through me has helped her, I'm glad.

"Always I have said that all Gretchen wanted was peace; and if she's found that, I'm happy for her."

And my final word? As Bishop Goodson said, "there are three people buried in a plot that has my family name on the stone, and I often stop to talk to them . . . [because I] believe that God enables us to live in that mysterious realm of the universe that is out beyond the far cliffs where only free spirits . . . are permitted to fly."

Dolores and I have ventured in spirit to the far cliffs, and we have heard from those who have gone on before, and I am glad.

Often I have been forced to stand in the pulpit as a minister of the gospel and deliver a eulogy to a group of people who had come to grieve for a dear departed body that lay in a casket before them. I have wept for those people, saddened that they could not really believe there was no one in the casket, that the real person who had been one with and among them had been translated by God's grace to a land we can never know in this life. Even as I grieved for the family, I was happy in my own mind, for I was certain that their spirits had soared into a land far more glorious than we shall ever see this side of heaven. Yes, those that have gone on before do live, and they are far more alive now than we shall ever be in this life.

But where oh where is that land out beyond the far cliffs? Really, I don't know, but I often think of my childhood days, when I first heard my mother read the story of Adam and Eve in the Garden of Eden, and ever before me has been the memory of how the Lord "placed at the east of the garden Cherubims with flaming swords which turned every way, to keep the way of the tree of life" (Genesis 3:24). And you know what? I seriously believe that someday I shall be a cherubim or some other form of being working for my Lord in another life, in another world, just as I have in this.

This says that I expect to live forever. I'm not just some little old country boy plunked down on this earth who just loves to stay down on the farm forever. Always I have been a get-up-and-go type of guy, and I guess I always will be. I presume that is true of all of us—we ain't gonna stay here forever. Good old St. Peter tells us in II Peter 3:10-12, "But the day of the Lord shall come as a thief in the night; in the which the heavens shall pass away with a great noise, and the elements shall melt with fervent heat, the earth also and the works that are therein shall be burned up. Seeing then that all these things shall be dissolved, what manner of person ought you to be?"

Yes, someday this old world is going to end, and a sad day it will be for many. A woman once told me in regression that she had died and tried in every possible way to contact her loved ones on earth and make them see the error of their ways. As she said, "I wasn't in heaven and I wasn't in hell—not good enough for heaven, nor bad enough for hell." Then she went on to explain, "If only I could go back and make them see the light . . . make them know that this life is real!"

Gretchen was, I believe, like that lady—not good enough for heaven and not bad enough for hell. I can only say to Gretchen, "Please, Gretchen, quit looking to Dolores and me for help. Look for the One who comes and preaches to you in Spirit. I know you want peace, but peace can only come from the One who said, 'Come, ye blessed of my Father, inherit the Kingdom prepared for you from the foundation of the world. Peace be unto you; peace I leave with you; my peace I give unto you.' "

It seems to me that because of all the stars and planets and universes around us we should realize this is not the first and only inhabited planet made by God, and while many theologians are of the opinion that angels, seraphim, and cherubim were creatures created specifically by God for service to Him, we should also consider that someday we too, also created by God, may be referred to by other creatures on other planets in another time and another place as angels, seraphim, and cherubim, as His servants who minister to others in their time of time.

Gretchen lives, that I know. And someday Dolores and I and all our friends, loved ones, and relatives will join her, because life, you see, is forever!

BIBLIOGRAPHY

BERNSTEIN, MOREY. *The Search for Bridey Murphy.* New York: Lancer Books, Inc., 1956.

BLYTHE, PETER. *Hypnotism: Its Power and Practice.* New York: Taplinger Publishing Co., 1971.

CHAMPION, SELWYN GURNEY, and SHORT, DOROTHY. *Readings from World Religions.* Boston: Beacon Press, 1951.

DAUVEN, JEAN. *The Powers of Hypnotism.* Briarcliff Manor, N.Y.: Stein and Day, Scarborough House, 1969.

EBON, MARTIN. *Reincarnation in Twentieth Century.* New York: Signet Books, New American Library, 1969.

EBON, MARTIN. *Communicating with the Dead.* New York: New American Library, n.d.

FAUST, FLOYD. *Life/Death/Life.* Nashville: The Upper Room, 1977.

FORD, ARTHUR, and ELLISON, JEROME. *The Life Beyond Death.* New York: G. P. Putnam's Sons, 1971.

GOLDENSON, ROBERT M. *The Encyclopedia of Human Behavior: Psychology, Psychiatry and Mental Health,* volumes 1 and 2. New York: Doubleday & Co., Inc., 1970.

KAPLEAU, PHILIP. *The Wheel of Death.* New York: Harper & Row, 1971.

KINKEAD, EUGENE. "Is There Another Life?" *Look,* October 20, 1970.

LECRON, LESLIE M. *Experimental Hypnosis.* New York: Macmillan Co., 1954.

LECRON, LESLIE M., and BORDEAUX, JEAN. *Hypnotism Today.* North Hollywood, Calif.: Wilshire Book Co., 1947.

MARCUSE, F. L. *Hypnosis, Fact and Fiction.* Baltimore: Penguin Books, 1959.

McTaggart, John, and McTaggart, Ellis. *Some Dogmas of Religion*. London: Edward Arnold, 1906.

Montgomery, Ruth. *Here and Hereafter*. New York: Fawcett, 1968.

Platt, Nathaniel, and Drummond, Muriel Jean. *Our World Through the Ages*. Englewood Cliffs, N.J.: Prentice-Hall, Inc., 1967.

Rhodes, Raphael H. *Hypnosis: Theory, Practice and Application*. New York: Citadel Press, 1950.

Science News, articles from vol. 102, no. 7 (Aug. 12, 1972); vol. 101, no. 21 (May 29, 1972); vol. 100, no. 19 (Nov. 6, 1971). Washington, D.C.: Science Service, Inc.

Stevenson, Ian. *Twenty Cases Suggestive of Reincarnation*. Hempstead, N.Y.: American Society for Psychical Research, 1966.

Stevenson, Ian. *Xenoglossy*. Charlottesville, Va.: University of Virginia Press, 1974.

Stevenson, Ian. "A Preliminary Report of a New Case of Responsive Xenoglossy: The Case of Gretchen," *Journal of the American Society for Psychical Research*, American Society for Phychical Research, vol. 70, 1976.

Stevenson, Ian. "Some Questions Related to Case of Reincarnation Type," *Journal of the American Society for Psychical Research*, American Society for Psychical Research, vol. 68, no. 4, 1974.

Stevenson, Ian. "A Communicator of the 'Drop In' Type in France: The Case of Robert Marie," *Journal of the American Society for Psychical Research*, American Society for Psychical Research, vol, 67, no. 1, 1973.

Weatherhead, Leslie D. *The Case for Reincarnation*. Surrey, England: M. C. Peto, 1957.

Weatherhead, Leslie D. *After Death*. Nashville: Abingdon Press, n.d.

Weitzenhoffer, Andre M. *General Techniques of Hypnotism*. New York: Grune & Stratton, Inc., 1957.

Wittels, Fritz. *Freud and His Time*. New York: Liveright Publishing Corp., 1931.